THE *Ulysses* GUIDE

Robert Nicholson was born in 1954 in Dublin,
where he now lives. He studied English Language
and Literature at Trinity College, Dublin, where
he was active in the Dublin University Players.
Since 1978 he has been the curator of the James
Joyce Museum at the Joyce Tower in Sandycove,
and he lectures and writes on Joyce. He is the
Chairman of the James Joyce Institute of Ireland
and a director of the James Joyce Cultural Centre.
In addition to *The Ulysses Guide* he has published
The James Joyce Daybook.

ROBERT NICHOLSON

THE *Ulysses* GUIDE

TOURS THROUGH JOYCE'S DUBLIN

Mandarin

A Mandarin Paperback
THE ULYSSES GUIDE

First published in Great Britain 1988
by Methuen London Ltd
This revised edition published 1991
by Mandarin Paperbacks
Michelin House, 81 Fulham Road, London SW3 6RB

Mandarin is an imprint of the Octopus Publishing Group,
a division of Reed International Books Limited

A CIP catalogue record for this title
is available from the British Library
ISBN 0 7493 0937 7

Acknowledgements
No work relating the action of *Ulysses* to its locations can be
complete without reference to Clive Hart and Leo Knuth's
excellent *Topographical Guide to James Joyce's Ulysses*, which
identifies all addresses mentioned in the book and supplies
some useful comment on the timing of each chapter. I am also
indebted to Danis Rose's article in the *James Joyce Quarterly*,
establishing the timing of *Nestor* and *Proteus* and the itinerary
of the latter. Other sources are listed in the bibliography.

For permission to quote extracts from *Ulysses: The Corrected
Text* I am grateful to the executors of the Estate of James Joyce,
and to the Bodley Head, London. For permission to quote
from Joyce's letters and other works I am grateful to the
Society of Authors, as the literary representatives of the Estate
of James Joyce.

My particular thanks are due to Patrick Johnston, Curator of
the Dublin Civic Museum, and to Peter Walsh, Curator of the
Guinness Brewery Museum, for photographs and valuable
information; to Des Gunning, administrator of the James Joyce
Cultural Centre, for helpful research; to Gerard O'Flaherty,
Vincent Deane and other members of the James Joyce Institute
of Ireland, for points of information; to the Photographic
Department, Bord Failte, for assistance; and to the Dublin and
Eastern Regional Tourism Organisation for various good offices.

Printed in England by Clays Ltd, St Ives plc

Contents

Illustrations

Photographs, except where otherwise stated, are reproduced by courtesy of the National Library of Ireland from the Lawrence Collection. The maps were drawn by Neil Hyslop.

A Note on the Maps

For the sake of clarity, only the most useful and essential details are included on the maps. The reader may find it helpful to study an Ordnance Survey street map of Dublin for additional information on street names and peripheral detail. The principal route on each map is indicated with a bold line, while a broken line signifies a detour or link route. Alternate arrows pointing in opposite directions indicate that this part of the route is retraced in reverse.

Introduction

THE GUIDE: When James Joyce wrote *Ulysses*, he did so with a copy of Thom's Dublin Directory beside him and a precise idea in his head of the location of every action described in the book. The city of Dublin, perhaps more than any scholarly work of reference, is the most valuable document we have to help us appreciate the intricate craftmanship of *Ulysses*. To follow the steps of Leopold Bloom, Stephen Dedalus and their fellow-Dubliners from one landmark to the next has become an act, not merely of study, but of homage. It is, in effect, a sort of pilgrimage.

This guide is intended to enable pilgrims, be they scholars, students or ordinary readers, to follow the action of *Ulysses* as near as possible to the locations in which it is set. To facilitate the traveller it is arranged on an area-by-area basis rather than taking the episodes in sequence. The eight itineraries, which vary in length from one to two hours, occasionally overlap, and indications are given of how to link one route with others nearby. All are designed to be followed on foot except those of the funeral procession (Tour 2) and the viceregal cavalcade (Tour 7). Some of them begin or end conveniently near to a DART station. At certain points detours or extensions are suggested to places of Joycean or general interest.

Incorporated in the guide is an outline of the action of *Ulysses* as it is presented in each episode. It concentrates on the activities and movements of the characters throughout the day that is described (as distinct from memories, imaginings and ideas) and is, of course, intended neither as a substitute for, nor as an interpretation of, *Ulysses* itself. Page numbers in the margin refer to the standard Corrected Text of *Ulysses* (see Appendix II).

There are many popular misconceptions about *Ulysses*, one of them being that the book describes a walk by Leopold Bloom which can be followed continuously from one chapter to the next like some sort of tourist trail. Bloom's day is no stroll. He covers a total of about eight miles on foot and a further ten by tram, train and horse-drawn vehicle. Of certain periods of the day there is no definite account at all, and much occurs between chapters which is simply not described. The guide fills in these gaps as far as possible, and a table is appended charting the known movements of Bloom and Stephen over the course of the day.

Finally, there is one puzzle in *Ulysses* which this guide makes no attempt to solve, namely how to 'cross Dublin without passing a pub'. Maybe you will be in one when you read this.

THE CHANGING CITY: Since 1904, Dublin has altered considerably. Buildings have gone, streets have been renamed, and shops and businesses continue to change hands. Some – but only a part – of this transformation is due to the destruction caused by the Easter Rising of 1916, the War of Independence which followed, and the Civil War of 1922–3. The ravages of these events were confined to certain streets and public buildings, some of which have been restored to their original appearance. Much more widespread is the effect of the gradual removal of old houses, sometimes piecemeal and sometimes by entire blocks, which has been taking place increasingly since the mid-1960s to make way for new property developments.

In Bloom's time the streets were laid with cobbles or setts; main thoroughfares had tram-tracks, standards and overhead cables; motor cars were a rarity (only one appears in *Ulysses*) and many people walked, cycled or took the tram. Without the roar and fumes of present-day motor traffic, it was possible to converse in the street as so many of Joyce's characters do, and to cross the roadway at any point without the benefit of traffic lights. Horse-drawn vehicles, however, were plentiful, and the streets were presumably foul with dung, except at the established crossings, where a line of granite setts would be kept clean by sweepers. Dublin was lit by gas; façades were not obscured by plastic and neon signs; there were no television aerials. Shopfronts were more discreet, less flashy; most shops had awnings to shade them from the sun. Plastic bags, parking meters, traffic signs, drink cans, bilingual street signs and burglar alarms were other unknowns.

Letterboxes were red, bearing the royal cipher VR or EviiR; now painted green, some of these older boxes may still be found here and there in Dublin. Coins of the period, particularly the larger copper pennies, were still in circulation up to decimalisation in 1971 – twelve pence to the shilling, twenty shillings to the pound. The guinea, worth twenty-one shillings, was a unit frequently used for fees and prices.

Number 7 Eccles Street has gone. Barney Kiernan's has gone, and so have the *Freeman's Journal* office and Bella Cohen's brothel. Much, however, remains – the banks, the public buildings, all the churches and nearly all the pubs mentioned in *Ulysses* are still there. Even Olhausen's the butcher's and Sweny's chemist shop still survive. Many of the original buildings have altered little, despite changes of ownership. Businesses move or disappear so frequently nowadays that street numbers are included in many of the addresses given in the Guide to aid identification.

It is easy to fall into the nostalgic trap of thinking of 'Joyce's Dublin' as a city in a golden age – a time of sepia photographs, parasols, penny tramfares and the leisurely clop of horses' hooves. What we rarely see in the old photographs are the barefoot children, the rampancy of tuberculosis and rickets, the squalor of tenement life and the infamous brothels of Nighttown. Standards of hygiene and personal cleanliness were lower. The shirt which Bloom wears throughout that hot day under his black waistcoat and funeral suit will probably be worn again the next day with the cuffs turned over and a clean detachable collar. Public toilets were of the most rudimentary kind and were not provided for women. Drunkenness and poverty were widespread. If Dublin has changed, it is not altogether for the worse.

Those who read *Ulysses* will know that Joyce was recording not merely the Dublin of 16 June 1904, but the quality of Dublin that survives through everchanging forms. This guide provides the facts of Bloomsday; by using it the reader may also discover the enduring Dublin of then and of today.

Robert Nicholson

Ulysses: The Episodes

Telemachus, Nestor

Telemachus, 8 a.m.

The Sandycove Martello Tower, known as the Joyce Tower, stands on a rocky headland one mile southeast of Dun Laoghaire, off the coast road. To get there, take the train to Sandycove Station or the No. 8 bus to Sandycove Avenue and walk down to the sea, where the Tower on Sandycove Point will be clearly visible. Cars should be parked by the harbour as the Tower is on a narrow road. Turn off Sandycove Avenue at the harbour and walk up past the distinctive white house designed as his own residence by the Irish architect Michael Scott, who also designed the present Abbey Theatre, the central bus station in Store Street and other notable public buildings. Follow the path behind the house leading to the Tower.

> They halted while Haines surveyed the tower and said at last:
> —Rather bleak in wintertime, I should say. Martello you call it?
> —Billy Pitt had them built, Buck Mulligan said, when the French were on the sea. But ours is the *omphalos*.

Coincidentally enough, the order for the building of this tower, and about thirty others of similar design around Dublin and other strategic points on the Irish coast, was dated 16 June 1804. The name 'Martello' comes from Mortella Point in Corsica, where the original tower was captured, and later copied, by the British. The expected Napoleonic invasion, however, never took place, and most of the towers were demilitarised in 1867. The

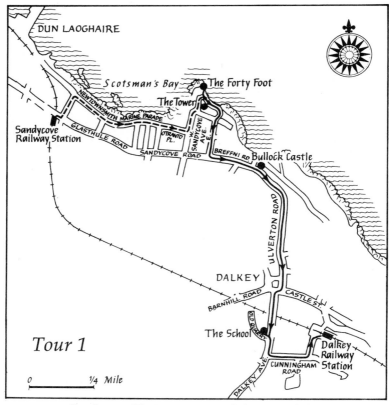

Tour 1

0   ¼ Mile

Sandycove Tower was one of those retained, along with
the nearby battery where frequent artillery practice was a
source of discomfort, according to Weston St John Joyce
(no relative), to nearby residents whose windows were
shattered by the concussions.

To their relief the positions were demilitarised in 1900,
and in 1904 the Tower was available for rent at the sum of
£8 a year. The letting was taken by Joyce's friend and the
model for Buck Mulligan, Oliver St John Gogarty, in
August 1904. Gogarty's plan was to establish the Tower as
an *omphalos* or new Delphi where he could invite other
young writers and kindred spirits to join him in the
preaching of a modern Hellenism and more convivial
pursuits. James Joyce, who arrived on 9 September, was

1. Sandycove Point in 1904. A rare photograph from *The Neighbourhood of Dublin*, looking eastwards from the coast road. The ladder may be seen beneath the door of the tower, and the structure visible to the left of the tower, behind the rooftop, was an outdoor privy.

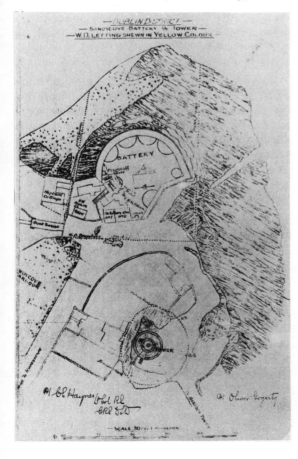

2. Sandycove Point in 1904: A map from the lease signed by Oliver Gogarty. The dotted line around the Tower and Battery shows the War Department boundary line with its boundary stones. The 'creek' of the bathing place can be seen to the right of the Battery.

probably more interested in having a roof over his head. His friendship with Gogarty was already cooling and he left precipitately during the night of 14–15 September, never to return.

Gogarty stayed in the Tower regularly, and continued to pay rent up to 1925. Many literary friends visited him there, including George Russell ('A.E.') who painted a picture on the roof, Padraic Colum, Seamus O'Sullivan, Arthur Griffith and possibly also W. B. Yeats, who was reluctantly persuaded to take a swim in the Forty Foot. The Tower might well be known now as 'Gogarty's Tower' had Joyce not used it as the setting for the opening of *Ulysses*. His implication that he himself had paid the rent effectively meant that he stole the Tower for posterity.

The James Joyce Museum, run by the Joyce Tower Society, was officially opened by Sylvia Beach, the publisher of *Ulysses*, on Bloomsday 1962. It is now owned and run by Dublin Tourism and is open daily from April to October (Monday–Saturday 10 a.m.–1 p.m., 2 p.m.–5 p.m.; Sunday 2.30 p.m.–6 p.m.) and by appointment with the Tourism Organisation (tel. 808571) during the rest of the year. The modern exhibition hall and entrance were added in 1978.

Pay admission at the entrance desk and go inside the Tower. At the back of the gunpowder magazine in the base is a narrow spiral staircase leading up to the top of the tower, where *Ulysses* begins.

3 'Stately, plump Buck Mulligan came from the stairhead, bearing a bowl of lather on which a mirror and a razor lay crossed. A yellow dressinggown, ungirdled, was sustained gently behind him on the mild morning air.' Around the central gunrest, which Mulligan mounts for his parody of the Mass, and the step beneath the parapet run two rails which supported a gun carriage, swivelling from the pivot in the centre.

Stephen Dedalus, 'displeased and sleepy', follows Mul-

4 ligan from the stairs and talks with him while he shaves, about their companion Haines and his nightmare about a black panther. Haines's real-life counterpart was

Gogarty's Anglo-Irish friend Samuel Chenevix Trench, and Joyce, as we shall see, had good cause to remember the nightmare. Mulligan then calls Stephen to look at 'The snotgreen sea. The scrotumtightening sea.'

5   'Stephen stood up and went over to the parapet. Leaning on it he looked down on the water and on the mailboat clearing the harbourmouth of Kingstown.' Kingstown, named to celebrate the departure of King George IV in 1821, reverted to its original name of Dun Laoghaire with the coming of Irish independence in 1922. To the east can be seen the Muglins, a small island with a beacon, and on the next point at Bullock is another Martello tower of almost identical design. To the north, on the far side of the bay, is Howth Head, where Bloom proposed to Molly. Nearby on Sandycove Point is the half-moon battery built with the Tower, beside the Forty Foot bathing place. According to Thom's Directory, most of the houses presently on Sandycove Point were there in Joyce's time. Stephen, however, can only look at 'the ring of bay and skyline' and compare it in his mind to the bowl into which his dying mother had vomited. Mulligan's teasing about

6 his appearance only makes his mood worse as they walk around the Tower arm in arm.

7   'They halted, looking towards the blunt cape of Bray Head that lay on the water like the snout of a sleeping whale.' Bray Head is not, in fact, visible from the Tower – it is to the south beyond Killiney, whose hill with an obelisk is on the skyline – and scholars continue to agonise over whether this is a genuine slip or a deliberate error. Some diehards have drawn comfort from the possibility that the word 'towards' does not necessarily mean that they were looking *at* the Head.

8   Following his argument with Stephen, Mulligan goes downstairs, leaving Stephen to brood alone while the sun, by now somewhere over the Muglins, disappears behind a

9 cloud. His reverie about his mother reaches an anguished climax just as Mulligan returns to bid him to breakfast.

10   Stephen descends halfway down the stairs to 'the gloomy domed livingroom of the tower'. To the left is the fireplace between the two window shafts (called 'barba-

cans' by Joyce); to the right is the heavy door opened by Haines to let in 'welcome light and bright air' from the sunny side of the building. It is locked now, and the huge key is on display downstairs. None of the original furniture (mainly supplied by Gogarty from his family home in Parnell Square) remains, but apparently there were shelves on the walls, a cooking range, and beds around the room.

It was here, on the night of 14 September 1904, that Joyce, Gogarty and Trench were sleeping when Trench had a nightmare about a black panther which he dreamed was crouching in the fireplace. Half-waking, he reached for a gun and loosed off a couple of shots to scare the beast away before going back to sleep. Gogarty promptly confiscated the gun. 'Leave the menagerie to me,' he said when Trench's nightmare returned, and fired the remaining bullets at the saucepans over Joyce's head. Joyce leapt out of bed, flung on his clothes and left the Tower immediately. He walked all the way into Dublin and appeared at the National Library at opening time. He never returned to the Tower.

The big door was the only way in and out of the Tower, and was approached by a step ladder attached to the
11 outside wall. As the three men begin their breakfast Haines sees the old woman coming with the milk, and they have time to exchange a page of dialogue before she reaches the top of the ladder.

The doorway was darkened by an entering form.
—The milk, sir!

12 Haines, anxious to try out his Irish on a native, speaks to her in Gaelic which Joyce does not attempt to reproduce. Haines's original, Trench, was a keen student of the Gaelic Revival and took every opportunity to air his Connemara Gaelic, which was unfortunately marred by a strong Oxford accent.
13 The milkwoman is paid her bill (somewhat reluctantly) by Mulligan and leaves. Mulligan, obviously hopeful of getting money or drink from his friends, urges Stephen to 'Hurry out to your school kip and bring us back some

14 money' and encourages Haines to add Stephen's Hamlet theory to his collection of Irish studies. Stephen embarrasses him by asking tactlessly 'Would I make any money by it?'

15 Mulligan gets dressed and the three leave the Tower to walk to the Forty Foot. Before following their path, it is worth lingering in the Tower to view the collection, which includes several of Joyce's possessions and manuscripts, first editions of *Ulysses* and other works, and all sorts of photographs, paintings and miscellaneous Joyceana. Joyce's piano, guitar and waistcoat may be seen, and one of the two death masks made by the sculptor Paul Speck in Zurich. Among the *Ulysses* trivia are a Plumtree's Potted Meat pot and an original photograph of Throwaway, the outsider which won the Ascot Gold Cup and indirectly led to Bloom's hasty departure from Barney Kiernan's. Literature, posters, cards etc. are available at the desk.

Leave the museum and turn left down the path along
16 the top of the cliff, where Mulligan chants his 'ballad of Joking Jesus' on the way to the bathing place.

17 Stephen follows with Haines, foreseeing correctly that Mulligan will obtain the key from him and prevent him returning to the Tower. He explains to Haines how he is the servant of two masters – Britain and the Roman Catholic Church – and a third 'who wants me for odd jobs'; this last, though unspecified, is probably Irish nationalism. In his mind he has a vision of the Church and its banishment of all those who dared contest its dogmas.

18 'They followed the winding path down to the creek. Buck Mulligan stood on a stone, in shirtsleeves, his unclipped tie rippling over his shoulder. A young man clinging to a spur of rock near him, moved slowly frogwise his green legs in the deep jelly of the water'.

The sign at the entrance to the bathing place once read, ambiguously, 'FORTY FOOT GENTLEMEN ONLY'. Nobody knows for certain why it is called the Forty Foot, since nothing in it has this measurement, but Mervyn Wall, who wrote a book about it, has suggested that it was named after the Fortieth Foot Regiment, which was once stationed at the battery, and whose soldiers may have established it. Visitors are generally less startled by the nudity of its elderly *habitués* than by their hardiness in braving the chilly waters at all seasons of the year. 'Gentlemen Only' is the custom rather than the rule.

19 As Stephen expected, Mulligan demands the key.

'—And twopence, he said, for a pint. Throw it here.' Mulligan and Haines arrange to meet him again at the Ship pub, where presumably he will be expected to buy them drink. He leaves them and walks back up the path on his way to Dalkey.

The most direct route, and the one which Stephen probably took, goes by way of Sandycove Avenue East and left along Breffni Road and Ulverton Road, passing Bullock Castle on the left. The castle, built in the thirteenth century, dates from the time when Bullock Harbour was the principal port of entry to Dublin for traders from abroad. Several castles in this area guarded the port and the lands of rich monasteries round about. The castle is now attached to Our Lady's Manor, a home for elderly people.

At the far end of Ulverton Road is the village of Dalkey. In Joyce's day it was the last stop on the tramline from Dublin; nowadays the No. 8 bus, running on the same route, has its terminus here. Dalkey has been celebrated by two later Irish writers, Flann O'Brien and Hugh Leonard. Flann O'Brien's comic novel *The Dalkey Archive* (1964) involves a demented scientist named De Selby who plans to destroy the world with a patent substance known as DMP; also featured is James Joyce, who is discovered alive and well and claiming that *Ulysses* was a smutty book compiled under his name by a ghostwriter. Hugh Leonard's plays *Da* (1973) and *A Life* (1980) and his autobiography *Home Before Night* (1979) lovingly recreate the Dalkey of his childhood in the 1930s.

Stephen's route continues up Dalkey Avenue as far as the corner with Old Quarry on the right.

Nestor, 9.45 a.m.

20   —You, Cochrane, what city sent for him?
        —Tarentum, sir.

On the corner of Dalkey Avenue and Old Quarry, just a mile from the Tower, is a large very rambling house named 'Summerfield'. It was once the home of the poet Denis Florence McCarthy (1817–82), whose *Poetical Works* are among the volumes on Bloom's bookshelf (p. 582). McCarthy was given to begetting children as well as verses, and the multiple extensions to the house were added as his family grew.

In 1904 part of the house was used by the Clifton School, run by Mr Deasy's original, Francis Irwin, where Joyce taught for a short while. It is convenient to imagine that the handsome porch was the one referred to by Joyce, that the playfield was situated on the tennis court behind the trees to the right of the gate, and that the stone pillars once bore 'lions couchant'. In fact, the school-house was at the other end of the building, in the section now called 'Greenbanks' with a separate gate on Old Quarry. The playfield was where Old Quarry road is now, but of porch, path, pillars and trees there is no sign on this side. The house and grounds are private.

As the opening episode was imbued with religion, so this one is preoccupied with history. Stephen is teaching history to a class of boys whose names – Cochrane, Armstrong, Talbot and so on – reflect their background. They are all of wealthy middle-class 'West British' families, Protestant probably and more English than Irish. 'Welloff people, proud that their eldest son was in the navy. Vico road, Dalkey.'

21   Neither Stephen nor his pupils are particularly interested in the lesson, and they switch to English and a
22   passage from Milton's *Lycidas*. When the lesson ends he asks them a riddle which they cannot answer and to which the solution is a baffling one:

Stephen, his throat itching, answered:
—The fox burying his grandmother under a hollybush.

He stood up and gave a shout of nervous laughter to
which their cries echoed dismay.

As countless Joyce scholars have skirted quietly round this
one it seems clear that the boys were not expected to
understand it either.

23   The boys leave for hockey and Stephen stays to help
24 Sargent with his sums before joining Mr Deasy in his
study to get paid. In the study, which resembles a little
25 museum with its cases of exhibits and curios, the theme of
26 history dominates their conversation. Mr Deasy is proud
of his unionist background and the traditions inherited
from the English; Stephen thinks of it as a pageant of
bigotry and violence.

27   Mr Deasy finishes a letter for the newspapers which he
wishes Stephen to pass on to *The Evening Telegraph*. It
proposes a solution to the foot-and-mouth disease and is
28 phrased in a series of time-worn clichés. He then delivers a
diatribe against the jews which prompts a direct compari-
son of their views of history. To Stephen, it 'is a nightmare
from which I am trying to awake'. For Mr Deasy, 'All
human history moves towards one great goal, the man-
ifestation of God.'

29   Stephen takes his leave of Mr Deasy, and has got as far
30 as the road when Deasy follows him with a final word:

—Ireland, they say, has the honour of being the only
country which never persecuted the jews. Do you know
that? No. And do you know why?
He frowned sternly on the bright air.
—Why, sir? Stephen asked, beginning to smile.
—Because she never let them in, Mr Deasy said
solemnly.

Leaving the school, Stephen in all probability walks to
Dalkey Station via Dalkey Avenue and Cunningham
Road, and takes the train to Lansdowne Road Station.
From here he would turn right along Lansdowne Road
and Newbridge Avenue (where *Hades* begins) to Sandymount Road, where he walked down Leahy's Terrace to
the sea. Tour 2a begins at this point.

Nausikaa, Proteus
Hades, Wandering Rocks (vii, iv)

Stephen Dedalus probably arrives on the train from Dalkey at Lansdowne Road Station just opposite the celebrated rugby ground. James Joyce was living quite near
this station in June 1904, at rented rooms in 60 Shelbourne
Road, just west of the railway line.

Turn right on leaving the station and follow Lansdowne
Road across the River Dodder. Taking the most direct
route towards the beach would have brought Stephen
along the next road to the left, Newbridge Avenue, and
past No. 9 on the left hand side, where, a short while later,
the mourners were to gather in the coaches to follow
Paddy Dignam on his last journey. Tour 2b, along the
funeral route, starts from this point. To follow Tour 2a,
continue across Tritonville Road and along Sandymount
Road as far as Leahy's Terrace.

2a *Nausikaa*, 8.25 p.m.

284   The summer evening had begun to fold the world in its
mysterious embrace. Far away in the west the sun was
setting and the last glow of all too fleeting day lingered
lovingly on sea and strand . . .

Mr Bloom, who at this stage of the story was last seen
leaving Barney Kiernan's at high speed with the citizen's
dog in hot pursuit, has spent the past couple of hours
visiting Paddy Dignam's widow in Newbridge Avenue.
Afterwards he makes his way, presumably by Leahy's
Terrace, to the beach. It is now almost sunset, which took
place at 8.27 p.m.

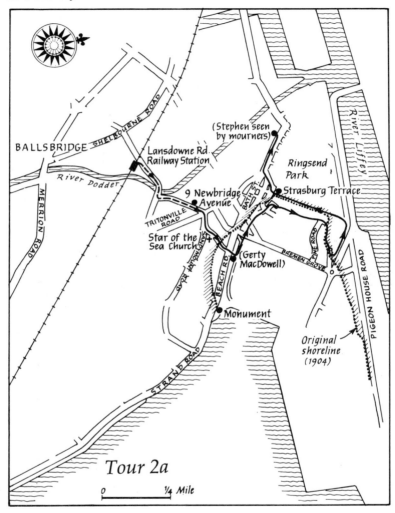

In 1904 the present Beach Road did not exist. Leahy's Terrace was shorter than it is now, stretching about as far as the wall of Cosy Lodge, and ended in a set of steps leading down to the beach. All of the strand between Beach Road and Pigeonhouse Road has since been re-claimed and built on, making it difficult to locate precisely any of the activities described in this area. Press on, however, across the Beach Road and over the low wall on the other side.

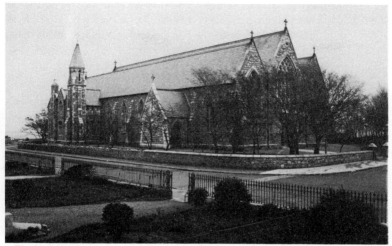

3. The Star of the Sea Church, Sandymount. Five trees, no longer young, now stand alongside the railings of Leahy's Terrace in the foreground. On the extreme left of the picture can just be seen the gap in the wall at the top of the steps leading to the strand.

It seems clear that this chapter is set opposite Leahy's Terrace, within sight of the church of St Mary, Star of the Sea, and close enough to hear the singing inside. Gerty MacDowell, Cissy Caffrey and Edy Boardman are seated here on the rocks with baby Boardman in his pram and the twins Jacky and Tommy Caffrey at work on a sandcastle.
285 '. . . and Master Tommy would have it right go wrong that it was to be architecturally improved by a frontdoor like the Martello tower had.' The Martello tower in question, similar in pattern to the one in Sandycove, would probably be the Sandymount Tower, some distance away just round the corner of the shore on Strand Road.

The first half of the episode is told from the point of view of Gerty MacDowell, in what Joyce described to his friend Frank Budgen as 'a namby-pamby jammy marma-lady drawersy (alto là!) style with effects of incense, mariolatry, masturbation, stewed cockles, painter's pal-ette, chitchat, circumlocutions, etc. etc.' It reads in the same way as the cheap romantic magazines which

286 obviously take up a large part of Gerty's reading time. As the heroine, she is described in detail both in appearance
287 and in dress. 'Gerty was dressed simply but with the instinctive taste of a votary of Dame Fashion . . .' These details extend as far as her undergarments, a subject for
288 which Joyce had a special affection.
289 Gerty's reverie of romance is interrupted by Tommy Caffrey's bold behaviour and the remarks of her companions.

290 —I'd like to give him something, she said, so I would, where I won't say.
—On the beeoteetom, laughed Cissy merrily. Gerty MacDowell bent down her head and crimsoned at the idea of Cissy saying an unladylike thing like that out loud she'd be ashamed of her life to say, flushing a deep rosy red, and Edy Boardman said she was sure the gentleman opposite heard what she said.

291 The gentleman opposite turns out to be Leopold Bloom, who participates more actively soon afterwards
292 when Jacky Caffrey kicks the ball towards him; he throws it back and it lands at Gerty's feet. She looks at him and
293 their eyes meet. 'And while she gazed her heart went pitapat. Yes, it was her he was looking at, and there was meaning in his look.'
294 The background to their exchange is the Benediction
295 in the Star of the Sea church nearby. Gerty swings her foot in time to the *Tantum Ergo*, showing off her stockings, and realises 'that she had raised the devil in him'.
296 Bloom's hand is in his pocket and he removes it nervously when Cissy Caffrey approaches to ask him the time. It is getting dark. 'Edy began to get ready to go and it was high time for her [. . .] because it was a long way along the strand to where there was the place to push up the pushcar . . .'
Access to the beach from the higher shore was limited to a number of points where roads or public land met the beach. The steps from Leahy's Terrace were unsuitable for a pushcar so a gentler slope had to be found, possibly in the direction of Bath Street.

297 Cissy and Edy get the children ready to go. 'And she
298 could see far away the lights of the lighthouses so picturesque . . .' The lighthouses, now out of view behind trees
and buildings, include the Bailey lighthouse on Howth
Head, the Poolbeg lighthouse on the South Wall and the
lighthouses on Dun Laoghaire harbour to the southeast.

299 As they prepare to leave, the twins see the fireworks
shooting up into the sky behind the church, from the
bazaar in Ballsbridge to the southwest. Everyone runs
down the strand for a better view, except for Gerty, who
remains behind, aware that Bloom is gazing at her. 'His
hands and face were working and a tremour went over
her'. Leaning back to look at the fireworks, she knowingly
reveals her legs to him.

300 As a Roman candle flies over the trees Gerty leans
further back, displaying 'her other things too, nainsook
knickers, the fabric that caresses the skin'. Bloom is given
'a full view high up above her knee' and can contain
himself no longer. The fireworks express his sensations.
'And then a rocket sprang and bang shot blind blank and
O! then the Roman candle burst and it was like a sigh of O!
and everyone cried O!O! in raptures and it gushed out of it
a stream of rain gold hair threads and they shed and ah!
they were all greeny dewy stars falling with golden, O so
lovely, O, soft, sweet, soft!'

301 Cissy calls Gerty and she rises to go. 'She walked with a
certain quiet dignity characteristic of her but with care and
very slowly because – because Gerty MacDowell was . . .
Tight boots? No. She's lame. O!'
Joyce, no doubt with tongue in cheek, labelled the technique of this chapter 'Tumescence and detumescence'.
Everything mounts up to a climax in a grand explosion;
deflation swiftly follows, beginning with the revelation
of Gerty's defect and the switch from her thoughts
302 to Bloom's point of view. He is left alone, thinking
303 about the ways of women and recomposing his wet
304 shirt. 'My fireworks. Up like a rocket, down like a stick'.
305 Thoughts of women put him in mind of babies and he
reminds himself to visit Mrs Purefoy in the maternity
306 hospital. Some of Gerty's perfume lingers in the air. 'What

is it? Heliotrope? No. Hyacinth? Hm. Roses, I think. She'd like scent of that kind. Sweet and cheap: soon sour.'

307 He muses about perfume and personal odours and smells himself. 'Almonds or. No. Lemons it is. Ah no, that's the soap.'

308 His eye is caught by the flashing of the Bailey light-house, and he recalls proposing to Molly on Howth Head.

309 'Where we. The rhododendrons.' Watching the bat flying about, he thinks sleepily about animals, migrating birds

310 and sailors. 'A last lonely candle' explodes over the bazaar as nine o'clock approaches. On the shore, the postman does his round, the lamplighter lights the gaslight outside the church, and a newsboy circulates with the *Evening Telegraph*, attracting the attention of someone in the Dignam house, probably Master Patrick Dignam, who was looking forward on page 206 to seeing the account of the funeral in the paper.

Joyce was particular enough about his details to write a letter to his Aunt Josephine Murray (Aunt Sara's original) asking 'whether there are trees (and of what kind) behind the Star of the Sea church in Sandymount visible from the shore'.

Another light twinkles at him, from the Kish lightship far out on the horizon. It has since been replaced by a permanent lighthouse, which was built in Dun Laoghaire harbour and towed out to be sunk in position on the sandbank.

311 Tired, Mr Bloom considers his plans. 'Go home. Too late for *Leah*. *Lily of Killarney*. No. Might be still up. Call to the hospital to see. Hope she's over. Long day I've had.'

312 Finding a bit of stick, he idly starts to write a message in the sand for Gerty in case she comes that way again: 'I . . .

313 AM. A. . . .', then stops and rubs it out. The noise of the cuckoo clock striking nine in the priest's house as the chapter ends suggests that 'CUCKOLD' is the word he left unwritten. Meanwhile Bloom has allowed himself to nod off for a few minutes. Later he will leave the beach and take the tram as far as Holles Street for his intended visit to Mrs Purefoy.

Proteus, 10.40 a.m.

31 'Ineluctable modality of the visible: at least that if no more, thought through my eyes. Signatures of all things I am here to read, seaspawn and seawrack, the nearing tide, that rusty boot.'

We return to the morning and Stephen Dedalus, who passes on his way across the strand from Leahy's Terrace the very spot where Bloom was later to come to rest. His thoughts are dominated by the theme of change, as it relates to space (the modality of the visible) and time (the modality of the audible).

The strand itself has been subject to a great deal of change since 1904. Then, it was bounded to the north by the Pigeonhouse Road and to the west by the main drainage embankment along the edge of Ringsend Park, which was at that time in the process of construction. Now, the nearest sand is a good hundred yards away to the southeast, where a standing stone on the shore, designed by Cliodna Cussen and erected in 1983, is dedicated to James Joyce. A smaller stone aligned with it points in the direction of sunrise on the winter solstice. The nearby strand was investigated by Danis Rose, who used the evidence of its seawrack, seaspawn, shells and shingle to plot the course of Stephen's walk.*

'Stephen closed his eyes to hear his boots crush crackling wrack and shells. You are walking through it howsomever. I am, a stride at a time. A very short space of time through very short times of space.'

Stephen is walking away from Leahy's Terrace. By the time he opens his eyes he is below the tidemark, about as far as the path now running parallel to Beach Road. The tide, approaching steadily across the flat strand, is still two hours from its full at 12.42. Looking about him, he observes the two women, the *Frauenzimmer*, who have followed him down from the terrace. 'Number one swung
32 lourdily her midwife's bag, the other's gamp poked in the

*'The Best Recent Scholarship in Joyce', *James Joyce Quarterly*, vol. 23, no. 3. (1986).

beach.' Prompted by the sight of the midwife, Stephen imagines himself connected back through all humanity to Eve by a succession of navelcords. 'The cords of all link back, strandentwining cable of all flesh.'

Meanwhile he is walking approximately northwestwards, following the line of the shore. Keep walking along the footpath towards Irishtown. 'His pace slackened. Here. Am I going to Aunt Sara's or not?' Stephen is heading in the direction of his aunt's house in Strasburg Terrace in Irishtown. In his mind's eye he pictures the scene if he should visit.

> I pull the wheezy bell of their shuttered cottage: and wait. They take me for a dun, peer out from a coign of vantage.
> —It's Stephen, sir.
> —Let him in. Let Stephen in.

His uncle Richie is the same Richie Goulding with whom Bloom dines at the Ormond hotel later in the day.

33 'Houses of decay, mine, his and all. You told the Clongowes gentry you had an uncle a judge and an uncle a general in the army. Come out of them, Stephen. Beauty is not there.'

34 Musing about the failure of his family and of his own aspirations, Stephen walks onward. Cross Bremen Grove to a triangular patch containing the Irish Mercantile Marine Memorial, and cross again towards the nearest of the brightly painted Corporation houses. Nicknamed 'Toytown', this development won a major European environmental award when it was built in 1982. Follow Kerlogue Road towards Ringsend Park.

> The grainy sand had gone from under his feet. His boots trod again a damp crackling mast, razorshells, squeaking pebbles . . .

The backdoors which he sees are probably those in the area ahead and to his left in Strand Street. Ahead, across Ringsend Park, he can see the 'wigwams' of Ringsend on the Liffey docks. 'Ringsend', wrote Weston St John Joyce in 1912, 'though now presenting a decayed and unattractive appearance, was formerly a place of considerable importance, having been nearly two hundred years in conjunction with the Pigeonhouse harbour, the principal packet station in Ireland for communication with Great Britain. The transfer of the packet service, however to Howth and Kingstown in the early part of last century, deprived Ringsend of its principal source of revenue, and consigned it henceforth to poverty and obscurity.'

'He halted. I have passed the way to aunt Sara's. Am I not going there? Seems not. No one about. He turned northeast and crossed the firmer sand towards the Pigeonhouse.' Although Strasburg Terrace is now only a short distance ahead of Stephen, he appears to have overshot the access point – a set of steps or a ramp – leading from the beach up to the shore. The route northeast leads across the present sports ground, parallel to the boundary of Ringsend Park, in the direction of the Pigeonhouse Road. The name 'the Pigeonhouse' refers variously either to the fort or to a house standing in the grounds of the electricity power station. Originally on the site was a large strongly constructed wooden house built by the port authorities in the early eighteenth century to hold stores and serve as a watch house. The caretaker, a man named Pidgeon, made his fortune by developing the premises as a popular and exclusive hostelry whose name outlived both Pidgeon and the house.

35   The name reminds Stephen of a passage from Léo Taxil's blasphemous *La Vie de Jésus*, and in turn of his Paris friend Patrice Egan who told him about it. He recalls his year in Paris and his return, summoned by

a blue French telegram, curiosity to show:
—Nother dying come home Father.

The 'misprint' was restored only in the Corrected Text.

'His feet marched in sudden proud rhythm over the sand furrows, along by the boulders of the south wall. He stared at them proudly, piled stone mammoth skulls. Gold light on sea, on sand, on boulders.' Cross Pine Road and follow the footpath which runs along the boundary below

the pumping station. This is the route that Stephen takes alongside the boulders of the south wall, while he thinks of
36 Paris and Patrice's father Kevin Egan, the exiled Fenian.
37 This leads him directly towards the sea and he soon stops when his feet begin to sink in the wet sand. 'Turning, he scanned the shore south, his feet sinking again slowly in new sockets. The cold domed room of the tower waits.' The Sandycove Tower is out of sight beyond Dun Laoghaire, but Stephen's thoughts may have been prompted by the sight of the similar tower on the other side of the strand. Now, of course, the entire view is obscured by the nearby houses.

'The flood is following me. I can watch it flow past from here. Get back then by the Poolbeg road to the strand there. He climbed over the sedge and eely oarweeds and sat on a stool of rock, resting his ashplant in a grike.' How far along the edge of the beach Stephen has walked is uncertain, but it is unlikely in the limited time span of this episode that he has got much further than the point where Pine Road now meets Bremen Grove, south of the old coastguard station which stands nearby. Beyond here the original coastline is lost under new roads and a fenced-off field. Behind Stephen as he sits is the long mole running out to the Pigeonhouse. In front of him he sees a dead dog and a sunken boat; approaching from the distance he sees a live dog and, further off, two figures whom he takes at first for the two midwives until he realises that the dog
38 belongs to them. Gradually they come near enough for him to distinguish 'A woman and a man. I see her skirties. Pinned up, I bet.' He sees from their activities that they are cocklepickers. This area, as Weston St John Joyce noted, 'was at one time noted for its cockles and shrimps'. The shrimps disappeared after the hard winter of 1741. 'The cockles, however, still remain for those who have the courage to eat them, and occasionally yield a rich harvest to the professional cocklepickers.'

39 The dog passes nearby and digs in the sand, its claws reminding Stephen of a panther and Haines's nightmare; he then recalls his own dream: 'Open hallway. Street of harlots. Remember, Haroun al Raschid. I am almosting it.

That man led me, spoke. I was not afraid. The melon he had he held against my face . . .'

The cocklepickers pass, 'the ruffian and his strolling mort', and Stephen thinks of a verse written in the 'rogues'
40 rum lingo' of these gypsy folk. A moment later a poem of his own begins to form in his mind.

He comes, pale vampire, through storm his eyes, his bat sails bloodying the sea, mouth to her mouth's kiss.

Hunting in his pockets for paper, he finds Deasy's letter and tears off the blank end on which to write the poem.
41 When it is finished, he lies back contemplating the toes of his borrowed boots, and notices the rising tide flowing in from Cock Lake, a pool out in the Strand. 'In long lassoes from the Cock lake the water flowed full, covering green-goldenly lagoons of sand, rising, flowing. My ashplant will float away. I shall wait. No, they will pass on, passing, chafing against the low rocks, swirling, passing. Better get this job over quick. Listen: a fourworded wavespeech: seesoo, hrss, rsseeiss, ooos.'

The 'wavespeech' reproduces the sound of a wave breaking, spreading and receding back across the flat strand; though some scholars have conjectured that Stephen has stood up and is taking the opportunity to urinate. Looking at the water, his thoughts turn to the drowned man, 'Bag of corpsegas sopping in foul brine,'
42 and the 'seachange' he is undergoing. Finally he takes his ashplant, preparing to go. He has left his handkerchief in the Tower, and picks his nose rather than blowing it. Looking behind him over the road, he sees the 'high spars of a threemaster', moving up the Liffey into the port of Dublin, 'a silent ship'.

Stephen plans to return by going up onto 'the Poolbeg road', i.e. the Pigeonhouse Road which also leads out along the two-mile pier to the lighthouse which Joyce elsewhere calls 'the Poolbeg flasher'. Now painted bright red, it was black in 1904. From the road, he can follow the directions advised by Weston St John Joyce. 'Returning along the Wall, we take the turn on the left along the Rathmines and Pembroke Main Drain embankment [i.e.

along the edge of Ringsend Park], which has reclaimed from the sea a considerable tract now being laid out as a public park.' (Nowadays it is not so easy to follow this route. Instead, turn back along the path you are on directly towards the boundary of the Park.)

This route is the most direct one to lead him to Irishtown via Strand Street and the Irishtown Road. It also happens to bring him straight past Aunt Sara's front door in Strasburg Terrace. He reaches Irishtown in time to be spotted by Mr Bloom between Watery Lane (now Dermot O'Hurley Avenue) and the library on the corner. From here he walks into town in the trail of the funeral procession, stopping in College Green to send a telegram to Mulligan before going on to the newspaper office.

To follow the entire route of the funeral cortège, start by returning from Strasburg Terrace to 9 Newbridge Avenue and then provide yourself with a carriage or other vehicle.

2b *Hades*, 11 a.m.

72 'Martin Cunningham, first, poked his silkhatted head into the creaking carriage and, entering deftly, seated himself.'

With the introduction of one-way traffic systems it is no longer possible to follow the entire route of the funeral procession by car or horse-drawn cab. Ideally, it may be done by bicycle, dismounting to follow one-way streets on foot where they occur.

The hearse and carriages leave from outside 9 Newbridge Avenue and turn left onto the cobbles of the tramline along Tritonville Road. Carole Brown and Leo Knuth, in a special study of this chapter* have worked out that in all likelihood Bloom is sitting on the left hand side, facing forward. Opposite him is Simon Dedalus, facing rearwards. Jack Power is sitting beside Bloom and Martin Cunningham is in the seat diagonally opposite.

—What way is he taking us? Mr Power asked through both windows.

—Irishtown, Martin Cunningham said. Ringsend, Brunswick street.

Bloomsday: The Eleventh Hour – A Quest for the Vacant Place (A Wake Newslitter Press, 1981).

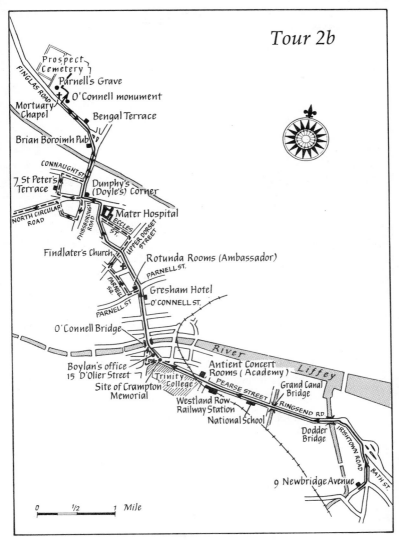

Tour 2b

Prospect Cemetery
Parnell's Grave
FINGLAS ROAD
O'Connell monument
Mortuary Chapel
Bengal Terrace
Brian Boroimh Pub
CONNAUGHT ST.
7 St Peter's Terrace
Dunphy's (Doyle's) Corner
NORTH CIRCULAR ROAD
PHIBSBOROUGH ROAD
ECCLES ST.
Mater Hospital
UPPER DORSET STREET
Findlater's Church
Rotunda Rooms (Ambassador)
PARNELL ST.
PARNELL SQ.
Gresham Hotel
O'CONNELL ST.
PARNELL ST.
O'Connell Bridge
River Liffey
Boylan's office
15 D'Olier Street
Antient Concert Rooms (Academy)
Site of Crampton Memorial
Trinity College
Grand Canal Bridge
L. PEARSE STREET
RINGSEND RD.
Westland Row Railway Station
National School
Dodder Bridge
IRISHTOWN ROAD
BATH ST.
9 Newbridge Avenue

0   1/2   1 Mile

73   Proceeding along Irishtown Road into Ringsend, the carriage passes Watery Lane (now Dermot O'Hurley Avenue) on the left and then swerves from the tramtrack to travel to the left of the island where a public library now stands. This was probably to avoid the major road works

consequent upon the laying down of the new main drainage scheme. At this point 'Mr Bloom at gaze saw a lithe
young man, clad in mourning, a wide hat.' He recognises
Stephen Dedalus and points him out to his father.

4. Irishtown Road. Rattling along this 'cobbled causeway', the funeral carriages pass Dodder
Terrace here on the left. At the junction with Bath Street a little further on, the road veers left into
Irishtown. Behind the houses in the background, Ringsend Park is under construction.

74   The carriage turns the corner onto Ringsend Road and
crosses the humpbacked bridge over the Dodder. A little
further on it stops.

> —What's wrong?
> —We're stopped.
> —Where are we?
> Mr Bloom put his head out of the window.
> —The grand canal, he said.

The bridge over the grand canal was designed to be
raised to allow access to the inner canal dock, and this was
presumably the reason for the brief halt. On the left beside
the bridge is Boland's Mill, one of the buildings occupied
by rebel troops in the Easter Rising in 1916. The comman-
der of this stronghold, born in the same year as Joyce, was
Eamon de Valera, who later became Ireland's foremost
political leader. The gasworks were across the canal to the

right, and the Cats' and Dogs' Home is ahead and to the left.

75 Resuming their journey, the mourners travel over the canal and along Great Brunswick Street (now Pearse
76 Street). They pass on the left St Andrew's National School and Meade's timberyard on the corner of South Cumberland Street, then the 'hazard' or cab rank beside the railway station. 'An hour ago I was passing there,' thinks Bloom.

On the right is the Academy Cinema, formerly the Antient Concert Rooms, which features in Joyce's story 'A Mother' in *Dubliners*. Joyce himself sang there in a concert on 27 August 1904, sharing the bill with such notables as J. C. Doyle and the great Irish tenor John McCormack – both of whom are to take part in Blazes Boylan's concert tour with Molly Bloom. A project is at present under way to restore the building as a theatre, concert hall and function venue as it was in Joyce's time.

Next to the Academy is 'the bleak pulpit of saint Mark's' where Oscar Wilde was baptised in 1854. Further up the street on the left was the Queen's Theatre, now replaced by a modern office block. The Abbey theatre company took up a fifteen-year residence there in 1951 after the old Abbey was destroyed by fire. On the right at No. 27, on the wall above the shop-front, may be seen bas-relief portraits of the 1916 leader Patrick Pearse and his brother Willie, who lived here. The soaring florentine tower beyond it belongs to the Fire Station.

As they near Boylan's office Bloom thinks helplessly about Molly's assignation. 'He's coming in the afternoon. Her songs. Plasto's. Sir Philip Crampton's memorial fountain bust. Who was he?' The Crampton Memorial, one of Dublin's more extraordinary monuments, stood in the junction at the end of Pearse Street until its semi-collapse in 1959. Because of the botanical nature of the structure, it was popularly known as 'the Cauliflower'. It commemorated Sir Philip Crampton (1777–1858), the Irish Surgeon General. In its place now stands a stone pillar by Cliodna Cussen, commemorating the fact that this was the original site of the 'Long Stone' erected by the Vikings.

5. The Crampton Memorial. This late photograph shows the back of the sculpture. On the other side, Sir Philip's bust faced up Pearse Street, towards the approaching funeral cortège.

The procession turns right along D'Olier Street (traffic nowadays must continue to Westmoreland Street), passing Blazes Boylan outside the Red Bank Restaurant on the right. The restaurant has since been transformed into the shrine of the Blessed Sacrament, but careful observers may see the carvings of lobsters and other delicacies on the wall outside.

(188)   *Wandering Rocks vii* is set in Boylan's office, believed to be the Advertising Co. Ltd. at 15 D'Olier Street, now part
(189) of the *Irish Times* office on the left next to Fleet Street. His secretary, Miss Dunne, takes a phone call from Boylan, who is ringing from Thornton's fruit shop. She takes his instructions and passes on a message: 'Mr Lenehan, yes. He said he'll be in the Ormond at four.'

Detour for drivers: keep straight on from Pearse Street along College Street, turn right along Westmoreland Street and rejoin the funeral route at O'Connell Bridge.

77   'Smith O'Brien. Someone has laid a bunch of flowers there. Woman. Must be his deathday.' The statue of William Smith O'Brien, which once stood at the junction

of D'Olier Street, Westmoreland Street and O'Connell Bridge, has been moved further down O'Connell Street to stand between 'the hugecloaked Liberator's form' of Daniel O'Connell and the statue of Sir John Gray.

Passing over O'Connell Bridge, celebrated for being as wide as it is long, they proceed down O'Connell Street (formerly Sackville Street), Dublin's premier boulevard, now heavily occupied by fast-food restaurants. Recent moves to improve the standard of shop-fronts in the street are gaining ground. Outside Elvery's Elephant House, now Kentucky Fried Chicken, on the corner of Middle

78 Abbey Street, they spot Reuben J. Dodd and a story is told about the rescue of Dodd's son from the Liffey when he tried to drown himself. The BBC broadcast this section of the novel in the 1950s and thought it was a great joke when someone claiming to be Reuben J. Dodd Junior brought a libel suit against them. Dodd won his case.

79 'Dead side of the street this.' Bloom is looking at the west side of O'Connell Street north of the GPO as they approach the foundation stone of the present Parnell Monument (the statue by Augustus Saint Gaudens was unveiled in 1911, twenty years after Parnell's death). The dead are so dominant in this episode that it is appropriate to note the Gresham Hotel on the opposite side, where Gabriel and Gretta Conroy spent the night in 'The Dead'.

Another *Dubliners* location is the Rotunda Concert Rooms (now occupied by the European Mercantile Exchange) where Mr Duffy met Mrs Sinico in 'A Painful Case'. 'Two Gallants' starts here on 'the hill of Rutland Square', now Parnell Square. Oliver Gogarty's family home at No. 5, opposite the Gate Theatre, is marked by a plaque.

80 The men in the carriage discuss the morality of suicide; only Martin Cunningham knows that Bloom's father poisoned himself. They pass Findlater's Church on the left and continue up North Frederick Street, over Dorset Street and along Blessington Street into Berkeley Street.

Detour for drivers: turn left at the Parnell Monument and take the first turn right up Parnell Square West and Granby Row (where the National Wax Museum has a figure of James Joyce in its collection). Turn right again onto Dorset Street, pass Blessington Street and turn left up Eccles Street to rejoin the funeral route beside the Mater Hospital. 'The *Mater Misericordiae*. Eccles street. My house down there.'

As they turn the corner left onto the North Circular Road they are delayed by a herd of cattle being driven to 81 the docks. They drive onwards to the Phibsborough Road. 'Dunphy's corner. Mourning coaches drawn up drowning their grief. A pause by the wayside. Tiptop position for a pub.' Dunphy's Corner is now known as Doyle's Corner, and the pub bears the grandiose name of Sir Arthur Conan Doyle, an author of Irish descent whose Sherlock Holmes stories did for London what *Ulysses* was later to do for Dublin. The carriages turn right here onto the Phibsborough Road.

Detour for motorists: Wandering Rocks iv. Continue to the next turn right onto St Peter's Road. The Joyce family lived on the left-hand side at No. 7 (St Peter's Terrace) in 1904, and it is apparently here that the Dedalus family is in residence.

(186)   Katey and Boody Dedalus shoved in the door of the closesteaming kitchen.

– Did you put in the books? Boody asked.

Katey and Boody have come from the pawnbroker's in Gardiner Street via Eccles Street, and are given soup by their sister Maggy.

Turn right again round Dalymount Park and rejoin the funeral route on Phibsborough Road.

82   'In silence they drove along Phibsborough road. An empty hearse trotted by, coming from the cemetery: looks relieved. Crossguns bridge: the royal canal.'

The carriages cross the canal and pass the Brian Boroimhe pub. More commonly spelt Brian Boru, this ancient Irish king is another of the commemorated dead who punctuate the funeral route. He is famous for beating the Danes at the Battle of Clontarf in 1014, during which he himself was killed by a Dane who entered his tent while he was praying. Steering left for Finglas Road, they pass the Childs murder house at 36 Bengal Terrace (Mr Power wrongly points to the last house, number 38) on the right next to the graveyard. The murder of seventy-six-year-old Thomas Childs took place in September 1899; Childs's brother Samuel was charged but acquitted.

83   Finally they draw to a halt at the gate of the graveyard
84   and the mourners walk inside. 'First the stiff: then the friends of the stiff.' The cemetery is open Monday to Friday, 8 a.m.–5 p.m., on Saturday 8 a.m.–4 p.m. and on Sunday 10 a.m.–4 p.m.

Dominating the entrance to the cemetery is the O'Connell Monument, a round tower with a 'lofty cone'. To the left is the mortuary chapel, opposite to the tombs of priests and bishops and 'the cardinal's mausoleum'. The cardinal in question was Archbishop McCabe, referred to by Mr Dedalus in *A Portrait* as 'the tub of guts up in Armagh'. 'Billy with the lip' – Archbishop William Walsh – lies nearby.

Bloom meets Tom Kernan and Ned Lambert, who
85   were in the other carriage, and the mourners enter the
86   chapel for the funeral service. When it is over they follow the coffincart outside and to the left 'along a lane of sepulchres' and walk towards Dignam's grave. Whereabouts he is buried Joyce does not specify, but the probable area may be reached by walking down the cypress avenue by the chapel, turning left at the bottom, and right
87   at the next intersection. Bloom and Kernan follow Ned
88   Lambert and John Henry Menton, Dignam's employer, and they meet John O'Connell, the caretaker, on the way.
89   By the graveside Bloom looks towards the Botanic Gardens just behind the cemetery and muses about the effect
90   of the corpses on the soil. Nearby he sees the mystery mourner whose identity has intrigued Joyceans ever since. 'Now who is that lankylooking galoot over there in the macintosh? Now who is he I'd like to know?'
91   In the silence after the coffin is lowered he thinks about his own grave nearby: 'Mine over there towards Finglas, the plot I bought. Mamma, poor mamma, and little Rudy.'
92   Joe Hynes of the *Evening Telegraph* approaches Bloom, collecting a list of names.

—And tell us, Hynes said, do you know that fellow in the, fellow was over there in the . . .

He looked around.

—Macintosh. Yes, I saw him, Mr Bloom said. Where is he now?

—M'Intosh, Hynes said scribbling. I don't know who he is. Is that his name?

He moved away, looking about him.

The erratic results of Hynes's scribblings may be found on p.529.

Returning by the same route, turn right at the intersection and walk a short distance along the path. On the left is a mound surrounded by an iron railing and surmounted by a huge boulder of Wicklow granite inscribed simply PARNELL. A stone plaque reads 'The Chief's Grave'. Parnell was buried here in 1891. Mourners leaving his funeral plucked ivy leaves from the cemetery wall, and the anniversary of his death on 6 October was celebrated
93 every year thereafter as Ivy Day. Hynes and Mr Power go round this way. Just before Parnell's grave, on the opposite side of the path, is the grave of Joyce's parents. The tombstone, which stands three away from the path, was inscribed according to Joyce's own instructions after his father's death in 1931.

Mr Bloom meanwhile walks along 'by saddened angels, crosses, broken pillars, family vaults, stone hopes praying with upcast eyes, old Ireland's hearts and hands', musing over the tombstones and remembering that he will be visiting his father's grave in Ennis on 27 June, the anniversary of his death.

The centenary of Rudolph Bloom's suicide in 1986 was observed by the James Joyce Institute of Ireland, who travelled to Ennis to visit the grave. Unfortunately, as the gardener had long since stopped receiving his annual ten shillings, Rudolph's resting-place could not be found in the undergrowth.

94 'The gates glimmered in front; still open. Back to the world again. Enough of this place. Brings you a bit nearer every time. Last time I was here was Mrs Sinico's

funeral.' Mrs Sinico's funeral, as we learn elsewhere, took place on 17 October 1903. The story of her death under a train at Sydney Parade Station is related in 'A Painful Case' in *Dubliners*.

95   On the way to the gates Bloom joins Martin Cunningham and John Henry Menton. He points out a dinge in Menton's hat but is treated coldly by Menton, who dislikes him. 'Chapfallen', he follows them to the gates.

It is worth staying awhile to explore the cemetery. Many of Joyce's family, friends and associates lie here, along with famous Irish men and women of the past 150 years. Some of the most celebrated are to be found by the east side of the O'Connell Monument.

6. Glasnevin Cemetery. The picture shows the O'Connell Monument and the chapel.

From Glasnevin the mourners return by coach to the city centre, where *Aeolus* (Tour 6) takes place. Alternatively, retrace the funeral route to Doyle's Corner, continue through the crossroads and turn right at the next lights along Monck Road and Avondale Road. At the top of Avondale Road turn left to follow the North Circular Road as far as Phoenix Park to begin Tour 7.

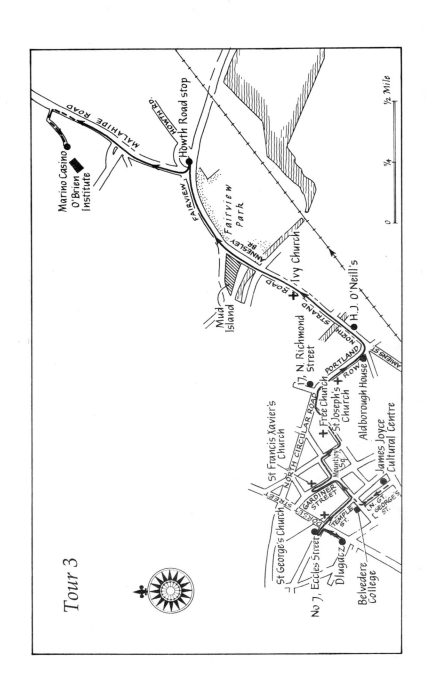

Tour 3

Marino Casino
O'Brien Institute

MALAHIDE ROAD

HOWTH RD.

Howth Road stop

FAIRVIEW

ANNESLEY BR.

Fairview Park

Ivy Church

Mud Island

STRAND ROAD

NORTH STRAND ROAD

H.J. O'Neill's

17, N. Richmond Street

PORTLAND ROW

Free Church

St Joseph's Church

Aldborough House

AMIENS

St Francis Xavier's Church

NORTH CIRCULAR ROAD

Mountjoy Sq.

James Joyce Cultural Centre

GARDINER STREET

DORSET STREET

TEMPLE ST.

LN. GT. GEORGE'S ST.

GT. GEORGE'S ST.

St George's Church

No 7, Eccles Street

Dlugacz

Belvedere College

0   ¼   ½ Mile

*Calypso, Ithaca, Penelope,
Wandering Rocks (iii, i, ii)*

Calypso, 8 a.m.

45 'Mr Leopold Bloom ate with relish the inner organs of beasts and fowls. He liked thick giblet soup, nutty gizzards, a stuffed roast heart, liverslices fried with crustcrumbs, fried hencods' roes. Most of all he liked grilled mutton kidneys which gave to his palate a fine tang of faintly scented urine.'

Leopold Bloom's house at 7 Eccles Street, one of the most famous addresses in world literature, is now no more. It was situated on the right hand side as you approach from Dorset Street, opposite No. 76. The front door was more or less exactly where the name of the Mater Private Hospital is displayed. Once the residence of Joyce's friend J. F. Byrne (the 'Cranly' of *A Portrait*), it was officially listed as vacant in the 1904 Thom's Directory. In later years it became derelict and was half-demolished in 1967. In 1982 it was finally levelled to make way for the present building. Bricks and other relics are scattered throughout the Joycean world.

The houses opposite give some idea of its appearance. The kitchen, where Mr Bloom appears at breakfast, was in the basement. He prepares his wife's breakfast tray, gives

46 the cat some milk, goes upstairs to the hall beside the bedroom on the ground floor, and comes out through the front door. 'He pulled the halldoor to after him very quietly, more, till the footleaf dropped gently over the threshold, a limp lid. Looked shut.'

The footleaf, a hinged flap serving as a draught excluder, may be seen on other doors nearby or indeed on the original door of 7 Eccles Street itself, which is preserved in the Bailey Restaurant in Duke Street.

'He crossed to the bright side, avoiding the loose cellar-flap of number seventy-five. The sun was nearing the steeple of George's Church.'

7. The Mater Hospital, Eccles Street. Bloom's house is near the bottom of the street in the terrace on the left-hand side, which has now been replaced by the private wing of the hospital.

The cellarflap was a heavy iron disc in the pavement covering the coalhole, through which coal deliveries could thus be made directly from the street. Some of the older Dublin cellarflaps are particularly ornate and of various styles. St George's Church in Hardwicke Place was designed by Francis Johnston in 1802, and Arthur Wellesley, the future Duke of Wellington, was married here in 1806 just before his involvement in the Peninsular War. The bells which chimed on every quarter hour of day or night are now reserved for times of worship. At the time of writing it seems likely that St George's will be relinquished by the Church of Ireland and its future role is uncertain.

47   Bloom approaches Larry O'Rourke's on the corner,
48 where he turns right into Dorset Street. The pub is now the James Joyce Lounge, no less. He passes St Joseph's

National School at No. 81–84, now occupied by the Garda Credit Union, and enters Dlugacz's the pork butcher's between the school and Blessington Street. This establishment, of which no record exists, was apparently invented by Joyce.

49   Bloom buys a pork kidney and returns towards Eccles Street, reading a pamphlet, picked from the butcher's pile of wrapping paper, which advertises a scheme by a planter's company named Agendath Netaim to buy land near

50 Galilee. A cloud – the same one, apparently, which Stephen sees from the Tower on page 8 – covers the sun and sheds gloom on his thoughts. Further gloom awaits him at his front door. 'Two letters and a card lay on the hallfloor. He stooped and gathered them. Mrs Marion Bloom. His quickened heart slowed at once. Bold hand. Mrs Marion.' He realises that the letter to his wife is from Blazes Boylan to make an assignation – a suspicion which is borne out when Molly does not open the letter in his presence.

51   His own letter, which he glances at in the kitchen, is from his daughter Milly in Mullingar. He puts the kidney on to cook and brings Molly's breakfast upstairs. Here he

52 pauses to explain the word 'metempsychosis' which she has found, strangely enough, in a trashy novel named *Ruby: the Pride of the Ring* (identified as a novel by Amye Reade in which, however, the word does not appear*).

53 Smelling the burning kidney, he hurries downstairs to eat

54 breakfast and reread Milly's letter. After breakfast he goes

55 out through the backdoor, armed with an old number of

56 *Titbits*, and heads for the outdoor lavatory in the garden rather than 'fag up the stairs to the landing'. 'Asquat on the cuckstool' he reads the prize story by Philip Beaufoy

57. before using it to wipe himself. As he emerges, the church bells chime at quarter to nine.

    Soon afterwards he leaves to walk to the quays, probably by the same route which he and Stephen follow in reverse in *Ithaca*.

*'The Discovery of *Ruby*', Mary Power, *James Joyce Quarterly*, vol. 18, no. 2.

Ithaca, 1 a.m.

544 'What parallel courses did Bloom and Stephen follow returning?'

545 The itinerary described at the beginning of the episode, leading from Beresford Place via Gardiner Street, Mountjoy Square, Gardiner Place, Temple Street and Hardwicke Place to Eccles Street, may be taken as a variation from Tour 4.

The chapter, written in the form of a catechism, is at times ludicrously pedantic in style. It also supplies us with the vast bulk of the factual information that can be obtained about Bloom and, to a lesser extent, Stephen.

546 Arriving at his front door, Bloom realises that he has forgotten to transfer his latchkey to the pocket of his funeral suit (a fact of which he was aware when he went to the butcher's in the morning). 'Bloom's decision?' – 'A stratagem.' He climbs over the railings, down into the
547 area, and enters through the basement door. Stephen is brought in through the front door and down into the
548/9 kitchen. Bloom puts on the kettle, finally uses the lemon
550 soap to wash his hands, and offers Stephen a wash which he declines ('his last bath having taken place in the month
551 of October of the preceding year'). On the dresser he
552 discovers traces of Boylan's visit: the fruit basket, a half empty bottle of port, and 'Four polygonal fragments of two lacerated scarlet betting tickets, numbered 8 87, 88 6.' He realises at this point the coincidences during the day which prophesied Throwaway's victory in the Gold Cup race.

553 Bloom makes cocoa and they drink it. We learn of
554 Bloom's early literary compositions, the relationship be-
555 tween his age (thirty-eight) and Stephen's (twenty-two),
556–8 and other comparisons and links between them. Bloom
559 talks of his ideas for effective advertising; Stephen sug-
560 gests an advertisement featuring a piece of paper with 'Queen's Hotel' written on it. Unknown to him, Bloom's father poisoned himself in the Queen's Hotel in Ennis, of
561 which he was the proprietor. Stephen tells Bloom 'The

562 Parable of the Plums' which he related earlier in the day
563 outside the newspaper office; they discuss famous Jews
564 and compare the Jewish and Irish alphabets and languages
565 (of which neither of them has any practical knowledge).
566 Stephen chants 'in a modulated voice a strange legend,'
567 the tale of little Harry Hughes, who had his head cut off by
568 'a jew's daughter, all dressed in green.' Disturbed, Bloom
569 thinks about his own daughter Milly.

570 Bloom invites Stephen to stay overnight, but his invita-
571 tion is declined. He returns Stephen his money, and they
discuss the possibility of meeting for further conversations
572 and mutual instruction. They go out through the back-
573 door into the garden and observe the clear summer night
sky, 'The heaventree of stars hung with humid nightblue
fruit.'

574 Bloom's scientific mind discards this artistic spectacle
575 and views it prosaically enough as '. . . an infinity render-
able equally finite by the suppositious apposition of one or
more bodies equally of the same and of different magni-
576 tudes.' His contemplation of the universe is interrupted
577 by the sight of a light in the bedroom window. 'At
Stephen's suggestion, at Bloom's instigation both, first
Stephen, then Bloom, in penumbra urinated, their sides
contiguous, their organs of micturition reciprocally ren-
dered invisible by manual circumposition.'

578 Bloom lets Stephen out by the door into Eccles Lane.
Where he goes for the rest of the night is never even stated.
579 Alone, Bloom returns indoors, ascends the stairs and
enters the living room at the front, to find that the
580 furniture has been rearranged. He uses the Agendath
581 Netaim prospectus to light a cone of incense, and notices
582 that some of the books on the shelf are upside down. He
583 rearranges them, sits down and loosens his clothes.

584 The budget for 16 June 1904 is interesting. It reveals
that Bloom travelled by tram from town to Sandymount
after his bath, and from Sandymount to town between
Nausikaa and *Oxen of the Sun*. More intriguingly, the
account omits his trainfare to Nighttown, the ten shillings
he paid on page 455 and the further shilling for the
damaged lamp on page 478.

585-3   As a relaxation before retiring he lets himself think about his ultimate ambition to settle comfortably in a well-appointed residence, and about schemes to enable
592-3   him to afford it. He opens a drawer to place in it his letter from Martha Clifford, whose name and address are also in the drawer, written in a cryptogram which clearly translates as MARTHA/CLIFFORD/DOLPHINS/BARN. J. F. Byrne, a later occupant of Bloom's house, was an expert on cyphers. This drawer contains a multitude of miscellaneous objects, from cameo brooches to erotic
594   postcards. The other drawer is reserved for certificates
595   and important documents, some relating to Bloom's
596   father, whom they bring to his mind. The financial docu-
597   ments are a security against a situation of poverty, which can only be precluded by death or departure. The possibi-
598   lities of his departure are considered, including a Missing Person advertisement with his description ('height 5 ft 9½ inches, full build, olive complexion').

599-600   He reviews the day briefly and, 'gathering multi-coloured multiform multitudinous garments', goes into
601   the bedroom where he puts on his nightshirt and enters the bed. He and Molly have their heads at opposite ends of the bed. 'What did his limbs, when gradually extended, encounter? New clean bedlinen, additional odours, the presence of a human form, female, hers, the imprint of a human form, male, not his, some crumbs, some flakes of potted meat, recooked, which he removed.' Bloom finally finds himself able to consider Boylan's intrusion with equanimity. He is, after all, merely
602-3   one of a series of men who have found Molly attractive. Bloom feels no sense of having 'been outraged by the adulterous violator'. It is, in a strange way, a victory for him.

604   He wakes Molly by a display of affection – 'He kissed the plump mellow yellow smellow melons of her rump, on each plump melonous hemisphere, in their mellow yellow
605   furrow' – and treats her to a carefully modified account of the day's activities. It is only now that we learn that Bloom and his wife have not had complete sexual intercourse
606   since before Rudy's birth more than ten years ago, and

that in recent months Molly has taken to questioning Bloom every time he goes out.

607   Finally Bloom's thoughts melt into confusion and he drifts off to sleep, dreaming about another traveller, Sinbad the Sailor. 'Where?' the last question asks. The answer is a full stop.

Penelope, 1.45 a.m.

608–44   'Yes because he never did a thing like that before as ask to get his breakfast in bed with a couple of eggs . . .' Molly Bloom's soliloquy, which has been seen or heard in performance more often than any other episode of *Ulysses*, begins where *Ithaca* leaves off. It is divided into eight so-called sentences and is totally unpunctuated apart from one full stop at the end of the fourth sentence and one at the end of the final sentence, ending the book. The full stop on page 624 was in fact, only 'rediscovered' in the Corrected Text, and the appropriate thesis about its significance has still to appear. Its position suggests that it acts as a central hinge of some sort.

Because, as Frank Budgen remarks, 'her thoughts jostle one another like the citizens of an egalitarian republic', it is difficult to summarise the episode coherently. Her thoughts swirl about, returning frequently to Boylan and the events of the afternoon, but more and more consistently towards Bloom, whom she finds at turns irritating and endearing.

Much of Molly's day can be pieced together from her thoughts. During the morning, besides rearranging the furniture, she burned a lot of old newspapers and magazines, put the remainder up in the WC, and cleared some old overcoats out of the hall (p.621). In preparation for Boylan's visit she spent 'hours dressing and perfuming and combing' (p.611). At quarter past three, when Katey and Boody Dedalus passed by and the onelegged sailor was begging in the street, she was still in a state of undress whistling 'There is a charming girl I love' in the living room (p.615). Soon afterwards the messengerboy from Thornton's arrived with the port and peaches, and 'I was just beginning to yawn with nerves thinking he was trying to make a fool of me when I knew his tattarrattat at the door' (p.615).

Whether Boylan and Molly paused to rehearse the concert programme before getting down to the main business of the afternoon is not clear. The activity in the bedroom is graphically recalled on pages 611, 617, 620, 621, 633, 638 and 641, the general impression being one of action rather than affection. At some stage they took a break to drink port and eat potted meat. '. . . he had all he could do to keep himself from falling asleep after the last time after we took the port and potted meat it had a fine salty taste yes . . .' (p. 611)

Boylan also went out to buy an *Evening Telegraph* for the result of the race and came back 'swearing blazes because he lost 20 quid'. He tore up the betting tickets on the dresser where Bloom found them later.

Boylan left, slapping Molly's behind familiarly. After his departure she had a pork chop from Dlugacz's for tea and returned to bed, where she slept soundly until woken by the thunder at ten o'clock.

Boylan occupies relatively little of Molly's thoughts, which revolve mainly round her husband, day-to-day trivia and memories of her girlhood in Gibraltar, her boyfriend Harry Mulvey who kissed her under the Moorish wall, and another early lover, lieutenant Gardner. Her mind shifts from one man to another and the word 'he' can refer to two different men in one line. Her reverie is interrupted by her period – 'O jesus wait yes that thing has come on me yes now wouldnt that afflict you' – and pages 633–4 are delivered from the chamberpot. On page 637 she starts thinking about Stephen Dedalus and the possibility of his becoming a regular visitor. 'I suppose hes 20 or more Im not too old for him if hes 23 or 24'.

The unrefined Boylan is a write-off as far as romance is concerned – 'of course hes right enough in his way to pass the time as a joke' – and in the end it is Bloom that she thinks of and the day in 1888 when he proposed to her on Howth Head. '. . . and I thought well as well him as another and then I asked him with my eyes to ask again yes

and then he asked me would I yes to say yes my mountain
flower and first I put my arms around him yes and drew
him down to me so he could feel my breasts all perfume yes
and his heart was going like mad and yes I said yes I will
Yes.'

Wandering Rocks iii, 3.15 p.m.

185 'A onelegged sailor crutched himself round MacConnell's
corner, skirting Rabaiotti's icecream car, and jerked himself up Eccles street.'

The sailor has come from Gardiner Street via Dorset
Street. MacConnell's the chemist's at 112 Dorset Street
was not actually on the corner itself. He passes the Dedalus girls and stops outside 7 Eccles Street. Molly Bloom,
inside in her underwear, flings a coin from the window on
the ground floor; the sign *Unfurnished Apartments* refers to
the rooms on the floor above.

The line referring to J. J. O'Molloy is an interpolation
of a simultaneous event taking place in Meetinghouse
Lane, setting of *WR viii* (p. 189). In a similar interpolation
on page 205, the sailor reappears in Nelson Street, off
Eccles Street.

From Eccles Street, cross Dorset Street and proceed
through Hardwicke Place past St George's Church to the
bottom of Temple Street North. Here you may make a
detour to the right to Belvedere College, the Jesuit school
attended by James Joyce from 1893 to 1898 and described
in *A Portrait of the Artist as a Young Man*. The college
stands at the head of North Great George's Street, a
distinctive Georgian thoroughfare where lived Sir Samuel
Ferguson, the poet, Sir John Pentland Mahaffy, a famous
Provost of Trinity College who associated with Oscar
Wilde and Oliver Gogarty, and John Dillon, the Irish
Nationalist MP. No. 35, formerly the dancing academy of
'Mr Denis J. Maginni, professor of Dancing, &c' (who
appears in an interpolation near here on page 181, and
later on page 208), is to be opened as The James Joyce
Cultural Centre.

Back at Temple Street, follow Gardiner Place as far as
Mountjoy Square. Opposite and to the left is St Francis

Xavier's Church (scene of the retreat in 'Grace', the *Dubliners* story). Beyond the church is the presbytery from which Father Conmee emerges at five to three.

8. St Francis Xavier's Church. Father Conmee passes the church just after five to three.

Wandering Rocks i, 2.55 p.m.

180 'The superior, the very reverend John Conmee S . J. reset his smooth watch in his interior pocket as he came down the presbytery steps. Five to three. Just nice time to walk to Artane.'

Father Conmee (1847–1910) was appointed Rector of Clongowes Wood College in 1885, and appears in that position in *A Portrait of the Artist as a Young Man*. He left Clongowes in 1891, the same year that Joyce did (because his father could no longer afford to pay the fees), and was later instrumental in having the Joyce boys educated for free at Belvedere (rather than suffer the awful fate of being educated with 'Paddy Stink and Micky Mud' in the Christian Brothers). In 1898 he was appointed superior of the St Francis Xavier's community in Gardiner Street, in which role he appears here.

He meets the sailor outside the convent on the corner and crosses to Mountjoy Square, where he meets the wife of Mr David Sheehy M.P. under the trees on the north side. The Sheehys were well known to Joyce, who was a frequent visitor to their home at 2 Belvidere Place. He was particularly friendly with Mary Sheehy, who later married the poet Thomas Kettle. Another sister, Hannah, married Joyce's friend Francis Skeffington, who appears as 'McCann' in *A Portrait*. Skeffington, an ardent pacifist, was arrested and summarily executed during the Easter Rising; Kettle died in the war in France. A younger brother, Eugene Sheehy, one of the boys in Belvedere, became a prominent judge. His memoir, *May it Please the Court*, contains some entertaining memories of Joyce.

181   At the corner of Mountjoy Square he meets some schoolboys and gets one of them to post a letter in 'the red pillarbox at the corner of Fitzgibbon Street'. The pillarbox has gone, but a circular mark indicates the spot. The Joyce family moved to Fitzgibbon Street from Blackrock in 1892; their house at No. 14 has since been demolished. From Mountjoy Square east Father Conmee turns left onto Great Charles Street, where he passes the free church (now the Travellers' Resource Centre) on the left. At the end of the street he turns right down the North Circular Road and Portland Row, passing North Richmond Street on the far side with its Christian Brothers school (17 North Richmond Street, another former Joyce residence, was the setting for 'Araby' in *Dubliners*). On the right he passes St Joseph's Church.

182   'Near Aldborough house Father Conmee thought of that spendthrift nobleman. And now it was an office or something.' Aldborough House, one of Ireland's last Palladian mansions, was built in 1793–6 in the style of William Chambers. It is now occupied by a department of An Post.

At the Five Lamps, a well known landmark among Dublin illuminations, he turns left onto the North Strand Road, passing Gallagher's at No. 4. Grogan's at No. 16,

Bergin's and Youkstetter's vanished suddenly one night in May 1941 when they were hit by a German bomb from an aeroplane which had gone very much astray. They have since been replaced by Corporation housing, as was H. J. O'Neill's funeral establishment across the road at No. 164.

9. Aldborough House. Lord Aldborough, 'that spendthrift nobleman', was imprisoned in Newgate Gaol for contempt of the House of Lords. The last of Dublin's great townhouses, this building became the Post Office Stores Department.

(184)   *Wandering Rocks ii* takes place at the undertaker's soon
(185)   afterwards at 3.15. Constable 57C, who saluted Father Conmee, now approaches Corny Kelleher, an ex-policeman who maintains his links with the force (he comes in handy later in Nighttown when he persuades the policemen to leave Stephen alone). Some information is then exchanged.

Father Conmee crosses the Royal Canal at Newcomen Bridge beside Charleville Mall, and steps into an outward bound tram 'for he disliked to traverse on foot the dingy way past Mud Island'. Mud Island on the left hand side of Annesley Bridge Road, according to Weston St John Joyce, 'was a locality of evil repute in former times . . . inhabited by a gang of smugglers, highwaymen, and desperadoes of every description, and ruled by a heredit-ary robber chief rejoicing in the title of "King of Mud

Island".' The tram journey to the Howth Road stop, a distance of about 1 km., cost one penny, rather less than the equivalent bus journey today.

There is a bus stop on the left shortly after Newcomen Bridge. From here follow Father Conmee's tram journey by bus (Nos. 24, 51 or 53), passing the 'ivy church' on the 183 left just before the railway bridge. Crossing the Tolka river by Annesley Bridge, pass Fairview Park (still to be constructed in 1904) on the right. On the left, off Fairview Strand, is Windsor Avenue, where the Joyces lived at No. 29 (one of their several Fairview addresses). Father Conmee alights at the Howth Road stop just past the Malahide Road on the left, and within view of 15 Marino Crescent, home of Bram Stoker, the author of *Dracula*.

10. The O'Brien Institute. Father Conmee's destination is now the Dublin Fire Brigade Training Centre. On the right of the picture is the celebrated Marino Casino, now open to the public.

'The Malahide Road was quiet. It pleased Father Conmee, road and name.' Father Conmee walks up the Malahide Road on his way to the O'Brien Institute, an orphanage where he will arrange for Paddy Dignam's son to be admitted. While walking he thinks of 'his little book *Old Times in the Barony*', a memoir of the Athlone area which 184 was published in 1895. The fields of the Marino estate on his left (now built over) remind him of earlier years in Co. Kildare, and he imagines himself reading his office on the

Clongowes playing fields. This prompts him to reach for his breviary.

> A flushed young man came from a gap of a hedge and after him came a young woman with wild nodding daisies in her hand. The young man raised his cap abruptly: the young woman abruptly bent and with slow care detached from her light skirt a clinging twig.
>
> Father Conmee blessed both gravely . . .

The young man, as we learn on page 339, is Lynch, who turns up later in the maternity hospital.

On the left, just past Griffith Avenue, is the O'Brien Institute, a large building set well back from the road. The next turn to the left leads to the Marino Casino, a gem of eighteenth-century architecture designed by Sir William Chambers for Lord Charlemont in 1762, recently restored and open to the public daily during the summer and at weekends in the winter. It is worth a visit before returning along the North Strand Road to Amiens Street (Connolly) Station. The No. 24 bus goes all the way from Malahide Road near the Casino.

The station is the starting point for Tour 4.

Circe, Eumaeus, (Ithaca),
Lotuseaters,
Wandering Rocks (xvii),
Oxen of The Sun

Circe, 11.20 p.m.

350 '(*The Mabbot street entrance of nighttown, before which stretches an uncobbled tramsiding set with skeleton tracks, red and green will-o'-the-wisps and danger signals . . .*)'

The longest of all the episodes in *Ulysses*, this section is set in what was once the most notorious brothel quarter in Europe. Known at one time as 'Monto', after Montgomery Street, it was famous in its heyday for the establishments run by Mrs Mack, Bella Cohen and May Oblong. It declined in later years, and one night in 1925, at the instigation of the Legion of Mary, it was thoroughly raided by the Irish police. The Legion of Mary followed in the wake of the Gardai and took charge of the 'fallen women', many of whom were only too ready to find more respectable employment. Although most of the streets have been subjected to rebuilding and renaming, this remains one of Dublin's danger areas where street crime is common, and it should be treated with caution.

Throughout this chapter the 'real' action is confusingly mingled with hallucinations generated in the minds of Bloom and Stephen. These hallucinations represent the enchantments of the witch Circe in the original *Odyssey*, who caused Ulysses' crew to be turned into animals (a theme echoed here in the continual descriptions of humans with bestial attributes). We will thread our way through this labyrinth, distinguishing reality from hallucination.

351 Among the grotesque figures in Talbot Street loom Cissy Caffrey, whom we last saw on Sandymount Strand,

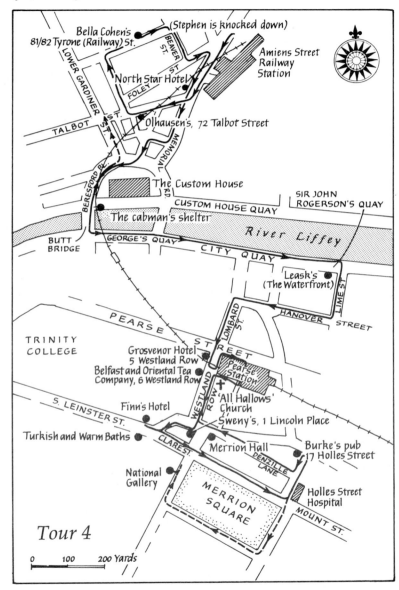

(Stephen is knocked down)

Bella Cohen's
81/82 Tyrone (Railway) St.

BEAVER ST.

LOWER GARDINER ST.

North Star Hotel

FOLEY ST.

Amiens Street
Railway
Station

TALBOT ST.

Olhausen's, 72 Talbot Street

MEMORIAL RD.

The Custom House

BERESFORD PL.

CUSTOM HOUSE QUAY

SIR JOHN
ROGERSON'S QUAY

The cabman's shelter

River Liffey

BUTT
BRIDGE

GEORGE'S QUAY

CITY QUAY

Leask's
(The Waterfront)

LIME ST.

PEARSE STREET

LOMBARD ST.

HANOVER STREET

TRINITY
COLLEGE

Grosvenor Hotel
5 Westland Row

Belfast and Oriental Tea
Company, 6 Westland Row

Pearse
Station

WESTLAND ROW

'All Hallows'
Church

S. LEINSTER ST.

Finn's Hotel

Sweny's, 1 Lincoln Place

Turkish and Warm Baths

CLARE ST.

Merrion Hall

DENZILLE LANE

Burke's pub
17 Holles Street

National
Gallery

MERRION
SQUARE

Holles Street
Hospital

MOUNT ST.

Tour 4

0   100   200 Yards

and the two English soldiers Private Compton and Private Carr. Stephen Dedalus and Lynch now appear, having
352 taken the train from Westland Row to Amiens Street Station (now Connolly Station). They would have left the station by the side entrance, the other side of the bridge from the present DART Station, and crossed into Talbot
353 Street. As they proceed into Nighttown they pass 'a liver and white spaniel on the prowl'. The dog reappears constantly in the episode, as a different breed each time.

11. Amiens Street Station. Stephen and Lynch, and later Bloom, emerge from the suburban line station at the end of the Loop Line bridge and cross Amiens Street into Talbot Street, on the extreme left. Later on Bloom and Stephen approach down the near side of the street from beyond the bridge.

354 '(. . . On the farther side under the railway bridge Bloom appears, flushed, panting, cramming bread and chocolate into a sidepocket . . .)' Bloom, who got on the same train as Stephen and Lynch, missed the station and had to return from the next stop at Killester. Now, arming himself with

provisions, he follows in their tracks along the south side of Talbot Street, past Gillen's at No. 64, in and out of Rabaiotti's at No. 65, and into Olhausen's at No. 72 to buy a crubeen and a sheep's trotter. Olhausen's still has the same name and location, though the sign proclaims that it was established in 1935.

355   By Cormack's pub on the corner before the lane he stops to look at the glow of a distant fire, then crosses Talbot Street after nearly colliding with two cyclists and a sand-
356 strewer. He reaches O'Beirne's corner at the bottom of Mabbot Street (now Corporation Street), and enters
357 Nighttown. His hallucinations begin with a vision of his
358–9 father; his mother and wife also appear. He returns to
360 reality briefly when a bawd seizes his sleeve, but then he
361–7 has visions of Gerty MacDowell and Mrs Breen, who finally fades from his side. '(. . . *Followed by the whining dog he walks on towards hellsgates. In an archway a standing woman, bent forward, her feet apart, pisses cowily. Outside a shuttered pub a bunch of loiterers listen to a tale which their brokensnouted gaffer rasps out with raucous humour . . .*)' Bloom's path passes Foley Street (formerly Montgomery
368 Street) and Purdon Street. Nearby the two redcoats and a
369 drunken navvy are arguing with a shebeenkeeper. 'Wild-goose chase this. Disorderly houses. Lord knows where they are gone. Drunks cover distance double quick.' He
370 abandons the crubeen and trotter to the hungry dog and
371–86 drifts into another hallucination in which he is arrested, charged with a long list of crimes and condemned. When
387 the vision ends he has taken the third turn to the right into Railway Street (formerly Tyrone Street and Mecklen-burgh Street).

    '(. . . *All recedes. Bloom plodges forward again through the sump. Kisses chirp amid the rifts of fog. A piano sounds. He stands before a lighted house, listening . . .*)'

    He has reached Bella Cohen's house at No. 81/82, on the left-hand side just before the convent, where a block of Corporation flats now stands. Here he is accosted by 'Zoe
388 Higgins, a young whore in a sapphire slip'. Stroking him,
389 she discovers in his pocket a potato which he keeps as a
390–407 good luck charm, and takes it from him. Again he hallu-

cinates, becoming a popular figure, a successful national
leader and a worker of miracles. Dissident voices arise and
408 he is denounced and publicly burned at the stake. Zoe
409 invites him inside and they enter the house, passing
410 through the hall and into the musicroom, where they find
Stephen and Lynch with two whores, Kitty and Florry.
411 Stephen, drunk and confused, is making philosophical
412 speeches towards Lynch's cap, but is interrupted by the
noise of a gramophone in a nearby house. More phantom
413 visions arise, involving the End of the World ('a two-
414 headed octopus in gillie's kilts, busby and tartan filibegs'),
415-6 Elijah, and Stephen's listeners from the library. Zoe
417 adjusts the whistling gasjet, and as Bloom observes her
418-22 he has another hallucination, involving his grandfather
Lipoti Virag and an appearance by Henry Flower.

Stephen meanwhile is still at the piano, and touches the
keys. The others request a song but he declines. 'No voice.
I am a most finished artist.' His mind briefly divides into
'The Siamese twins, Philip Drunk and Philip Sober.'
423 Philip Sober reminds him of all the drinking he has
already done around town, in 'Mooney's en ville,
Mooney's sur mer, the Moira, Larchet's, Holles street
hospital, Burke's,' but Philip Drunk continues recklessly.
Florry asks him if he is out of the priests' college at
Maynooth, and Zoe tells of the priest who visited the
424-7 brothel recently. The conversation continues with hallu-
cinatory interruptions from Virag, the Philips, Henry
Flower, Ben Dollard and others.
428 '(A male form passes down the creaking staircase and is
heard taking the waterproof and hat from the rack. Bloom
starts forward involuntarily and, half closing the door as he
passes, takes the chocolate from his pocket and offers it
429 nervously to Zoe.)' Bloom speculates that the man in the
hall is Boylan but relaxes when he hears a 'male cough and
tread . . . passing through the mist outside.'
430 Bella Cohen, the whoremistress, now enters the room.
431-43 Bloom, awed by her dominating appearance, plunges into
a long and harrowing hallucination in which Bella becomes a man and he himself becomes a woman. He is
mistreated, dressed up, humiliated, put to work in the

brothel and auctioned to the highest bidder. In the depths
444 of his shame he is confronted by the nymph from the *Photo*
445–9 *Bits* print in his bedroom, who reproaches him with his
secret lusts and masturbations. Through his fantasies leak
450 sounds from the real world as Kitty asks Florry for a
cushion. Reality comes closer when his back trouser
button snaps, breaking the spell.

451 Suddenly restored to an awareness of his own virility,
452 Bloom gains confidence. The nymph flees, and a moment
later he is able to return the stare of the awesome Mrs
Cohen with composure and contempt. This is a turning
453 point for him. Bloom gains further ground by reclaiming
his potato from Zoe, and Bella descends on the swaying
Stephen for payment. Confused by drink, he hands her a
454 poundnote, a gold half sovereign and two crowns – a total
of two pounds, or ten shillings too much since the rate is
ten shillings a girl. Bloom insists on paying for himself,
455 and prevents Stephen being cheated.

BLOOM

(quietly lays a half sovereign on the table between Bella and Florry) So. Allow me. *(he takes up the poundnote)* Three times ten. We're square.

He returns the pound to Stephen, who drops a box of
matches and is still witty enough to make a remark about
456 falling Lucifers. Bloom offers to take care of Stephen's
money before he loses any more.

457 Zoe reads Stephen's and Bloom's palms, and sees in
458–9 Bloom's hand something which causes her to whisper and
giggle with Florry and the others. Excluded from the joke,
460–2 he slips into fantasy, imagining Boylan's visit to Molly
with himself as a compliant and ridiculous cuckold.
463 Stephen and Bloom gaze together into the mirror and
Shakespeare's face appears, horned and uttering incohe-
464 rent quotations. The whores persuade Stephen to 'give us
465 some parleyvoo' and he delivers a recital in broken English
promoting some of the seamier entertainments of Paris.
466 He tells them of his dream of the previous night – 'I flew.
467 My foes beneath me' – and in a fantasy he sees himself as a

fox, running from the hounds. The hunt turns into a horserace with Mr Deasy bringing up the rear.

468 *'(Private Carr, Private Compton and Cissy Caffrey pass beneath the windows, singing in discord.)'* On cue, Stephen is reminded of the definition of God which he gave Mr Deasy – 'Our friend noise in the street.' The song they are singing is 'My Girl's a Yorkshire Girl' and Zoe sets the

469–71 pianola going with the same tune. Stephen starts dancing with all the girls, surrounded by fantasy figures including

472 the music and dancing masters Professor Goodwin and Professor Maginni. The others form couples and he con-

473 tinues dancing wildly on his own, whirling giddily till the music ends and he stops dead. A horrible vision now confronts him – his mother, rising through the floor, her body dead and rotting. Buck Mulligan, who earlier ac-cused Stephen of killing his mother, appears in the back-

474 ground to reinforce her reproaches. The others only see

475 that Stephen has gone white, and Florry goes to get him some water. Stephen refuses to let his spirit be broken, and lashes out in rage.

'(. . . He lifts his ashplant high with both hands and smashes the chandelier. Time's livid final flame leaps and, in the following darkness, ruin of all space, shattered glass and

476 *toppling masonry).'* He dashes from the house, and the others rush towards the halldoor. Bella seizes Bloom's coat-tail and demands ten shillings for the broken lamp.

477 'There's not sixpenceworth of damage done,' retorts Bloom, throwing down a shilling and hurrying to the

478 door. On the doorstep the whores are pointing at a disturbance down the street, and a hackney car arrives outside bearing Corny Kelleher and 'two silent lechers'. Bloom hastens past them and turns left along the street, seeing in his imagination a great crowd rushing after him with hue and cry.

479 *'(At the corner of Beaver street beneath the scaffolding Bloom panting stops on the fringe of the noisy quarrelling knot . . .)'* Stephen, it appears, has addressed or accosted Cissy Caffrey while the soldiers were relieving themselves,

480 and a row has developed. Private Compton is urging Private Carr to hit Stephen. (Carr, incidentally, derived

his name from a British consular official in Zurich, Henry
Carr, with whom Joyce had a particularly ludicrous dis-
pute in 1917. The incident formed the basis for Tom
Stoppard's play *Travesties*.)

481   Bloom tries to pull Stephen away, but without success.
Stephen, still rebellious against any attempt to master
him, especially by his arch-enemies the Church and the
State, makes a rambling reference to killing 'the priest and
the king'. Carr seizes on this as an insulting reference to
482 King Edward VII, who immediately materialises, wearing
483 a white jersey and sucking a red jujube. Bloom tries
desperately to calm the soldiers and remove Stephen, but
484 the argument escalates, attended by the imaginary figure
485 of 'Old Gummy Granny' (a grotesque version of Kathleen
Ni Houlihan), symbolising the Irish nationalist cause. All
that is lacking now is the third of Stephen's would-be-
486 masters, the Church. 'How do I stand you? The hat trick!
Where's the third person of the Blessed Trinity? Soggarth
487-9 Aroon? The reverend Carrion Crow.' This body is duly
represented by Father Malachi O'Flynn and the Reverend
Mr Hugh C. Haines Love, MA (Mulligan and Haines in
disguise, it would seem) celebrating a black Mass.

490   Lynch, who has been watching with Kitty, sneaks off,
and while Bloom still tries to calm things down, Private
491 Carr rushes forward, strikes Stephen and knocks him out.
The lurking dog, now identified as a retriever, barks
492 furiously, and two policemen turn up. Private Compton
pulls Carr away, and Bloom is trying to explain matters to
493 the police when Corny Kelleher appears. Knowing Kel-
494 leher's influence with the police, Bloom enlists his help in
getting them to disperse the crowd and leave Stephen
495 alone. The policemen leave, followed by Kelleher on his
496 outside car, and Bloom stands by Stephen as he gradually
497 comes to. His last hallucination is of his dead son Rudy,
'. . . a fairy boy of eleven, a changeling, kidnapped,
dressed in an Eton suit with glass shoes and a little bronze
helmet, holding a book in his hand.'

Eumaeus, 12.40 a.m.

501 'Preparatory to anything else Mr Bloom brushed off the greater bulk of the shavings and handed Stephen the hat and ashplant and bucked him up generally in orthodox Samaritan fashion which he very badly needed.'

The new chapter begins where *Circe* ended, at the corner of Railway Street and Beaver Street. Fitting to the condition of the protagonists, the style is weary and clumsy, full of mixed metaphors, worn clichés and stumbling syntax. The first priority is refreshment.

'Accordingly [. . .] they both walked together along Beaver street or, more properly, lane as far as the farrier's and the distinctly fetid atmosphere of the livery stables at the corner of Montgomery street where they made tracks to the left from thence debouching into Amiens street round by the corner of Dan Bergin's.' Montgomery Street is now Foley Street, and Dan Bergin's pub is now Lloyd's. Many of the establishments which they pass can easily be identified. Mullett's and the North Star Hotel still bear the same names, the Signal House is now Cleary's and Amiens Street railway terminus is, of course, Connolly Station.

502 'They passed the main entrance of the Great Northern railway station, [. . .] and passing the backdoor of the morgue (a not very enticing locality, not to say gruesome to a degree, more especially at night) ultimately gained the Dock Tavern and in due course turned into Store street, famous for its C division police station.' The Dock Tavern, next door to the morgue, has now been re-

503 designed as The Master Mariner. Passing what is now the central bus station (one of Dublin's first public buildings in the modern style, designed in 1953 by Michael Scott), 'they made a beeline across the back of the Customhouse and passed under the Loop Line bridge'.

In one line Joyce mentions one of Dublin's most handsome constructions and one of its most abominable eyesores. The Custom House, designed by James Gandon and built 1781–91, appears at its most impressive from the far side of the river. The interior was destroyed by fire during the Troubles in 1921 and has since been restored.

12. The Custom House. After the fire of 1921, the Custom House was restored, but lost its chimney stacks and the statues over the portico. The wooden structure on the left is not, in fact, the cabman's shelter, which is just outside the picture.

Work is at present in progress on the exterior of the building. Just inside the railings near the railway bridge is a forlorn group of statues which formerly stood above the portico. The Loop Line bridge was built in 1891 to connect the stations in Westland Row and Amiens Street.

504   Under the bridge Stephen is hailed by an acquaintance, 'Lord' John Corley (who appears in *Dubliners* as Lenehan's companion in 'Two Gallants'). Corley is down on his luck and asks Stephen to lend him some money. Stephen

505   discovers that he has some halfcrowns in his pocket; obviously he did not put all his cash into Bloom's care.

506   Bloom continues on his way with Stephen, attempting to give him some advice about his choice of friends,

507   especially after the scene at Westland Row Station where Mulligan and Haines apparently made it obvious that they did not want Stephen to come back to the Tower.

508   'Mr Bloom and Stephen entered the cabman's shelter, an unpretentious wooden structure . . .' The shelter stood on Custom House Quay beside the railway bridge. Here Bloom orders coffee and a bun and they study the

other occupants of the shelter, including its keeper, who
509 may or may not be the celebrated Invincible, Fitzharris,
known as Skin-the-Goat.

In keeping with the original episode in the *Odyssey*,
where Ulysses appears in disguise, there are continual
references in this episode to mistaken and dubious identities, confused and disguised names and unreliable stories.
It begins with the redbearded sailor who asks Stephen's
name and claims to know a Simon Dedalus who turns out
510 to be a circus sharpshooter. The sailor's name is D. B.
Murphy; by an appropriate chance this appeared as W. B.
Murphy until the Corrected Text decided his real identity.
511 The picture postcard which he produces is addressed,
512 however, to Señor A. Boudin. He is full of colourful tales,
513 about the Chinese with his little pills and the stabbing
514 incident in Trieste, but is elusive when questioned. Even
515–16 the man's face tattooed on his chest is capable of being
changed.

517 Bloom is distracted from this entertaining spectacle by
the sight of a streetwalker looking in through the door –
the same one whom he saw earlier on Ormond Quay and
by whom he is scared of being recognised. He converses
with Stephen about the evils of prostitution and then asks
518 him 'as a good catholic' about his views on the soul.
Stephen's reply leaves Bloom a bit out of his depth and he
ventures instead to persuade Stephen to tackle the coffee
519 and bun. Their attention returns to the sailor and his
520 scarcely credible yarns, which are interrupted when the
521–2 mariner goes outside to 'unfurl a reef'.

523–4 The conversation in the shelter turns to the subject of
Irish Home Rule and an argument begins between the
sailor and the keeper. Bloom takes up the subject with
525 Stephen and tells him about the incident in Barney Kier-
526 nan's. Their views on nationality and nationalism differ,
527 and Stephen gets crosstempered, saying: '—We can't
change the country. Let us change the subject.'

528 Bloom picks up a nearby copy of 'the pink edition extra
sporting of the *Telegraph* tell a graphic lie' in which he is
momentarily jolted by misreading 'Hugh Boylan' for H.
529 du Boyes, and reads Hynes's report on the Dignam

funeral, which contains his own name, misspelt, and those of others who were not even there. Bloom is 'Nettled not a little by L. Boom (as it incorrectly stated) and the line of bitched type but tickled to death simultaneously by C. P. M'Coy and Stephen Dedalus B.A. who were conspicuous, needless to say, by their total absence (to say nothing of M'Intosh) . . .' The paper also contains Mr Deasy's letter and an account of the Gold Cup race.

530 The others in the shelter begin a conversation about
531 Parnell, the possibility of his not being dead after all, and
532 Kitty O'Shea, who Bloom recalls had Spanish blood. This
533 prompts him to show Stephen a photograph of Molly
534-5 which Stephen politely admires. Bloom thinks it a pity that Stephen should be wasting his time with 'profligate
536 women' and, further solicitous for his welfare, asks him 'At what o'clock did you dine?'

—Some time yesterday, Stephen said.
—Yesterday! exclaimed Bloom till he remembered it was already tomorrow Friday. Ah, you mean it's after twelve!
—The day before yesterday, Stephen said, improving on himself.

537 Bloom decides to offer Stephen 'a cup of Epps's cocoa
538 and a shakedown for the night'. He pays the fourpenny
539 bill and supports Stephen outside. Chatting about music, 'they made tracks arm in arm across Beresford place',
540 rounding the back of the Custom House inside the 'swing-chains' at the edge of the road. Nearby a horse, dragging a sweeper, is being used to clean the street after the horse
541 traffic of the day. They stop as it crosses their path. Stephen, showing signs of recovery, is illustrating the
542 conversation by singing; Bloom admires Stephen's voice and considers advising him to concentrate seriously on a
543 singing career. They take advantage of a pause when the horse stops to let fall 'three smoking globes of turds', and cross the wide roadway towards Gardiner Street Lower. The driver watches them as they disappear up the street in the direction of Bloom's house.

(Ithaca, 1 a.m.

The route from here to Bloom's house is described in Tour 3 and connects with it.) To continue this tour, cross Butt Bridge and turn left along George's Quay and City Quay, following the route presumably taken by Bloom between *Calypso* and *Lotuseaters*.

13. Eden Quay and Butt Bridge. The clock on the left belongs to 'Mooney's *sur mer*'. The centre section of Butt Bridge, in the middle of the picture, is mounted on a turntable.

Lotuseaters, 9.45 a.m.

58 'By lorries along sir John Rogerson's quay Mr Bloom walked soberly, past Windmill Lane, Leask's the linseed crusher, the postal telegraph office.'

Bloom's unnecessarily circuitous route from home, taking him almost as far as the gasometer, leads past Leask's, now the Waterfront Restaurant, the post office next door and the sailors' home on the corner of Lime Street, where he turns right, away from the quayside. Brady's Cottages, now demolished, were on either side of Lime Street. He turns right along Hanover Street and into Townsend Street, which he crosses to turn left up Lombard Street. 'Bethel', the Salvation Army hall on the right, has gone, but Nichols' the undertaker still flourishes on the same side.

Crossing Great Brunswick Street (now Pearse Street),
he goes up the right hand side of Westland Row and halts
before the window of the Belfast and Oriental Tea Company (now demolished) just beyond the railway bridge.
59 Finally, holding a *Freeman's Journal* which he has bought
on the way from Eccles Street, he crosses to the post office,
which was situated beneath the bridge just about where
the newsagent's is now, and collects a letter addressed to
'Henry Flower Esq'.

Strolling out of the post office and turning to the right,
60 he encounters M'Coy, and gazes idly past him during the
conversation at the woman entering the carriage outside
the Grosvenor Hotel, which stood until recently next to
the railway bridge on the opposite side to the station.
Conway's pub, to which M'Coy refers, is now Kenney's
61 on the corner of Lincoln Place. Eluding M'Coy at last,
62 Bloom strolls on towards Brunswick Street.

Wonder is he pimping after me?

Mr Bloom stood at the corner, his eyes wandering
over the multicoloured hoardings. Cantrell and
Cochrane's Ginger Ale (Aromatic). Clery's Summer
Sale. No, he's going on straight.

63 He turns right onto Brunswick Street and passes the
'hazard' or cab rank and the cabman's shelter, now transformed into a public toilet. 'He turned into Cumberland
street and, going on some paces, halted in the lee of the
station wall. No-one.'
64 Here in private he opens the letter. It is from Martha
Clifford, whom he has never met and with whom he is
65 carrying on a clandestine erotic correspondence. He tears
up the envelope under the railway arch, and reaches 'the
open backdoor of All Hallows' on the right beyond the
lane. This door is not always open, but there is a side door
on the laneway between Cumberland Street and Westland
Row. It is not certain why Joyce called the church All
Hallows, since it is in fact St Andrew's (by James Boulger,
1832–7); perhaps there is some connection with the
ancient monastery of All Hallows, which stood on the
grounds now occupied by Trinity College.

14. St Andrew's Church. Called 'All Hallows' by Joyce, the church has changed little since Bloom emerged and turned left towards Sweny's.

66   Entering the church, Bloom finds communion in progress and takes a quiet seat in the corner, observing the
67 proceedings. The original of this episode in the *Odyssey* described the Lotuseaters, a hopelessly addicted band of
68 dropouts; and the so-called 'opiate of the people' becomes the subject of Bloom's thoughts here. He decides to leave before they come round with the plate, and emerges by the front door into Westland Row, next to the post office. Outside, he turns left.

   'Sweny's in Lincoln place. Chemists rarely move.' The
69 'green and gold beaconjars' have gone, but Sweny's is still there in Lincoln Place, at the far end of Westland Row, complete with its original name-plate, shop-front and interior furnishings. Lemon soap is on sale there for the many imitators of Bloom who call in. The real purpose of his visit is to get some lotion made up for Molly; he arranges to call back later in the day but eventually omits to do so.

70   Outside Sweny's Bloom is accosted by Bantam Lyons, who has probably spotted him from inside Conway's. Lyons borrows Bloom's paper to look up the Ascot runners, and Bloom gets impatient. He tells Lyons he can keep the paper.

—I was just going to throw it away, Mr Bloom said.

Bantam Lyons raised his eyes suddenly and leered weakly.

—What's that? his sharp voice said.

—I say you can keep it, Mr Bloom answered. I was going to throw it away that moment.

Bantam Lyons doubted an instant, leering: then thrust the outspread sheets back on Mr Bloom's arms.

—I'll risk it, he said. Here, thanks.

Bloom thus unwittingly gives a tip for the eventual winner of the Gold Cup, Throwaway.

Turning left, he walks 'cheerfully towards the mosque of the baths'. The Lincoln Place Baths, on the site now occupied by the Norwich Union building, were designed in Oriental style by Richard Barter in 1859. However, this establishment, which had closed in 1899, was not the one where Bloom goes for his bath. We discover elsewhere in the book that he went further on to the Turkish and Warm Baths, 11 Leinster Street. On the other side of Lincoln Place he observes Hornblower the college porter standing outside his lodge at the back gate of Trinity College.

71   Continue along Lincoln Place into South Leinster Street, a short street connecting Nassau Street and Clare Street. The last building on the right before the College railings was once Finn's Hotel, where Joyce's wife Nora Barnacle worked as a chambermaid. The name may still be seen in faded white paint on the gable wall, half-hidden by a tree. Nearly opposite Finn's an office block at number 11 now occupies the site of the baths where Bloom foresees himself. 'He saw his trunk and limbs riprippled over and sustained, buoyed lightly upward, lemonyellow: his naval, bud of flesh: and saw the dark tangled curls of his bush floating, floating hair of the stream around the limp father of thousands, a

languid floating flower.' After his bath, Bloom takes the tram to Sandymount for the funeral.

Wandering Rocks xvii

205 'Almidano Artifoni walked past Holles street past Sewell's yard. Behind him Cashel Boyle O'Connor Fitzmaurice Tisdall Farrell, with stickumbrelladustcoat dangling, shunned the lamp before Mr Law Smith's house and crossing, walked along Merrion square. Distantly behind him a blind stripling tapped his way by the wall of College park.'

Artifoni, having missed the tram outside Trinity, is walking to Ballsbridge. Farrell is on his way from the National Library, where he was signing the readers' book on p.177. On p.201 he was seen passing the Kildare Street club as he turned the corner into Nassau Street. The blind stripling, whom Bloom saw about two hours previously approaching Levenston's Dancing Academy in South Frederick Street, has since been up to the Ormond Hotel to tune the piano. Shortly after we see him here he will realise that he has left his tuningfork behind, and will go all the way back to retrieve it.

Farrell walks all the way to the corner of Holles Street, then turns and retraces his steps so that when the viceroy passes he is outside Finn's Hotel, staring at the head of M. E. Solomons in his optician's shop where he also served as the Austro-Hungarian viceconsul (p.208). The shop, at 19 Nassau Street, just beyond the Dawson Street corner, cannot in fact have been easily visible from here.

From Finn's Hotel walk along Clare Street and Merrion Square North, passing the landmarks of Farrell's walk in reverse order. 'Mr Bloom's dental windows' were at 2 Clare Street, where M. Bloom had his practice, and Law Smith's house was on the next corner. Across the next street, on the corner of Merrion Square, was the former residence of Oscar Wilde's father Sir William Wilde. It was outside here that James Joyce had his first rendezvous with Nora Barnacle on 14 June 1904. She stood him up. Halting at this corner, Farrell frowns northwards at the notice on Merrion Hall, and southwards at 'the distant pleasance of duke's lawn' outside Leinster House (just beyond the National Gallery). 'Mr Lewis Werner's cheerful windows', on the corner house at the far end of Merrion Square North, are now preserved in the Kenny Gallery in Galway.

From here cross the street to the Maternity Hospital. The entrance is halfway down Holles Street.

Oxen of the Sun, 10 p.m.

314 'Deshil Holles Eamus. Deshil Holles Eamus. Deshil Holles Eamus.'

The National Maternity Hospital in Holles Street was opened in 1894, under the mastership of Dr Andrew Horne. Major rebuilding was carried out in 1934, including the neo-Georgian façade of the Nurses' Residence on the Merrion Square side. The Holles Street front was not greatly altered in style. Precisely in which room of the building most of the events take place is not specified.

The form of this episode was based by Joyce on the growth of the baby in the womb, from conception to birth. The language of the episode evolves historically as it goes along, beginning with primitive incantations, proceeding with what look like word for word translations from Greek and Latin and so through old and Middle English to a brilliant series of pastiches on the styles of the major writers in English literature, century by century.

315 After a short introduction dealing with medicine and maternity care, Bloom makes his appearance. 'Some man that wayfaring was stood by housedoor at night's oncoming. Of Israel's folk was that man that on earth wandering far had fared.' Bloom has arrived by tram from Sandymount, and has come to visit his friend Mrs Purefoy.

316 Lightning flashes as the nurse at the door, crossing herself, lets him in. She is Nurse Callan, who rented out a flat in Holles Street to the Blooms during their hard times some years previously. Bloom learns from her of the death of a young medical friend, Doctor O'Hare. He asks after Mrs Purefoy and learns that her long labour is nearly over.

317 Just then a medical student named Dixon, who treated

Bloom for a bee sting on Whit Monday at the Mater Misericordiae Hospital, appears and invites Bloom to join his colleagues and himself for a drink inside. Bloom is reluctantly persuaded to sit down and take his hat off,
318 though he takes care to drink little, unlike the rest of the company. Besides Dixon and four other students he finds Lenehan and Stephen Dedalus, who has been drinking all afternoon, all awaiting the arrival of Buck Mulligan.

Oxen of the Sun parallels an episode in the *Odyssey* in which Ulysses' crew kill and eat oxen sacred to Apollo. The students, too, show little respect for the sacred cows of medical ethics, and embark on a jocular discussion of
319 whether to save the mother or the child in a birth where it is a case of one life or the other. Bloom is painfully
320 reminded of the death of his baby son Rudy.

Stephen meanwhile, merry with drink, fills all the glasses, shows off some money which he claims to have received 'for a song which he writ', though in fact it appears to be the remains of the morning's pay from Mr Deasy, depleted by thirteen shillings which would seem to have been spent on drink for himself and others. Ready to show that for him especially nothing is sacred, he poses a theosophical conundrum to prove that whether Mary conceived Jesus wittingly or unwittingly, there is nothing
321 special in her by herself to be venerated. Punch Costello, one of the students, starts up a bawdy song but is silenced first by Nurse Quigley and then by his colleagues.

322 Tales of Stephen's womanising are told, while he himself reflects on his treatment by Mulligan which symbolises his treatment by Ireland as a whole: 'Remember, Erin, [. . .] how thou settedst little by me and by my work and broughtedst in a stranger to my gates [. . .] and hast made me, thy lord, to be the slave of servants [. . .]. Why hast thou done this abomination before me that thou didst
323 spurn me for a merchant of jalaps . . .?' Even as he jeers at the futility of any attempt to relate our life to any sort of immortality, the thunderstorm breaks over them. 'A black crack of noise in the street here, alack, bawled back. Loud on left Thor thundered: in anger awful the hammerhurler.'

Stephen, interpreting the 'noise in the street' as the voice of an angry God, is frightened, despite Bloom's assurance that it can all be explained scientifically. A 324 pastiche of *The Pilgrim's Progress* tells how Stephen and his fellows are less interested in godliness than in whoring, protected by 'a stout shield of oxengut and [. . .] they might take no hurt neither from Offspring that was that wicked devil by virtue of this same shield which was named Killchild'. Condoms are another desecration of this building devoted to the bringing forth of children.

325 Outside, as rain pours down on Dublin, Buck Mulligan, on his way from George Moore's in Ely Place, meets Alec Bannon outside Justice Fitzgibbon's at 10 Merrion Square North and invites him to come with him to the 326 hospital. Meanwhile a discussion has begun about the foot-and-mouth disease (the slaughter of oxen again being 327 relevant here), from which arises the tale of the two bulls, a fable about the two churches in Ireland. The first is the Roman Catholic Church, which arrived in Ireland in 1170 when the English pope Adrian IV (Nicholas Breakspear or 'farmer Nicholas') gave his blessing to Henry II's con- 328 quest of Ireland with his papal bull *Laudabiliter*. The second is the Church of England, founded with Henry VIII ('the Lord Harry') as its head.

329 Mulligan and Bannon now arrive, and Mulligan proposes his scheme to buy Lambay Island off the north 330 Dublin coast and set himself up as a stud farm. Bannon meanwhile accepts a drink from Crotthers, the Scottish 331 student, and displays to him a locket with a picture of his girlfriend (Milly Bloom, as it happens). The conversation once again turns to condoms – 'But at this point a bell tinkling in the hall cut short a discourse which promised so bravely for the enrichment of our store of knowledge.'

332 Nurse Callan enters to inform Dixon that Mrs Purefoy's labour is over and that the baby is a boy. Punch Costello makes ribald remarks about the nurse as soon as her back is turned, but he is rebuked by Dixon, who goes to attend 333–4 to his duties. Mr Bloom rejoices at the news but the others 335 are less respectful in their comments. They burst forth in a discussion of every type of abnormal birth from the

commonplace Caesarean section to monstrous and de-
336 formed births. Mulligan then conjures up for them a
ludicrous vision of Haines, who, it seems, made a brief
appearance at the soirée in Ely Place, witnessed by Moore
337 ('the dissipated host') and Russell ('the seer'), to tell
Mulligan 'Meet me at Westland Row Station at ten past
eleven.'

338   Bloom meanwhile is in a daydream about his youth, and
then appears to nod off into a strange dream about a
moving herd of beasts, about his daughter Milly and a
mysterious writing which transforms itself into 'Alpha,
a ruby and triangled sign upon the forehead of Taurus.'

Around him the others are discussing old times in
339 Clongowes, the horse race, and Lynch's encounter with
340 Father Conmee that afternoon. Lenehan, reaching for a
bottle of Bass, is restrained by Mulligan, who indicates
Bloom's dreamy gaze fixed on the red triangle on the label.
Bloom comes to and pours Lenehan some ale. The con-
341 versation continues and they discuss such matters as the
342 future determination of sex and, to a greater length, infant
mortality.

343   'Meanwhile the skill and patience of the physician had
344 brought about a happy *accouchement*.' The birth is over
and Bloom is observing Stephen, remembering the occa-
345 sion when he met him as a child at Matt Dillon's. Suddenly – 'Burke's! outflings my lord Stephen, giving the
cry, and a tag and bobtail of all them after . . .'

The revellers burst out of the hospital and turn right,
346 heading for the pub at the bottom of the street. 'Jay, look
at the drunken minister coming out of the maternity
hospital!' remark the boys in Denzille Lane across the
street, deceived by Stephen's 'Latin quarter hat'. They
reach Burke's on the corner of Holles Street and Denzille
(now Fenian) Street at ten to eleven. (The pub has been
demolished and replaced by a flower shop). Stephen
orders the drinks – absinthe for himself, ginger cordial for
Bloom, and five pints of Bass's No. 1 Ale, two pints of
347 Guinness and two whiskeys among the others. Snatches of
conversation are heard: Dixon telling someone about
Bloom, Mulligan remarking that Stephen's telegram

message of the morning was 'Cribbed out of Meredith'; and Stephen paying 'Two bar and a wing' (two shillings and sixpence) for the round of drinks. Someone, possibly Bloom, sees Bantam Lyons drowning his sorrows in the pub.

348   'You move a motion? Steve boy, you're going it some. More bluggy drunkables?' Stephen buys another round as closing time is called – absinthe all round, except for Bloom, who has a glass of wine. Bannon overhears Bloom's name and realises 'Photo's papli, by all that's gorgeous.' Mulligan has slipped away to the station. The mystery man in the mackintosh is noticed; apparently he is known as Bartle the Bread and has seen better days.

As they leave the pub Stephen and Lynch slip off up Holles Street and along Denzille Lane, trailed by Bloom, 349 and emerge from the lane by Merrion Hall with its notice 'Elijah is coming! Washed in the blood of the Lamb.' From Lincoln Place they proceed down Westland Row to the station, on their way to 'the kips where shady Mary is'.

From Pearse Station you may take the train to Sandymount for Tour 2 (a) or Sandycove for Tour 1.

Alternatively, from Holles Street return round the east, south and west sides of Merrion Square, passing the houses of Daniel O'Connell (No. 58), W. B. Yeats (No. 52 and 82), Sheridan Le Fanu (No. 70) and George Russell (A.E.) (No. 84), Leinster House, and the National Gallery, which has portraits of Joyce by Sean O'Sullivan, Wyndham Lewis and Jacques-Emile Blanche.

15. City Hall. Martin Cunningham, Mr Power and John Wyse Nolan come out of the Upper Castleyard gate, on the extreme right of the picture, and walk across Cork Hill, on the left, passing the councillors on the steps of City Hall.

| *Wandering Rocks* (xv, ix, xvi, x, xiii, xi, xiv, viii), *Sirens*

Wandering Rocks xv

202 '—The youngster will be all right, Martin Cunningham said, as they passed out of the Castleyard gate.'

Before setting out on this tour, it is worth visiting Dublin Castle, one of the city's most historic buildings, originally constructed in the early thirteenth century. Parts of it, including the impressive State Apartments, are open to the public when not in use for state functions.

Cunningham, Mr Power and John Wyse Nolan emerge from the Upper Castleyard gate, uphill from City Hall, with the list of subscriptions collected for Paddy Dignam's family. They pass City Hall and walk down Cork Hill into Parliament Street, meeting Jimmy Henry on the way.

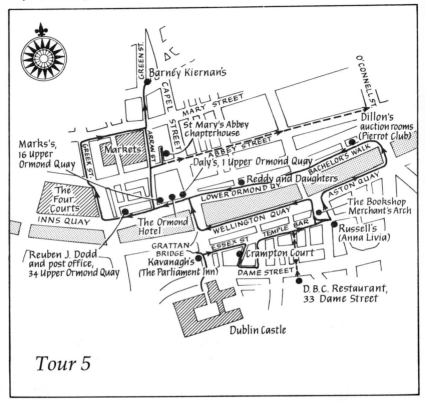

Tour 5

Passing the watchmaker's at 30 Parliament Street, they
203 turn the corner into Essex Gate and meet long John
Fanning in the doorway of James Kavanagh's winerooms.
This is now the door to the upstairs lounge of The
Parliament Inn. As they all go in and upstairs John Wyse
Nolan watches the viceregal cavalcade riding past up
Parliament Street. In interpolations we see the barmaids
looking out of the Ormond Hotel window, and Blazes
Boylan meeting Bob Doran in Grafton Street.

From the Parliament Inn, cross Parliament Street to
Essex Street and take the second turn to the right into the
laneway which leads to Crampton Court, beside the Olympia Theatre. Built about 1740 by Philip Crampton, the
little square has now been almost entirely demolished.

Wandering Rocks ix

191 'Tom Rochford took the top disk from the pile he clasped against his claret waistcoat.'

It is not clear whereabouts in the court this exchange takes place – possibly at the side entrance to Dan Lowry's Empire Musichall (now the Olympia Theatre), or in the billiard rooms at No. 16 in the opposite corner (now demolished). Tom Rochford is demonstrating to Lenehan, M'Coy and Nosey Flynn his invention for showing what turn is on – presumably in the musichall programme. Lenehan is to canvass Boylan's support for the device.

Lenehan, who was last seen heading for Mooney's with Stephen, is now bound for another drink in the Ormond Hotel. He and M'Coy leave Crampton Court by the exit into Dame Street, turning left past the theatre and left again down Sycamore Street, past the stage door to the east corner of the Dolphin Hotel (now occupied by Bad Bob's Backstage Bar; but the west end has been preserved, complete with its carved dolphin, as an office building).

They turn right along Essex Street, pausing at the bottom of Eustace Street to check the time in 'Marcus

16. Eustace Street. Marcus Tertius Moses' office is on the right, with the triangular pediment over the door. The pub on the corner, Mullally Bros., was O'Neill's in 1904.

Tertius Moses' sombre office' and O'Neill's pub (now The Norseman). In the *Dubliners* story 'Counterparts', O'Neill's is the pub visited by Farrington when he slips out of Crosbie and Alleyne's office in the middle of the day for a quick drink.

192   In Temple Bar Lenehan calls into Lynam's betting shop (location unknown) to place his money on Sceptre. (The Gold Cup race, scheduled for 3 o'clock (GMT) had already been run by this stage, but bets were, apparently, still taken until the result was telegraphed through). Inside he meets Bantam Lyons about to back Throwaway on the strength of his 'tip' from Bloom, and (unfortunately for Lyons) talks him out of it. They continue along the street. The Temple Bar area in recent years has cultivated a 'Left Bank' atmosphere, with arts centres, restaurants and second-hand shops flourishing in a maze of narrow streets which were scheduled for demolition in an urban transport scheme. This scheme has now been dropped and efforts are being made to preserve the character of the area.

Detour: *Wandering Rocks xvi*

At Fownes Street turn right and up to Dame Street. Directly opposite the top of Fownes Street at 33 Dame Street is the site of the DBC restaurant. The present façade was built in 1989, replacing an ugly 1960s front.

As they trod across the thick carpet Buck Mulligan whispered behind his Panama to Haines:
—Parnell's brother. There in the corner.

204   Mulligan, having parted from Stephen on the way from the library, meets Haines, who has bought Douglas Hyde's *Lovesongs of Connacht* in Gill's bookshop in O'Connell Street (passed by the funeral cortège earlier in the morning).

'—We call it D.B.C. because they have damn bad cakes,' explains Mulligan. The letters actually stood for Dublin Bread Company, later Dublin Bakery Company. There were several of these DBC tearooms around the city; it was in this one that Boylan was introduced to Molly Bloom (who afterwards left her gloves in the ladies' lavatory). The window where they sat was a wide one, with a good view over the street. At the next table is John Howard Parnell, the city marshal and brother of the dead nationalist leader. Bloom saw him earlier opposite Trinity College, presumably on his way to the DBC. His unnamed opponent at the chessboard could well have been Joyce's friend J. F. Byrne ('Cranly'), who played chess here regularly with Parnell and devoted a section of his memoirs, *Silent Years*, to accounts of their matches.

205   Over scones and butter and cakes and *mélanges* (probably coffee with whipped cream) they discuss Stephen Dedalus and decide that he is a lost cause. A few minutes later (p.208) they watch the viceregal equipage going past. (The interpolations in this section feature the onelegged sailor, who has reached Nelson Street, and the crumpled piece of paper thrown into the river by Bloom on p.125, floating 'beyond new Wapping street past Benson's ferry', practically as far as the present East Link toll bridge.)

Return down Fownes Street to Temple Bar and Lenehan and M'Coy.

Wandering Rocks ix (continued)

'They went up the steps and under Merchants' arch. A darkbacked figure scanned books on the hawker's cart.' Merchants' Arch gives access leftwards from Temple Bar to the river, directly beside the Halfpenny Bridge. This picturesque little thoroughfare is still lined with second-hand bookshops, and it is outside one of these that Lenehan and M'Coy spot Bloom (see *WR x* below). While Lenehan tells the story of the Glencree Reformatory dinner they go through the arch, across to the riverwall and left along the river. Bloom will follow in their tracks (see Tour 5a below).

(Interpolations in *WR ix* describe Richie Goulding outside the Four Courts, the viceregal cavalcade emerging from the Lodge gates, Master Patrick Dignam leaving Mangan's in Wicklow Street, and Molly Bloom replacing the fallen card in 7 Eccles Street.)

Wandering Rocks x

193   'Mr Bloom turned over idly pages of *The Awful Disclosures of Maria Monk*, then of Aristotle's *Masterpiece*.'

Bloom, who left the library at the same time as Stephen, has travelled in the same direction – to the bookshops on the quays. Evidence suggests that he has already visited Clohissey's in Bedford Row, where Stephen browses a few minutes later. According to Hart and Knuth, Bloom is probably at Francis Fitzgerald's shop (now Halfpenny Bridge Books) on the corner of Merchant's Arch and

194   Temple Bar. He selects for Molly a book named *Sweets of Sin* (which the scholars have yet to identify) and rents it from the shopman, who appears from behind a dingy curtain strung across the back of the shop. '—*Sweets of Sin*, he said, tapping on it. That's a good one.' (Interpolations in this section refer to Denis J. Maginni, who has made his elegant way all along O'Connell Street to the Bridge, and to the 'elderly female' leaving the Four Courts.)

To follow Bloom on his way to the Ormond Hotel, see Tour 5a below. Otherwise continue along Temple Bar and Fleet Street to the junction with Bedford Row.

Wandering Rocks xiii

198   'Stephen Dedalus watched through the webbed window the lapidary's fingers prove a timedulled chain.'

Stephen, having left Buck Mulligan near the library and Almidano Artifoni outside Trinity College, is now outside Russell's the jewellers at 57 Fleet Street (now the lounge of

199   the Anna Livia pub). He hears 'the whirr of flapping leathern bands and hum of dynamos from the powerhouse' in the building next door, which is still operated by the Electricity Supply Board. Oppressed by the 'two roaring worlds' of time and space, he feels the urge to shatter them (as he does eventually, in Nighttown) but decides 'Not yet awhile.'

He turns and goes down Bedford Row. Clohissey's bookshop at Nos. 10–11 on the right has gone now, replaced by a garage entrance with large steel shutters. As

he pores over an interesting book of 'Charms and invocations' he is interrupted by his sister Dilly, who has crossed
200 the river from Dillon's auctionrooms and has just bought a French primer with one of the precious pennies she coaxed out of her father. (It is of interest to note that a French-English dictionary bearing the name 'John Stanislaus Joyce' and the address '7 St Peter's Terrace, Cabra' is in the collection at the Joyce Tower.) Stephen gives his approval, and inwardly stifles the urge to help his family, knowing that he will only sink with them.

This is the last we see of Stephen for some time. From here he goes to spend his money on drink in the Moira Hotel in Trinity Street and Larchet's in College Green, five minutes' walk from Bedford Row. (The interpolations in this section describe the two women whom Stephen saw on Sandymount Strand, returning from their expedition with their cockles, and Father Conmee, now walking through Donnycarney.)

Follow Bedford Row down to the river and turn right along Aston Quay, then cross the river by O'Connell Bridge and turn left along Bachelor's Walk, passing the entrance to Williams's Row.

Wandering Rocks xi

195 'The lacquey by the door of Dillon's auctionrooms shook his handbell twice again and viewed himself in the chalked mirror of the cabinet.'

The auctionrooms where Dilly has been loitering for the past couple of hours are now the Pierrot Club.

'Mr Dedalus, tugging a long moustache, came round from Williams's row.' Mr Dedalus has presumably come up Williams's Row from the Oval pub in Abbey Street, where he was drinking with Ned Lambert and other cronies. (Because the lane is obscured from this angle, Dilly cannot tell which direction he came from and thinks he may have been further away in the Scotch House on Burgh Quay.) Bloom would also have come this way earlier from the newspaper office when he went to talk to Alexander Keyes here in Dillon's.

196 Dilly persuades her father to hand over a shilling and

two pennies, and he walks on along the quays towards the Ormond Hotel, while she crosses the river to the bookshop in Bedford Row. (In the interpolations we see the runners in the College races, Mr Kernan in James's Street, and the viceregal cavalcade leaving the Park.)

Continue with Mr Dedalus along the quays past the metal bridge, known as the Halfpenny Bridge because when it was first erected a toll of one halfpenny was levied on those who used it. Beside the bridge is the shop of the Dublin Woollen Company, for whom Joyce worked as an agent when he was in Trieste. At the next corner is Swift's Row.

Wandering Rocks xiv

200 —Hello, Simon, Father Cowley said. How are things?
—Hello, Bob, old man, Mr Dedalus answered, stopping.
They clasped hands loudly outside Reddy and Daughter's.

Reddy's antique shop on Ormond Quay lower was on the east side of Swift's Row. Father Cowley is waiting for Ben
201 Dollard, whom they now see approaching from the metal bridge on his way from the Bodega in Dame Street. Ben Dollard is to intercede for Cowley with long John Fanning to call off the bailiffs placed on his house by Reuben J. Dodd. However it turns out that Cowley's landlord, the Reverend Hugh C. Love (who is not far away at that moment) has already distrained for rent and has the prior claim. Cowley's address, 29 Windsor Avenue, was a former residence of the Joyces in Fairview.

They continue along the quay, past Grattan Bridge. Mr Dedalus visits the 'greenhouse' or public urinal on the riverside pavement just beyond the bridge, and the others go on to the subsheriff's office further along Ormond Quay Upper. The subsheriff, long John Fanning, is in fact across the river in Kavanagh's at this time. Shortly afterwards they all meet up again in the Ormond Hotel. (Interpolations here describe Cashel Boyle O'Connor Fitzmaurice Tisdall Farrell, passing the Kildare Street

Club on the corner with Nassau Street, and the Reverend Hugh C. Love passing Kennedy's at the corner of Mary's Abbey and Capel Street.)

Tour 5a: Alternative route to the Ormond Hotel; *Sirens*, 3.40 p.m.

Bloom, leaving Merchant's Arch with *Sweets of Sin* in his pocket, follows in the wake of Lenehan and M'Coy along Wellington Quay, past what is now the Gallery of Photography (an interesting place to visit on the left). As the action of *Sirens* begins in the Ormond Hotel, we get glimpses of him approaching in the distance.

(212) 'Bloowho went by by Moulang's pipes bearing in his breast the sweets of sin, by Wine's antiques, in memory bearing sweet sinful words, by Carroll's dusky battered plate, for Raoul.' Wine's at No. 35 was just beyond the Gallery of Photography; it is now Wellington Office Supply Ltd. Moulang's (now Culliton's opticians) was at No. 31 (Hart and Knuth explain this inversion as typical of the musical techniques used throughout the episode), followed by Carroll's at No. 29 (now Little's).

(213) 'Bloowhose dark eye read Aaron Figatner's name. Why do I always think Figather?' He passes Figatner's the jewellers at No. 26 Wellington Quay and Prosper Loré the milliner at No. 22. 'Bassi's blessed virgins' are still there at No. 14; the religious statues remind him of his unsuccessful attempt to inspect the goddesses in the National

(214) Museum, interrupted by Buck Mulligan. He continues past Cantwell's at No. 12 and more religious goods at Ceppi's (Nos. 8–9). In between at No. 11 was, and still is, Roger Greene's the solicitor's office. Here, a few minutes earlier, Gerty MacDowell watched the viceroy passing by while Lenehan and M'Coy took leave of each other on the bridge. Bloom decides to eat before seeing Nannetti about the paragraph for Keyes; he considers the Clarence Hotel, which he is passing, and the Dolphin in the next street, but goes on.

(215) 'Yes, Mr Bloom crossed bridge of Yessex. To Martha I must write. Buy paper. Daly's.' Bloom crosses Grattan (formerly Essex) Bridge. At this point in the Liffey was

the entrance to the 'Dubh Linn' (Black Pool) which gave its name to the ninth-century Viking settlement that was formed on the river bank nearby at Wood Quay, location of the controversial modern Civic Offices which were built on top of the archaeological site.

(216)   In Daly's, the tobacconists on the corner of Capel Street and Ormond Quay Upper (now a branch of the Bank of Ireland), Bloom buys 'Two sheets cream vellum paper one

(217)   reserve two envelopes' for his letter to Martha. Catching sight of Blazes Boylan passing in a jaunting car, he moves on an impulse to follow it and almost forgets to pay for the stationery. He tenders a sixpence and gets fourpence change.

Boylan alights and enters the Ormond Hotel. Bloom,

(218)   hovering outside, sees Father Cowley outside Fanning's office and meets Richie Goulding approaching from the direction of the Four Courts. They decide to eat together and go into the hotel.

To find out what has been happening there in the

17. Grattan Bridge. Daly's, where Bloom buys notepaper, is on the corner at the extreme right. The Ormond Hotel, with its entrance and windows painted white, is at 8 Ormond Quay Upper; the 'greenhouse' is outside it by the riverwall. Marks's shop is to the left of the hotel on the next corner.

meantime, we return to the beginning of the chapter. 'Bronze by gold heard the hoofirons, steelyringing.'

210 Joyce said that he wrote this episode in the musical form of a *fuga per canonem*. Its technique represents in words a number of musical devices, and the episode begins with a sort of overture which previews the various themes of the

211 piece. The action proper starts on the next page with the two barmaids looking 'over the crossblind of the Ormond Bar' at the passing cavalcade.

The hotel has changed considerably since the first Bloomsday. In 1904, when it was run by Mrs Nora de Massey, the façade of the building was of a type with the surrounding houses. Considerable alterations, however, were carried out after a fire in the 1930s, and there have been further changes to the interior since its reopening as The New Ormond Hotel in 1987. The front entrance of the hotel is still in the same place. On the right as you enter, the present bar occupies the same area as the original, with its window onto the street, although the structure and decor are modern. On the left, in the modern 'Siren Suite', was the diningroom where Bloom and Goulding ate and where they could hear the music in the bar through the open door. The back bar, behind the diningroom, has been restored in its original style.

As the clatter of the viceregal hoofs dies away the boots

212 comes into the bar with a 'tray of chattering china', and Miss Douce and Miss Kennedy drink their tea despite a fit

213 of the giggles over the 'old fogey' in Boyd's the druggist's. (Boyd's was at 46 Mary Street, next door to Dublin's first cinema, the Volta, which was opened in 1909 with James Joyce himself as manager. Joyce returned to Trieste within weeks of the opening and the cinema had to be sold soon afterwards.)

214 'Into their bar strolled Mr Dedalus. Chips, picking chips off one of his rocky thumbnails.' Mr Dedalus appears not to have accompanied the others to the sub-sheriff's office, having found the hotel too tempting a lure to pass by. He has barely sat down with his whiskey and

215 water and filled his pipe when Lenehan comes in, looking for Boylan. He left a message with Boylan's secretary

earlier that he would see him here at four, his purpose apparently being to interest him in Tom Rochford's invention. Lenehan passes on greetings to Mr Dedalus from
216 Stephen, with whom he was drinking earlier in 'Mooney's *en ville*' (Abbey Street) and 'Mooney's *sur mer*' (now the Horse and Tram on Eden Quay).

(Lenehan's movements for the day are fairly well documented. He first appears in the newspaper office around 12.30, and then joins Stephen in the two Mooneys'. Afterwards he calls in to Boylan's office in D'Olier Street and then goes on up to Crampton Court to meet Tom Rochford. The stroll along Temple Bar with M'Coy fills in time before his rendezvous at the Ormond. From here he will go to find out the result of the race and then repair to Barney Kiernan's; later he meets up with Stephen and joins the others in Holles Street Hospital.)

Bald Pat the waiter comes into the bar to get a drink for a customer in the diningroom. Mr Dedalus, perhaps not too interested in hearing about his son, wanders into the saloon, a separate room probably situated at the back of
217 the bar, and fingers the piano. The instrument has just been retuned by the blind stripling who left his tuningfork behind. Mr Dedalus strikes 'its buzzing prongs'.

218 As he begins to play the piano, Blazes Boylan arrives in the bar and orders a sloegin for himself and a glass of bitter for Lenehan. 'Wire in yet?' he asks, referring to the result of the horserace. Both of them have put their money on Sceptre.

219 Richie Goulding and Bloom arrive in the diningroom and choose a table near the door. In the bar, Lenehan persuades Miss Douce '*Sonnez la cloche!*' and she performs her party trick of twanging her garter: 'Smack. She set free sudden in rebound her nipped elastic garter smackwarm against her smackable a woman's warmhosed thigh.' This is another sound to add to the many musical noises in this episode – the cavalcade, the teacups, the piano, Boylan's creaking shoes and so on. The organ of the body which Joyce assigned to *Sirens* was the ear, and there is plenty to entertain it.

Boylan, aware that he is already late for his four o'clock

meeting with Molly, tosses back his drink (a quick sloegin, it would appear) and makes for the door before Lenehan can raise the business of Tom Rochford's invention. Lenehan gulps his bitter and hurries after him. They 220 leave the hotel and a minute later Boylan sets off in the jaunting car, along the quays, up O'Connell Street and North Frederick Street, along Dorset Street and into Eccles Street. The jingling of the car will soon be echoed in the brass quoits of Molly's bed.

As Lenehan disappears outside, Father Cowley and Ben Dollard come in from the subsheriff's office. They have, of course, missed Fanning, but Dollard assures Cowley that 'Alf Bergan will speak to the long fellow.' As they join Mr Dedalus in the saloon, Richie Goulding and Bloom order Power's whiskey and a bottle of cider from Pat, who gets them from the bar. Miss Douce is at the window, watching Boylan leave and wondering why her 'cloche' sent him going so quickly.

221 The trio in the saloon, unaware of Bloom's proximity, are recalling the night when Ben Dollard went to Holles Street to borrow a pair of trousers from Bloom for a concert. The trousers, as Bloom himself recalls soon afterwards, were a revealingly tight fit. Bloom orders liver and mashed potatoes and Goulding has steak and kidney 222 pie. As they eat Ben Dollard launches into song: '—*When love absorbs my ardent soul . . .*' and Miss Kennedy serves two gentlemen at the bar. George Lidwell 'suave solicitor' enters the bar and is told that his friends (Mr Dedalus and 223 company) are inside. Rather than join them, he stays in the bar to have a Guinness and to flirt with Miss Douce. Lidwell was a real-life person whom Joyce engaged as his solicitor during the dispute over *Dubliners* with George Roberts, and with whom he had at least one meeting here in the Ormond Hotel bar; he was, however, ineffectual in the case and actually took Roberts' side.

Dollard and Cowley try to persuade Mr Dedalus to sing; 224 but at first he only plays '—*All is lost now*' on the piano, 225 overheard by the diners. At length he sings, '—*When first I saw that form endearing*', and Bloom signals to Pat 'to set ajar the door of the bar' so that they can hear better.

Listening, Bloom takes the elastic band off his packet of notepaper and winds it round his fingers. The song, he
226 realises, is from Flotow's *Martha*. '*Martha* it is. Coincidence. Just going to write. Lionel's song.'
227 Mr Dedalus finishes the song amid applause, and Tom Kernan turns up (we last saw him on page 207, vainly greeting the viceroy further along the quays at Bloody
228 Bridge). Half-listening to Richie Goulding, Bloom continues to fiddle with the elastic band until it snaps. He decides to write his letter to Martha here rather than in the post office, and asks Pat for a pen and ink and a blotter.
229 Pretending to be answering an advertisement, he produces his newspaper. 'He held unfurled his *Freeman*. Can't see now. Remember write Greek ees. Bloom dipped, Bloo mur: dear sir. Dear Henry wrote: dear Mady.'

Joyce himself used Greek E's when writing to a lady called Martha; this was Marthe Fleischmann, for whom he had a brief infatuation in Zurich in 1918–19. His letters to her, produced after his death, were at first believed to be fakes because of the unusual E's, but Richard Ellmann, Joyce's biographer, was able to verify them by reference to this passage.

Quickly calculating, he works out that he can enclose a postal order for two and six as a 'poor little pres'. Finishing
230 the letter, he murmurs, for Goulding's benefit, a false address while writing the real one. 'Messrs Callan, Coleman and Co, limited' come, of course, straight off the top of the Deaths column. He will buy the postal order at 'the postoffice lower down' on his way to Green Street where he has arranged to meet Martin Cunningham and the others for a lift to Dignam's house in Sandymount.
231 Through the bardoor he can see Lydia Douce holding to Lidwell's ear a shell which she brought back from her visit to the seaside. Bob Cowley is back at the piano, playing the
232 minuet from *Don Giovanni*. At that moment Boylan, of whom we have been given periodic glimpses (as we were earlier of Bloom) during his journey through the city, arrives at 7 Eccles Street and raps on the doorknocker. No more is heard of him, but the rap is echoed by a 'Tap,' the

sound of the blind stripling's cane, which is repeated over the next few pages as he returns towards the hotel to fetch his tuningfork.

Bloom prepares to leave and pays for his meal, but lingers when he hears Ben Dollard singing 'The Croppy 233 Boy'. The story of the song comes through, bit by bit – how the croppy boy makes his confession to the priest and asks for his blessing before he goes out to die for Ireland, only to discover that the 'priest' is a yeoman captain in 234 disguise. Bloom watches Miss Douce listening and thinks of the effect of music on people's thoughts and how 235 absorbed she looks. He then notices Lidwell and wonders if the absorption is really for him. Certainly the motions of her hand on the beerpull seem to indicate something not merely musical in her mind.

Bloom takes his hat, abandons his newspaper and goes out past Pat, glances at the barmaids through the bardoor, and scares the 'eavesdropping boots' in the hallway. As he 236 leaves the song ends and the trio return to the bar. Their conversation continues while Bloom, feeling lonely, turns right outside the door and walks off along Ormond Quay Upper. 'Wait. Postoffice near Reuben J's one and eight-pence too. Get shut of it. Dodge round by Greek street.'

237 The cider, and the burgundy from earlier in the day, are creating their own music as he walks past Barry's at No. 12, and he is wondering how and where he can exercise his 238 wind instrument when he sees 'A frowsy whore with black straw sailor hat askew' and recognises her; he had once approached her in a lane but had been scared off when she said that she had seen him with Molly. To avoid her he turns and looks in the window of Lionel Marks's shop on the corner of Arran Street (now a gift shop). As the blind man arrives at the Ormond Hotel Bloom views a print of Robert Emmet in the window with the famous last words of his speech in the dock: 'When my country takes her place among the nations of the earth, then and not till then let my epitaph be written. I have done.' The print is possibly a souvenir from the previous year's celebration of the centenary of Emmet's rebellion.

239 Taking the opportunity as a passing tram drowns the

noise, he lets his gases take their course. 'Pprrpffrrppffff.'

At this point one may follow Bloom's route from here to Barney Kiernan's, or take Tour 5b below to the location of *Wandering Rocks viii*.

Bloom passes Arran Street and goes on to the post office at 34 Ormond Quay Upper, below Reuben J. Dodd's office in the same building. From here he apparently takes another circuitous route towards Barney Kiernan's. He turns right either beside number 35 or at the next corner beside the Four Courts. (This imposing building by James Gandon, completed 1786–1802, housed the original four courts; Chancery, King's Bench, Exchequer and Common Pleas. In 1922 its occupation by anti-Treaty forces precipitated the outbreak of the Irish Civil War. The building was shelled and countless irreplaceable archives in the adjoining Public Record Office was destroyed. The Courts were restored and reopened in 1931.)

At the back of the Four Courts he crosses Chancery Street (formerly Pill Lane) and is seen on the corner of Greek Street by the narrator of *Cyclops*, 'with his cod's eye counting up all the guts of the fish' (p.244). He appears to have filled in some time hanging round the back of the markets before heading for Barney Kiernan's, perhaps by going up Greek Street, turning right along Mary's Lane and taking the third turn to the left into Little Green Street. This street crosses Little Britain Street, where Barney Kiernan's pub stood near the opposite corner on the right. The action of *Cyclops* is described in Tour 8.

By returning along Little Green Street as far as Mary's Abbey, you may connect with Tour 5b, which begins back on Ormond Quay Upper.

Tour 5b: *Wandering Rocks viii*

From the site of Marks's shop walk up Arran Street and turn right into Mary's Abbey. On the left hand side is Meetinghouse Lane, a narrow laneway in which is situated the old chapterhouse at St Mary's Abbey. Recently refurbished by the Office of Public Works, the chapterhouse now contains an exhibition on the history of the Abbey. It is open to the public during summer months (further information from the OPW at 613111, extension 2386).

189   Two pink faces turned in the flare of the tiny torch.
    —Who's that? Ned Lambert asked. Is that Crotty?

Ned Lambert, who has left the Oval pub after drinking with Mr Dedalus, is now showing a visitor around the chapterhouse, which is being used as a warehouse by his firm, Alexander and Co. J. J. O'Molloy, having failed to borrow any money from Myles Crawford (p.121), probably joined the drinkers in Mooney's before going in search of his next touch, Ned Lambert. He enquires in the office on Mary's Abbey and is directed to the chapterhouse (p.185), where he finds Lambert with the Reverend Hugh C. Love, Bob Cowley's landlord. 'Crotty' is probably another of Alexander's men.

    '—Yes, sir, Ned Lambert said heartily. We are standing in the historic council chamber of Saint Mary's Abbey where silken Thomas proclaimed himself a rebel in 1534. This is the most historic spot in all Dublin.' All these details, and more, are available within. The room once lit only by Love's vesta now has the benefit of electricity. The chapterhouse, with its present floor seven feet above its ancient level, is all that remains of a flourishing Cistercian Abbey, whose stones were used in 1678 to build Essex Bridge. The 'pillars' mentioned are probably a detail misremembered by Joyce. Love, who is writing a history of the Fitzgerald (or 'Geraldine') family, is interested in 'Silken' Thomas Fitzgerald, whose short-lived rebellion ended in his execution. A later scion of the family, Desmond Fitzgerald, a minister in the Irish Free State government in 1922, offered to propose Joyce for the Nobel prize for literature, but Joyce advised him against it, saying it would probably cost him his portfolio.

    (In interpolations we see John Howard Parnell in the DBC and Lynch's girlfriend in Marino.)

190   Ned Lambert shows his visitor out, and follows with

J. J. O'Molloy into Mary's Abbey. The clergyman turns left into Mary's Abbey and right into Capel Street towards City Hall (p.201), but then apparently turns left along Great Strand Street towards Cahill's corner on Liffey Street Lower and Lotts, where he is understandably 'unperceived' when the viceroy passes. The other two go round to the courthouse in Green Street, where J. J. O'Molloy apparently does Lambert a favour in return for a loan. Like most other earned or borrowed money in this book, it is promptly spent on drink, in Barney Kiernan's.

To follow their route, turn right into Mary's Abbey and right again along Little Green Street, which leads to Little Britain Street and to the courthouse just beyond it on the left hand side (see Tour 8). Alternatively, turn left and follow Abbey Street to O'Connell Street for Tour 6.

Aeolus, 12 noon

96 'Before Nelson's pillar trams slowed, shunted, changed trolley . . .'

Halfway along O'Connell Street on the west side is the General Post Office with its imposing portico. Designed by Francis Johnston in 1815, shortly after the erection of Nelson's Pillar nearby, it was occupied in Easter 1916 by the Irish Volunteers and became their principal stronghold in the week-long rebellion which left most of the street in ruins. The GPO, gutted by fire, was later restored, and the opening lines of the Proclamation of Independence are displayed outside where they were first read out by Patrick Pearse. Inside the main hall is a statue of the Irish hero Cuchulain by Oliver Sheppard (which receives unusual treatment in Samuel Beckett's *Murphy* at the beginning of chapter four).

On the south side of the GPO is the cul-de-sac of Prince's Street. The area now occupied by the British Home Stores was then the site of the ornate Metropole Hotel. Just behind the BHS, where the pavement angles into the street, was the entrance to the *Freeman's Journal* office. Prince's stores were further along the street.

Appropriate to its location, the episode is set like a newspaper in short sections under headlines. 'Aeolus' in the *Odyssey* was the controller of the winds, and Joyce chose the lungs as the organ of the body for the episode. Accordingly there are many references to wind and breath. People rush in and out, doors blow open and papers whirl about.

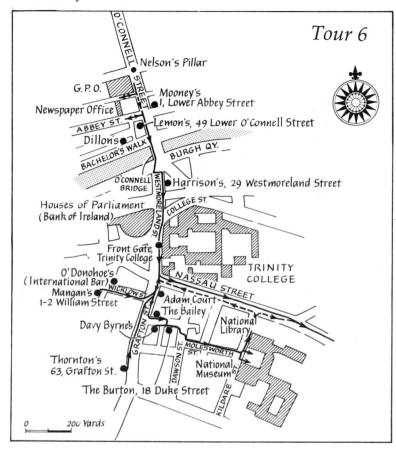

Tour 6

Nelson's Pillar

G.P.O.

Mooney's
I, Lower Abbey Street

Newspaper Office

ABBEY ST.

Lemon's, 49 Lower O'Connell Street

Dillon's

BACHELOR'S WALK

BURGH QY.

O'CONNELL
BRIDGE

WESTMORELAND ST

Harrison's, 29 Westmoreland Street

Houses of Parliament
(Bank of Ireland)

COLLEGE ST.

Front Gate,
Trinity College

TRINITY
COLLEGE

O'Donohoe's
(International Bar)

NASSAU STREET

Mangan's
1-2 William Street

WICKLOW ST

Adam Court

The Bailey

National
Library

Davy Byrnes

GRAFTON ST

MOLESWORTH
ST.

Thornton's
63, Grafton St.

DAWSON ST.

National
Museum

KILDARE

The Burton, 18 Duke Street

0   200 Yards

Bloom, who has returned to the city centre with the funeral carriages, is inside the *Freeman* office, where Red Murray cuts out a copy of the Alexander Keyes advertisement for him, and William Brayden, the owner, passes on the way to his office upstairs. Bloom takes the clipping through the building, 'along the warm dark stairs and passage', into the *Evening Telegraph* office, which backed onto the *Freeman*.

Here he sees Hynes getting his account of the funeral in to the evening edition. It is taken by the foreman, Councillor Nannetti. Nannetti, an Italian Irishman, was indeed a

18. O'Connell Street (formerly Sackville Street). While Stephen and his companions cross the street past Sir John Gray's statue (the small figure between O'Connell and Nelson's Pillar) Bloom walks up the west side of the street past Lemon's (the second shop beyond the nearest awning). On the right of the picture is the peaked roof of the Sackville Street branch of the DBC, built in 1901.

councillor in real life and, as Bloom foresees, later became Lord Mayor of Dublin.

99   As Hynes passes, Bloom drops an unsuccessful hint about the three shillings which Hynes has owed him for the past three weeks. Bloom approaches Nannetti with the
100 ad, which requires a change in design, and offers to run round and pick up a copy of the redesigned ad which has already appeared in a Kilkenny paper. The foreman
101 agrees to give Keyes a three months' renewal, and Bloom walks on through the caseroom towards the Abbey Street
102 exit. Passing the *Telegraph* editor's office, he goes in to phone Keyes and finds Ned Lambert, Mr Dedalus and Professor MacHugh laughing over Dan Dawson's speech in the newspaper.
103   J. J. O'Molloy, a declining barrister, enters behind Bloom. He has come to see Myles Crawford, the editor, in

104 hope of borrowing some money. Ned Lambert continues to read the Dawson speech until Mr Dedalus can take no more. '—O! Mr Dedalus cried, giving vent to a hopeless groan. Shite and onions! That'll do, Ned. Life is too short.'

Myles Crawford appears from the inner office, where he has been talking with Lenehan, the correspondent for
105 *Sport*. Ned Lambert and Mr Dedalus leave for a drink in the Oval pub (just outside the office in Abbey Street) and Bloom slips into Crawford's office to phone Keyes as
106 Lenehan joins the others. He is informed that Keyes is in Dillon's auctionrooms in Bachelor's Walk, and goes out to
107 see him (probably via Williams's Row on the other side, which leads directly to the quays). The others, at the window, watch in amusement as the newsboys follow Bloom across the street, imitating him.

108 'Mr O'Madden Burke, tall in copious grey of Donegal tweed, came in from the hallway. Stephen Dedalus, behind him, uncovered as he entered.' Stephen's companion is not to be confused with O. Madden, the rider of Sceptre, or Madden, the medical student in Holles Street Hospital. Stephen himself, who was last seen in Irishtown as the mourners went by, has stopped on his way here to
109 send a telegram from College Green post office. Now he delivers Mr Deasy's letter to Myles Crawford, who notices that a blank piece has been torn off the end. Stephen recalls to himself the lines which he wrote on the paper.

110 Lenehan, who seems determined to let the wind out of any conversation when it gets too serious, finally manages to parade his riddle: 'What opera is like a
111 railwayline? . . . *The Rose of Castile*.' Myles Crawford, surveying the array of talents gathered in his office, encourages Stephen to write him something. '. . . something with a bite in it. Put us all into it, damn its soul. Father, Son and Holy Ghost and Jakes M'Carthy.'

This was precisely the challenge which Joyce rose to in his own books, particularly *Ulysses*. The headline above this section, quoting Crawford's remark "YOU CAN DO IT!", has an unusual distinction in that it is the only occurrence in the entire book of conventional quotation

marks, which Joyce normally never used, preferring ital-
ics or an opening dash. Presumably employed here to
convey the form that a newspaper headline would have
used, the marks only appeared for the first time in the
Corrected Text.

112   Myles Crawford recalls a brilliant coup by the journalist
Ignatius Gallaher (who appears in 'A Little Cloud' in
Dubliners) when he reported on the Phoenix Park murders
of 6 May 1882 (not 'eightyone' as remembered here),
using an advertisement to provide map references. The
victims of this famous crime were Lord Frederick Caven-
dish, the Under-Secretary for Ireland, and Thomas
Burke, also of the viceregal staff. The attack was carried
out by a nationalist group called The Invincibles, and on
the evidence of an informer named James Carey, Joe
Brady and the other assassins were hanged. Fitzharris
(known as 'Skin-the-Goat'), driver of the getaway vehicle,
got twenty years in prison and was let out in time to appear
in *Ulysses*.

113   In the middle of Crawford's story Bloom rings up from
Dillon's to discuss the Keyes advertisement. The editor
refuses to be interrupted and Professor MacHugh advises
Bloom: 'Come across yourself.'

114   Meanwhile the conversation turns to the subject of
115   oratory. J. J. O'Molloy quotes a polished period from the
lips of a fellow barrister, Seymour Bushe, and Professor
116   MacHugh answers with the lofty speech of John F.
Taylor, which was delivered, not in the College Historical
117   Society in Trinity as stated, but in the Law Students'
Debating Society of Ireland in the King's Inns in October
1901. Joyce selected this passage for the only recording he
made from *Ulysses* – apparently because the acoustic
recording was more suitable to a declamatory speech than
to the quiet tones of interior monologue.

118   'I have money,' remembers Stephen, and he proposes
that they adjourn for a drink. As they proceed towards the
door, Myles Crawford goes back into the inner office for
his keys, and J. J. O'Molloy follows him in, seeing his
opportunity to ask for a loan.

119   The others emerge down the steps into Abbey Street

and turn left. (The newspaper office was destroyed in 1916. The entrance was situated where the Abbey Street door of Eason's is now.) As the newsboys burst out behind them with the freshly printed racing special, Stephen starts telling his story 'The Parable of the Plums' about the two Dublin women going up Nelson's Pillar. The tale is full of actions which are ultimately cancelled out by equal and negative ones. The money, for instance, is saved up, only to be spent; the plums are bought 'to take off the thirst of the brawn'; and when the ladies get to the top they get giddy looking down and a crick in their necks looking up, so they end up doing neither.

120 Myles Crawford appears on the steps just as Bloom returns from Dillon's. Why Bloom should be as far along the street as the offices of the *Irish Catholic* (now occupied by the *Irish Independent*) is not clear. Bloom breathlessly asks Myles Crawford if he will grant Keyes a free paragraph of editorial ('a little puff') in return for his renewal of the ad; but Crawford uncooperatively replies '—He can
121 kiss my royal Irish arse' and turns back to J. J. O'Molloy, whom he is also unable to oblige. (J. J. O'Molloy later gets money from Ned Lambert, but only in return for a favour.)

Leaving Bloom standing uncertainly in Abbey Street
122 (where we will return to him shortly), the pubgoers reach the corner, hearing the end of Stephen's story, and cross
123 O'Connell Street by way of 'sir John Gray's pavement island', where a statue commemorates the founder of the *Freeman's Journal* and inaugurator of the city waterworks. Here the professor peers aloft and to his left at Nelson on his Pillar, a doric column 134 feet high which was founded in 1808 to support a 13-foot statue by Thomas Kirk of 'the onehandled adulterer'. Despite numerous proposals for its removal, the Pillar survived until the night of 7–8 March 1966, when the top half was expertly blown off by persons unknown. Army engineers blew up the rest (and shattered numerous shop windows) two days later. For a while afterwards *two* heads of Nelson were on the market, but the real one is now on display in the Dublin Civic Museum in South William Street. The Pillar stood at

the intersection of O'Connell Street, Henry Street and Earl Street. Just north of the site is the statue of Anna Livia, Joyce's personification of the river Liffey. The female figure reclining amid jets of water has been dubbed 'the floosie in the jacuzzi' by the locals. Close by in Earl Street is a statue of Joyce himself by Marjorie Fitzgibbon.

Stephen and the others are bound for Mooney's pub, which was on the north side of Lower Abbey Street next to the O'Connell Street corner. The pub exterior survives, but a building society now operates within. Nearby at No. 5 was The Ship pub, where Mulligan and Haines were waiting vainly for Stephen to make his 12.30 rendezvous. Between Abbey Street and the National Library Stephen also visits 'Mooney's *sur mer*' on Eden Quay, travelling nearly on the same route as Bloom, to whom we shall now return.

Back outside the *Telegraph* office, Bloom turns right out of Middle Abbey Street and walks towards O'Connell Bridge.

19. O'Connell Bridge. Bloom buys Banbury cakes from the barrow in the foreground. Ahead of him, on the extreme right of the picture, the timeball on the Ballast Office shows that it is after one o'clock (and the shadows confirm it). On the far side of Westmoreland Street is Harrison's, to the left of the building with the two arched doorways.

Laestrygonians, 1.10 p.m.

124 'Pineapple rock, lemon platt, butter scotch. A sugar-sticky girl shovelling scoopfuls of creams for a christian brother.'

This chapter contains one of the most minutely detailed itineraries of the book and for that reason is especially rewarding to follow, so much so that in 1988 Bloom's lunchtime route was marked by a series of fourteen pavement plaques graced with the appropriate text. *Laestrygonians* begins outside Graham Lemon's sweetshop, where a sign reading 'The Confectioner's Hall' still exists above the modern shop-front. This stretch, between Abbey Street and the river, is the only complete block in O'Connell Street to have survived the destruction of 1916 and 1922; ironically, it has suffered more from an outbreak of garish shop-fronts and fast-food restaurants which have appeared in the last twenty years.

Reading a throwaway which advertises the gospel meeting in Merrion Hall, he reaches the corner with Bachelor's Walk and glances to the right towards the auctionrooms where he met Keyes earlier, noticing that Dilly Dedalus is still outside.

125 'As he set foot on O'Connell bridge a puffball of smoke plumed up from the parapet.' The brewery barges, plying to and from the Guinness brewery, had hinged funnels which were let down when they passed under a low bridge, releasing the 'puffball'. Bloom stops by the parapet, looks down at the gulls and throws them the crumpled throwaway (which is seen floating seawards in 'Wandering Rocks'). From an applewoman's stall on the pavement he buys two Banbury cakes (made of pastry and currants) and throws them also to the birds.

126 Stifling an uneasy thought that Blazes Boylan might have a venereal infection, Bloom looks ahead to the Ballast Office on the corner in front of him. Now Ballast House, it was taken down in 1979 and rebuilt with some alterations, including the moving of its famous clock from the east to the north side. This was the clock which, in *Stephen Hero*, Stephen told Cranly 'was capable of an epiphany'. The timeball was part of a mechanism on the roof involving a copper sphere which fell down a pole at 1 p.m. precisely.

Dunsink time (estimated from the observatory near Phoenix Park where Sir Robert Ball was the Astronomer Royal) was 25 minutes behind Greenwich time, and was official Irish time until 1914.

127 As he crosses Aston Quay to the Ballast Office the five 'sandwichmen' march towards him from Westmoreland Street, advertising Hely's in Dame Street where Bloom used to work. They spend the day walking up and down between the far end of Grafton Street and, probably, the far end of O'Connell Street.

'He crossed Westmoreland street when apostrophe S had plodded by. Rover cycleshop.' Crossing the street nowadays is a much more complicated business than in 1904. Bloom did not have to contend with cars, pedestrian lights, traffic islands and curbside railings on his way across to the cycleshop (where the new ICS Building Society office now stands).

128 Thinking of the old times when he was in Hely's, Bloom walks along the curbstone.

—O, Mr Bloom, how do you do?
—O, how do you do, Mrs Breen?

129 He meets Mrs Breen, an old friend, outside Harrison's Restaurant, now a newer establishment under the same name. The pavement grating outside, where the street arab stood breathing the smell of the food he could not buy, has gone, but something of the Edwardian interior remains at the back of the premises. Mrs Breen and her husband are on their way to John Henry Menton's office

130 in Bachelor's Walk to take an action over an anonymous postcard reading 'U.p: up'. The most that scholars have been able to make of this cryptic message is that Breen must have had some kind of urinary complaint. As Bloom learns that their friend Mrs Purefoy is in Holles Street hospital, 'A bony form strode along the curbstone from the river staring with a rapt gaze into the sunlight through a heavystringed glass'.

131 Cashel Boyle O'Connor Fitzmaurice Tisdall Farrell, also known as 'Endymion' was a well-known Dublin eccentric whose condition was reportedly due to a plunge into a vat in Guinness's Brewery (which was, in fact, full of

carbon dioxide rather than stout). One of his tricks was to let off an alarm clock outside the Ballast Office when the timeball fell, which may explain his presence at this point. Farrell continues on his way towards the National Library, dodging outside all the lampposts. Parting from 132 Mrs Breen, Bloom follows Farrell past the *Irish Times* office at No. 31 (now replaced by the EBS office) and the crossing at Fleet Street.

'Luncheon interval. A sixpenny at Rowe's? Must look up that ad in the national library. An eightpenny in the Burton. Better. On my way.' (Rowe's would have involved a detour to George's Street.) Bloom passes Bolton's on the corner of Fleet Street and walks on towards College Street.

133 'Before the huge high door of the Irish house of parliament a flock of pigeons flew. Their little frolic after meals. Who will we do it on? I pick the fellow in black.' The magnificent Houses of Parliament in College Green, designed in 1729 by Sir Edward Lovett Pearce and enlarged in 1785 by James Gandon, lost their occupation in 1800 when the Act of Union merged the Irish and British parliaments in Westminster, effectively ending the prosperous Georgian era in Ireland. The building now houses the Bank of Ireland, but the chamber of the House of Lords was preserved and may be seen on request.

Bloom passes the statue of the poet Thomas Moore with its 'roguish finger' and the nearby public toilet which gave rise to the joke about Moore's famous poem, 'The Meeting of the Waters'. In a less genial description in *A Portrait*, Joyce says of the statue 'sloth of the body and of the soul crept over it like unseen vermin', while Trinity College is a 'grey block . . . set heavily in the city's ignorance like a 134 dull stone set in a cumbrous ring'. For Bloom, the college has a 'surly front'. Founded in 1592 by Elizabeth I, Trinity has produced such distinguished graduates as Jonathan Swift, Oliver Goldsmith, Edmund Burke, Oscar Wilde and Samuel Beckett. Its elegant buildings include the Old Library, containing its most famous treasure, the Book of Kells, an intricately illuminated manuscript of the Gospels dating from the ninth century.

Wandering Rocks vi

(188) —*Ma!* Almidano Artifoni said.

He gazed over Stephen's shoulder at Goldsmith's knobby poll . . .

Here at the front gate of Trinity, Stephen, on his way from the National Library to Bedford Row, meets Almidano Artifoni, the professor of singing. (The character is based on Joyce's teacher Benedetto Palmieri, and the name is taken from the director of the Berlitz School in Trieste.) Artifoni is, apparently, advising Stephen against abandoning his singing career. He had ideas like Stephen's when he was young, he says, he too thought the world was a beast. He feels that Stephen is sacrificing himself. A

20. College Green. On the right is 'Goldsmith's knobby poll'. The Dalkey tram which Almidano Artifoni has just missed is on the left, and beyond it is the Grattan statue. The tram passing the Bank of Ireland is advertising Flower & M'Donald, Bloom's coal merchant.

bloodless sacrifice, Stephen claims. Artifoni begs him to consider his advice, and Stephen promises to do so. Spotting the Dalkey tram, Artifoni takes hasty leave and trots in vain after it. He is obliged to walk to Ballsbridge, and arrives there just as the viceroy does. 'The stern stone hand of Grattan' is raised aloft opposite the gate on the statue of the greatest member of the old Irish Parliament.

Laestrygonians (continued)

135 Bloom approaches the Provost's house on the left, built in 1760 and still lived in by the Provost of Trinity. A former incumbent of the office was Dean Salmon, whom Bloom remembers here. On the other side of the street he sees John Howard Parnell, the city marshal, with his 'Poached eyes on ghost', passing Walter Sexton's (now Thomas Cook's Travel) on his way towards the DBC in Dame Street for coffee and chess. George Russell, the poet (better known as A.E.) and a young woman pass Bloom on the curbstone; Russell, like Farrell, is on his way to the National Library.

136 'He crossed at Nassau street corner and stood before the window of Yeates and Son, pricing the fieldglasses.' The opticians on the corner moved some years ago and a new front was put on the premises by the ICS Building Society. Bloom looks up Grafton Street into the sun and holds up his hand to blot out the disk with his little finger. He

137 moves on past La Maison Claire, now a newsagent, and looks left into Adam Court, where he sees Bob Doran 'sloping into the Empire'. This is the back entrance of what is now Judge Roy Bean's bar restaurant on Nassau

21. Grafton Street. Bloom approaches up the right hand side of this fashionable thoroughfare, passing the entrance to Adam Court beneath the clock. On the left are Switzer's and the corner of Wicklow Street.

Street. The establishment's most famous phase began in 1926, when Jammet's Restaurant moved here from 27 Andrew Street (where in 1900 Jammet's purchased Corless's restaurant, the meeting-place of Chandler and Gallaher in 'A Little Cloud' in *Dubliners*). Jammet's became a favourite meeting-place of writers and artists and its closure in 1967 was the end of an era.

'Grafton street gay with housed awnings lured his senses.' Grafton Street, still one of the city's most fashionable shopping areas, is now pedestrianised and has recently been repaved in brick. In Joyce's day this street was paved, not with cobbles or setts, but with hexagonal wooden blocks which could be lifted out when repairs to pipes and other surfaces were necessary. Similar blocks can be seen inside Front Gate in Trinity. The wooden surface would have produced the 'hoofthuds lowringing' which Bloom hears.

138   Bloom passes Brown Thomas, still a premier department store, where he considers buying a pincushion for Molly for her birthday on 8 September (also the birthday, as Joyce was mischievously aware, of the Blessed Virgin Mary).

Frank Budgen wrote of meeting Joyce one day in Zurich and asking after the progress of *Ulysses*. Joyce said he had been working hard all day and had completed two sentences. The time was consumed, not in choosing the words, but in seeking 'the perfect order of words in the sentence'. The lines in question, which occur as the hungry Bloom, caught by the sight of silk petticoats, daydreams of seduction, are: 'Perfume of embraces all him assailed. With hungered flesh obscurely, he mutely craved to adore'.

The corner premises, formerly Combridge's the stationers, were taken over by Brown Thomas some years ago. Bloom turns left here into Duke Street.

On the left hand side of the street is the Bailey Restaurant, where Parnell and his supporters used to meet in the smoking room upstairs. In Bloom's time it was the haunt of Arthur Griffith and *his* nationalist followers, whom Gogarty later joined there. In the 1950s and 1960s it became a favourite meeting-place of Dublin writers. The door nearest to Grafton Street leads to the stairs, where halfway up on the return may be seen the original door of 7 Eccles Street, saved when the house was demolished, and officially unveiled by Patrick Kavanagh on Bloomsday 1967 with the words 'I hereby declare this door shut'.

Bloom's destination is the Burton Restaurant, beyond Duke Lane on the opposite side of the street at No. 18 (now the Gas Emporium). 'His heart astir he pushed in the door of the Burton restaurant. Stink gripped his trembling breath: pungent meatjuice, slush of greens. See 139 the animals feed.' Repulsed, however, by the crowd of dirty eaters, 'He came out into clearer air and turned back towards Grafton street.'

140   Instead he enters Davy Byrne's 'moral pub', still flourishing at No. 21 but greatly altered inside. The nicely planed curving oak counter and the shelves full of tins are gone, and the walls are decorated with elegant murals by Cecil Salkeld, in one of which Davy Byrne himself appears in his later years, bald and with a large white moustache. Gorgonzola cheese sandwiches and burgundy are popular on Bloomsday.

As Bloom orders his burgundy he is hailed by Nosey Flynn in his nook. His gaze wanders over the potted meat on the shelves, reminding him of the Plumtree's ad placed under the obituaries and prompting thoughts of cannibals. The Laestrygonians in the *Odyssey* were cannibals, and appropriately for this lunchtime episode full of food and eating the organ is the oesophagus.

141   He sits down with Flynn, who hears about the concert tour and asks 'Isn't Blazes Boylan mixed up in it?' Involuntarily Bloom glances up at the 'bilious clock'. There are still two hours to go before Boylan's meeting with Molly. (Joyce specified in his schema that this episode begins at about 1 p.m. If Bloom's observation 'Pub clock five minutes fast' is correct – and he checked his watch on entering the pub – he has taken at least three-quarters of an hour to walk from Abbey Street, a journey which should only take twenty minutes at most.)

142   Davy Byrne joins them from behind the bar on his way towards the window. Nosey Flynn is considering the runners in the Gold Cup, and appears already to have

scanned the edition of *Sport* which emerged from the newspaper office on page 120 with Lenehan's tip for
143 Sceptre. Bloom briefly considers the dewdrop coming down Flynn's nose again, then returns to his lunch. About six o'clock, he thinks, Boylan will be gone and he can head for home. In the event he lingers out much later.

144 He thinks of 'All the odd things people pick up for food'. The sunshine and the taste on his palate bring back memories of the day in May 1888 when he proposed to Molly on Howth Head – the same scene which is in her mind at the end of the book. Studying 'the silent veining' of the oak bar, he thinks of the shapely curves of the classical statues in the museum. In contrast to humans 'stuffing food in one hole and out behind', the goddesses,
145 he realises, are differently shaped. 'They have no. Never looked. I'll look today. Keeper won't see. Bend down let something drop. See if she.'

He rises and goes out to relieve himself in the yard at the back (probably where the exit to Creation Arcade is now). In his absence Nosey Flynn tells Davy Byrne that Bloom is
146 a freemason. Although everybody will admit that 'Bloom has his good points' nobody apparently seems to trust him entirely or to claim him as a close friend. It is perhaps significant that no one he meets is on first-name terms with him.

Paddy Leonard and Bantam Lyons enter, followed by Tom Rochford. As they talk about the Gold Cup race, Bantam Lyons claims to have a hot tip and indicates Mr
147 Bloom on his way out as the man that gave it to him. After their drink Tom Rochford and Nosey Flynn will go up to Crampton Court to show Lenehan and M'Coy the invention, while Bantam Lyons appears soon afterwards in the bookie's in Temple Bar.

Mr Bloom meanwhile turns right towards Dawson Street, avoiding the ravenous terrier choking up its cud in Duke Lane. He passes the Burton and William Miller the plumber's (where another Miller now sells medals), considering ways of watching the progress of material through the digestive tract and calculating how much he will earn if he can get Nannetti to insert Keyes's ad with the accom-
148 panying paragraph as requested. He passes Gray's at No.

13 (not, in fact, on the corner; Joyce was misled by Thom's Directory which listed it as the last number in Duke Street, the corner shop being in Dawson Street) and turns right into Dawson Street, passing Connellan's proselytising bookshop where the Tea Time Express is now.

'A blind stripling stood tapping the curbstone with his slender cane.' The street is clear save for the Prescott's van outside Drago's on the near corner of Molesworth Street. The driver, Bloom presumes, is in John Long's (where Graham O'Sullivan's is now), 'slaking his drouth'. He helps the blind man across the street and follows him along

149 the north side of Molesworth Street. The post office which he passes is gone now, but a pillar box of the period still stands outside.

The blind man turns left down Frederick Street towards the dancing academy at No. 35 on the right. Bloom, musing on whether it is possible to tell colour by touch, decides to experiment. 'Might be settling my braces' he thinks as he passes what is now the Jones Lang Wootton office. 'Walking by Doran's publichouse he slid his hand between his waistcoat and trousers, and, pulling aside his shirt gently, felt a slack fold of his belly. But I know it's whitey yellow. Want to try in the dark to see.'

Ahead of him he sees Sir Frederick Falkiner entering the freemasons' hall, on the left with its pillared doorway.

150 Passing a placard for the Mirus bazaar, he reaches Kildare Street and is just about to bear to the left towards the library when he sees Blazes Boylan approaching up the street. 'Straw hat in sunlight. Tan shoes. Turned up trousers. It is. It is. His heart quopped softly. To the right. Museum. Goddesses. He swerved to the right.' Anxious to avoid Boylan, he makes 'with long windy steps' for the gate of the National Museum.

This building, as Bloom recalls, was built in 1890 to the design of Sir Thomas Deane, along with the matching library on the other side of the courtyard. Before 1925, when Leinster House became the home of the Irish parliament, it was possible to walk straight across between the museum and the library.

To conceal his disquiet Bloom pretends to be searching his pockets for something. The various contents of his pockets are unearthed – the Agendath Netaim leaflet, his handkerchief and newspaper, his potato good luck charm and finally the soap. Reaching the gate, he is 'Safe!'

Inside the entrance rotunda of the museum were the plaster casts of antique statues (since removed) which Bloom proceeds to examine, presumably using his subterfuge of dropping something behind the backside of Venus Kallipyge. Unfortunately, as we gather later, just before he can 'certify the presence or absence of posterior rectal orifice in the case of Hellenic female divinities' he is surprised by Buck Mulligan, who addresses a remark to him. After this expedition he crosses to the library.

Before following him it is worth visiting the museum, despite its lack of divinities. Its most impressive room is the Treasury, where some of the finest examples of Celtic art are on display, including the famous Ardagh and Derrynaflan chalices and the Tara Brooch.

Continue to the National Library by the gate from Kildare Street and the door beneath the portico, and climb the stairway at the back of the rotunda. At the head of the stairs is a monument to T. W. Lyster, the Quaker librarian. To your right as you face the monument is the entrance to the reading room. Behind the counter inside the door is another door which leads to the office where *Scylla and Charybdis* is set. This room may normally only be seen by those applying for a reader's card.

Scylla and Charybdis, 2.15 p.m.

151 'Urbane, to comfort them, the quaker librarian purred . . .'

In the librarian's office are gathered William Lyster, Stephen Dedalus, John Eglinton and George Russell (A.E.). Stephen, who has had three whiskeys in two pubs since we saw him last in the newspaper office, has come to expound his theory on *Hamlet*. John Eglinton (a pen-name; his real name was W. K. Magee) was the editor of *Dana* magazine and a member of the library staff. It was he who met Joyce at the library on the morning after he left the Tower in September 1904. George Russell (who passed Bloom in Grafton Street on the way here) was a key figure in the Irish literary renaissance and a close associate of W. B. Yeats. As editor of the *Irish Homestead* (disrespectfully known as 'The Pigs' Paper') he was the first to publish stories from *Dubliners*. His pseudonym was originally intended to be 'AEON' but a printer's error determined the name by which he was to become known.

The discussion which is in progress becomes a conflict between Stephen's Aristotelian logic and the Platonist approach of the others. Stephen's approach to Shakespeare to a certain extent reflects the approach which Joyce has presented to his own readers, that of seeing his writing as a 'portrait of the artist', filled with the experiences of his own life.

Lyster is only destined to hear the conversation in part. Almost immediately he is summoned away to the reading
152 room by a 'noiseless attendant'. His assistant, Richard Best, 'tall, young, mild, light', joins the group, having just
153 seen off Haines, who has gone to Gill's bookshop in O'Connell Street. Best in later years was asked to give an interview on this chapter. 'After all, you *are* a character in *Ulysses*,' said the interviewer. Best retorted that he was no character but a real person.

154 Best raises the subject of *Hamlet*, and Stephen launches into his theme. He sails a difficult course, as Ulysses did in the *Odyssey* when he took his ship between Scylla, the monster on a rock, and Charybdis, the whirlpool. Almost inevitably he sees himself between 'the devil and the deep sea'. Carefully he sets his scene with a description of the Globe Theatre. 'Local colour. Work in all you know. Make them accomplices'.

155 Shakespeare, it is known, played the part of the Ghost in *Hamlet*. Stephen claims that he wrote the part for himself because he too had been betrayed by his wife with his brother. Russell feels that 'This prying into the family life of a great man' is unnecessary, 'interesting only to the parish clerk'. Joyce scholars would think otherwise. Stephen thinks of the pound he owes Russell, most of which he spent on a whore in Bella Cohen's (the same one whom he goes to see later, only to learn that she is
156 married). Because the molecules of his body have renewed themselves since he borrowed the money, 'I am other I

now. Other I got pound'. On the other hand, his memory gives him continuity; he remains himself. 'A.E.I.O.U.', he concludes.

Stephen argues that Shakespeare's wife, Ann Hathaway, was of major importance to his work, though the others feel that she was merely a mistake. '—Bosh! Stephen said rudely. A man of genius makes no mistakes. His errors are volitional and are the portals of discovery.' This is a very useful remark with which to explain the occasional discrepancies which appear in *Ulysses*.

157 Lyster returns to the room as Stephen reminds his listeners that Ann Hathaway was older than Shakespeare and seduced him in a cornfield. 'And my turn? When?' he wonders secretly. Stephen, for all his self-confidence, is a lonely young man and longing for love. When he looks at the book of charms in Clohissey's later on, it is the one for winning a woman's love that interests him. He is ready for someone to come into his life as Nora Barnacle did into Joyce's at this time.

Russell rises; he is 'due at the *Homestead*'. A meeting of the Theosophical Society may prevent him attending 158 George Moore's soirée later on. Stephen listens as the others talk about the evening and mention several of Dublin's prominent writers who are invited. His own name is conspicuously absent, though Mulligan has been asked to bring Haines. Moore is proposed as the man to write 'our national epic', a task which many would claim fell eventually to Joyce. Hart and Knuth have pointed out that Moore's soirées were usually held on Saturdays, not Thursdays.

159 A.E. leaves, taking with him a copy of Mr Deasy's letter for the *Homestead*, and the discussion is resumed. John Eglinton rightly points out that we know next to nothing about Shakespeare's life. The books by George Brandes, Sidney Lee and Frank Harris which provide the sources for Stephen's argument are based very largely on supposi-160 tion and very little on hard fact. Stephen is aware of the claim that Sir Francis Bacon was really the author of Shakespeare's plays and that 'cypherjugglers' like Ignatius Donnelly, author of *The Great Cryptogram*, had worked out that the printed texts of Shakespeare's works were

in a cypher telling the real story of Bacon's identity (he was, it seems, a son of Elizabeth I by a secret marriage to Robert Dudley). However, he sails by this particular whirlpool and sticks to his theory. The period of Shakespeare's great tragedies indicates a time of sorrow and turmoil; 'the shadow lifts' at the time of the birth of his first grandchild, which revives in him his feeling for love.

161   Stephen claims that Shakespeare lost 'belief in himself' when he was 'overborne' by Ann Hathaway. Something in him was killed and he became, in a way, a ghost.

162   '—Amen! was responded from the doorway.' Buck Mulligan, the last person Stephen wants among his audi-
163 ence, appears in the room. Best tells him that Haines just missed him and Mulligan explains that he came through the museum. Again the conversation veers off course into a discussion of Oscar Wilde's *The Portrait of Mr W. H.* which Best describes as 'the very essence of Wilde'. 'Tame essence of Wilde,' thinks Stephen, watching Best.

'You're darned witty. Three drams of usquebaugh you drank with Dan Deasy's ducats'. It is worth noting that from this episode onwards we never see Stephen entirely sober. Others, however, were not so lucky. Mulligan
164 produces the telegram which Stephen sent him from College Green and describes the terrible scene in the Ship when Haines and he were waiting with '. . . our tongues out a yard long like the drouthy clerics do be fainting for a pussful'.

Having parodied Synge, he goes on to tell Stephen that the playwright is 'out in pampooties' for revenge after an insult to his front door (31 Crosthwaite Park, Dun Laoghaire, fifteen minutes' walk from the Tower). Stephen recalls Synge's 'harsh gargoyle face' from their
165 meeting in Paris. Lyster is summoned again, this time to attend to Mr Bloom, whom he conducts to consult the *Kilkenny People* for Keyes's ad. Buck Mulligan recognises Bloom and tells them what he saw him doing in the museum.

John Eglinton and Best invite Stephen to continue.
166 Stephen explains that Shakespeare spent twenty years living it up in London while Ann (left like Ulysses'

Penelope) stayed in Stratford. We hear nothing of her in all that time save that 'she had to borrow forty shillings from her father's shepherd'. Stephen claims that she had cause and occasion for adultery. If Shakespeare had not been wronged, he adds, why in his famous will did he leave her none of his possessions but his secondbest bed?

167

Stephen reinforces his idea that Shakespeare wrote from experience. A money-lender himself, he knew how Shylock operated. 'All events brought grist to his mill.' Current affairs and topical events provided the themes and material for his plays.

168

'I think you're getting on very nicely. Just mix up a mixture of theolologicophilolological.' The theory, it seems, is more of a clever game than a serious belief. Diverted briefly by Eglinton's challenge to prove Shakespeare a jew, Stephen steers back to Ann Hathaway, 'laid out in stark stiffness in that secondbest bed', and her return to religion in her old age. Eglinton, however, still feels that 'Russell is right. What do we care for his wife or father?' Stephen, considering briefly the alienation between himself and his own father, describes a father as 'a necessary evil'. Shakespeare's father was dead when *Hamlet* was written; Shakespeare himself was a father, no longer a son. His role in the play and in his life as playwright was that of a father and begetter.

169

170

171

Mulligan seizes on one of Stephen's remarks and has an idea. Lyster returns, and Stephen introduces Shakespeare's three brothers, of whom two, Edmund and Richard, are named in his plays, both in the role of villain. Shakespeare uses his own name, Will or William, here and there as well. '—You make good use of the name, John Eglinton allowed. Your own name is strange enough.'

172

173

Joyce chose the name 'Dedalus' for himself with care. In Greek mythology Dedalus was the 'fabulous artificer' who built the labyrinth in Crete and later made himself wings to escape from that country. The Dublin described in Joyce's books was his labyrinth, and he was destined to escape from it. Stephen, however, only has an abortive attempt to recall: 'Newhaven-Dieppe, steerage passenger. Paris and back.'

Lyster is called away again, this time for Father Dineen, the Irish scholar who is famous for his authoritative Irish-English dictionary, and Eglinton asks Stephen to continue his story of the brothers. Stephen thinks briefly of his own brother in the Apothecaries' Hall in Mary Street, on whom he sharpened his theories as he has since done on 'Cranly, Mulligan: now these', and presses on,

174 pointing out that '. . . the theme of the false or the usurping or the adulterous brother of all three in one is to Shakespeare, what the poor are not, always with him'.

He goes beyond this to claim that all Shakespeare's characters arise from different aspects of Shakespeare's mind. Their sins are his sins. 'His unremitting intellect is the hornmad Iago ceaselessly willing that the moor in him

175 shall suffer.' Shakespeare is a parable for all men, concludes Stephen.

Mulligan's idea comes to fruition and he begins to scribble on a slip of paper. Eglinton realises that Stephen's whole construction may be merely a *jeu d'esprit*.

—. . . You have brought us all this way to show us a French triangle. Do you believe your own theory?
—No, Stephen said promptly.

176 Eglinton feels that if this is the case Stephen need hardly expect *Dana* to pay him for the privilege of printing the theory. He is the only contributor who insists on payment. '—For a guinea, Stephen said, you can publish this interview.'

Mulligan draws him away from the Shakespeare fans (who remind Mulligan that he is invited to Moore's) with the hopeful suggestion 'Come, Kinch, the bards must

177 drink'. They leave the office and pass through the readers' room where Cashel Boyle O'Connor Fitzmaurice Tisdall Farrell is writing his name in the book. As they reach the turnstile at the door, Stephen thinks he sees a girl acquaintance in a 'blueribboned hat', but they pass on to the staircase with its 'curving balustrade' while Mulligan tells of the visit he and Haines made that morning to the Abbey Theatre. (By taking a train from Sandycove Station

after their swim, they could have reached Tara Street or Amiens Street station soon after ten o'clock and stopped at the theatre on their way to the Ship in the same street. How long they spent in the pub is uncertain, but Haines must have left some time before Mulligan and visited Best in the library.) The Abbey Theatre was at that time still in the process of formation, with the movement of the Irish Literary Theatre society into new premises at the former Dublin Mechanics' Institute ('the plumbers' hall'), and the first opening night did not take place until 27 December 1904.

Stephen recalls a couple of points he should have made in his theory, but is swept on by Mulligan with his droll remarks and news about the literary people in the theatre. '—Longworth is awfully sick, he said, after what you wrote about that old hake Gregory. [. . .] She gets you a
178 job on the paper and then you go and slate her drivel to Jaysus.' It is small wonder that Stephen is not invited to Moore's.

In 'the pillared Moorish hall' Mulligan reveals the subject of his scribblings, a so-called 'play for the mummers', and laughingly reminds Stephen of a recent incident when he was discovered lying drunk in the corridor of the Literary Theatre's previous venue, the Camden Hall. This was based on a real incident. The 'daughter of Erin' who stumbled over Joyce's sprawled body was a Miss Esposito. When he was ejected by the Fay brothers Joyce recovered somewhat and began beating on the door and shouting 'Open up, Fay, we know you've got women in there.'

179   As they reach the exit door someone passes between them. It is Bloom, making his way like Ulysses between these two obstacles. Mulligan greets him a second time and notices that Bloom has taken an interest in Stephen, which he jokingly interprets as lust. They walk out under the portico and through the gate into Kildare Street.

From here all three travel in the direction of College Green, either by the same route by which Bloom approached the museum, or via Kildare Street and Nassau Street. Somewhere on the way Stephen shakes off Buck

Mulligan, who goes to meet Haines in the DBC while Stephen encounters Almidano Artifoni outside Trinity. Bloom heads for the bookshops off Temple Bar, followed a few minutes later by Stephen.

Turn right from the library gate and follow Kildare Street to Nassau Street. On the right hand corner is the former Kildare Street Club, now the office of the Alliance Française. The magnificent interior of this gentlemen's club (designed by Woodward and Deane, 1861) has alas been removed but the witty carvings by C. W. Harrison (often attributed to the O'Shea brothers) may be seen on the exterior.

Here you may turn right to join Tour 4 at Finn's Hotel, or left towards the Grafton Street area to trace the routes of two Wandering Rocks.

Tour 6a: *Wandering Rocks v*

187 'The blond girl in Thornton's bedded the wicker basket with rustling fibre.'

Blazes Boylan, whom Bloom saw in Kildare Street about an hour previously, is now in Grafton Street at Thornton's fruit and flower shop beside Tangier Lane (now Cassidy's), buying pears and peaches for Molly. At the bottom of the basket go the port and potted meat, which he has presumably bought elsewhere. Outside the shop the Hely's men plod 'towards their goal' at the corner of Stephen's Green, where on p.188 they turn round and retrace their steps behind the intended site for Wolfe Tone's statue (eventually placed at a different corner).

'—Can you send them by tram? Now?' he asks, while in an interpolation we see Bloom in Merchant's Arch. A messenger boy on a tram from the corner of Nassau Street would reach Dorset Street and Eccles Street in about ten minutes. Boylan tells the girl 'It's for an invalid' and asks to use the telephone. His call (on p.189) is to his secretary Miss Dunne, who informs him of his appointment with Lenehan in the Ormond. Boylan then walks along Grafton Street towards Trinity College. Outside La Maison Claire he meets Bob Doran coming out of the Empire (p.202) and is seen by Master Dignam (p.206). When the viceregal cavalcade passes on p.208 Boylan is outside the Provost's house. Soon afterwards – possibly near O'Connell Bridge – he takes a hackney car (number 324, driver Barton James) along the south quays and over Essex Bridge to the Ormond Hotel (Tour 5).

Tour 6b: *Wandering Rocks xviii*

206 'Opposite Ruggy O'Donohoe's Master Patrick Aloysius Dignam, pawing the pound and a half of Mangan's (late Fehrenbach's) porksteaks he had been sent for, went along warm Wicklow street dawdling.' Master Dignam, who came out of Mangan's (now Hobo's) on the corner of Exchequer Street and South William Street on p.192, is dawdling along the south side of Wicklow Street, opposite the International Bar, still with its fine interior and O'Donohoe's initials in mosaic on the doorstep. At No. 33, Madame Doyle's (now the Taverna restaurant), he looks in at the poster for the Keogh-Bennett boxing match. On the opposite side of the street is the doorway of No. 15a Wicklow Street, where according to Bidwell and Heffer★ the action of the *Dubliners* story 'Ivy Day in the Committee Room' is set in an upstairs room. On the same side of the street, the building now containing Casper and Giumbini's Restaurant used to be the Wicklow Hotel, where young Stephen in *A Portrait* heard the sound *suck* in the washroom.

In Grafton Street he sees Blazes Boylan, with a flower in his mouth, listening to Bob Doran outside La Maison Claire. Reaching the tramline at Nassau Street, he sees 'No Sandymount tram' and follows Artifoni's example by walking along Nassau Street in the wake of Artifoni himself, Farrell, and the blind stripling. Farrell, returning on his tracks, passes Master Dignam but the fact is not recorded. Finally, the viceroy passes him in Merrion Square as he stands waiting to see the parade go by. His route home, by foot or tram, brings him via Haddington Road (Tour 2).

★Bruce Bidwell and Linda Heffer: *The Joycean Way –*
A Topographic Guide to Dubliners and A Portrait of the Artist
as a Young Man (Wolfhound Press, 1981).

Wandering Rocks XIX –
The Viceregal Cavalcade

207 'William Humble, earl of Dudley, and lady Dudley, accompanied by lieutenantcolonel Heseltine, drove out after luncheon from the viceregal lodge.'

As with *Hades*, this long route is best followed by bicycle, or by car with occasional detours.

The viceregal lodge in Phoenix Park, where this tour begins, was originally built in 1751–4 to the design of Nathaniel Clements. Now known as Aras an Uachtarain, it is the residence of the President of Ireland and is not open to the public. Some minor roads in Phoenix Park have recently been closed and it is best to take up the route at the Phoenix monument halfway along the main road.

22. Parkgate. 'Saluted by obsequious policemen', the viceregal cavalcade sets off across the city. To the left stands the Wellington Testimonial.

The park itself is the largest city park in Europe and one of the most beautiful. It derives its name from a spring of clear water (Irish *Fionn Uisce*) rising near the entrance to the present Zoological Gardens. Acquired by the Government in 1618, the grounds were first enclosed in 1660. The monument was erected in 1747 by the then Viceroy, Lord Chesterfield, who also laid out the grounds.

Drive from the monument towards Dublin. On the right hand side of the road, just before the next junction and opposite the Viceregal Lodge, is the site of the Phoenix Park murders. Also on the right, shortly before Parkgate, is the Wellington Testimonial, a 205-foot obelisk designed in 1817 by Sir William Smirke. This monument is prominent in *Finnegans Wake*, as are the Magazine Fort, also in this part of the park, and the Mullingar House Inn in Chapelizod, south of the park.

'The cavalcade passed out by the lower gate of Phoenix park saluted by obsequious policemen and proceeded past Kingsbridge along the northern quays.' The gates at the Parkgate entrance were removed, together with their piers, for the Eucharistic Congress in 1932. Two of the piers were re-erected recently as part of a plan to restrict traffic through the Park.

The cavalcade follows Parkgate Street past Kingsbridge (leading to Heuston Station, formerly Kingsbridge Station, on the other side of the river) and proceeds along the northern quays. On the opposite side of the river is the Guinness Brewery, followed by 'Bloody Bridge', a metal bridge erected in 1863 (see Tour 8). At the far side of the bridge is Tom Kernan, saluting 'vainly from afar'. Next comes Queen's Bridge. At the next corner on the left, outside the pawnshop at 32 Arran Quay, they pass Dudley White. After Whitworth Bridge the viceroy reaches the Four Courts, where Richie Goulding, emerging on his way to the Ormond, 'saw him with surprise'. Reuben J. Dodd's office, near the corner of Charles Street just after Richmond Bridge (the next block but one to the Four Courts) was above the post office at 34 Ormond Quay Upper; King's the printer's was on the west side of Charles Street at number 36. Opposite is Wood Quay,

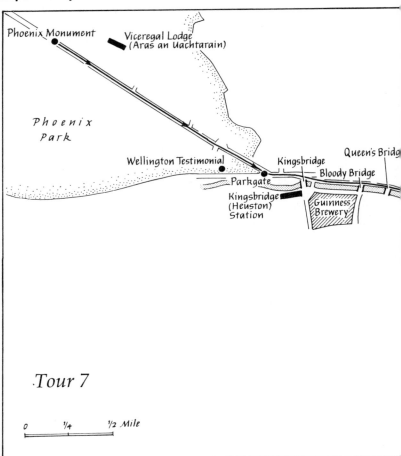

Tour 7

0   ¼   ½ Mile

site of Dublin's oldest Viking settlement, where the Dublin Corporation offices now stand in front of Christ Church Cathedral. (The river Poddle, which 'hung out in fealty a tongue of liquid sewage', in fact emerges about halfway along Wellington Quay from an arched conduit in the river wall; it may be seen from Grattan Bridge.)

The viceroy passes the admiring barmaids in the Ormond, and Mr Dedalus on his way across the street from the urinal on the quay. (Hart and Knuth suspect that

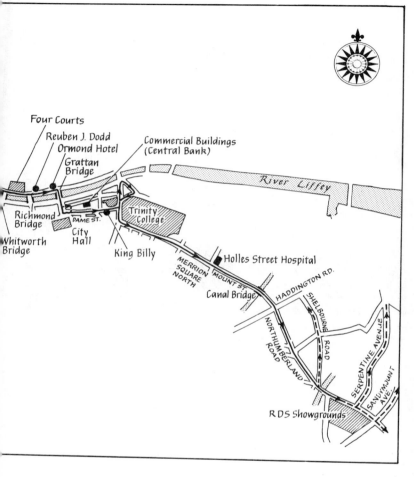

his hat is brought low to cover an open trouserfly.) The
reverend Hugh C. Love at Cahill's corner can neither see
208 nor be seen by the viceroy, who is watched by Lenehan
and M'Coy as the carriages turn right across Grattan
Bridge (also referred to in *Sirens* by its earlier name of
Essex Bridge). To the left on Wellington Quay, beside
Dollard House, is Gerty MacDowell, whose view of the
cavalcade is obscured by the vehicles stopped in front of
her. To the right, on the corner of Essex Quay, may be

seen Sunlight Chambers, formerly the offices of a soap company, where a coloured frieze around the wall displays the various stages in the manufacture and use of soap. Straight ahead is City Hall, built in 1769 as the Royal Exchange by Thomas Cooley.

23. The Four Courts. The viceroy surprises Richie Goulding here on his journey along the north quays. Note the brewery barges on the river.

'Beyond Lundy Foot's from the shaded door of Kavanagh's winerooms John Wyse Nolan smiled with unseen coldness towards the lord lieutenantgeneral and general governor of Ireland.' John Wyse Nolan is at the back door of the Parliament Inn in Essex Gate, on the right. The viceroy goes straight on here, but motorists should turn left here into Essex Street (see detour below). Anderson's the watchmaker's was at No. 30 on the right, and Henry and James the tailor's shop was on the left at the corner with Dame Street. Also on the left, and worth noting, is Read's the cutler's at No. 4, Dublin's oldest shop. On display inside are swords made by the firm in the seventeenth century.

Tom Rochford and Nosey Flynn, who have just come from Crampton Court nearby, are at the top of Parliament Street (site of Dame Gate in the old city walls) watching the viceroy approach. Here the cavalcade turns left (a privilege now reserved for buses and bicycles) and proceeds down Dame Street.

Detour for motorists: turn left from Parliament Street onto Essex Street, and take the first right turn up a narrow street beside the Dolphin. Turn left at the top to rejoin the viceregal route on Dame Street. (If the lane is blocked by an inconsiderately parked car you will have to drive on as far as Fownes Street.)

The viceroy and his equipage pass the poster of Marie Kendall outside the theatre, and the DBC tearooms at No. 33 Dame Street on the right. Directly opposite the DBC is Fownes Street, where 'Dilly Dedalus, straining her sight upwards from Chardenal's first French primer, saw sunshades spanned and wheelspokes spinning in the glare'.

Dilly has come by Temple Bar from her encounter with Stephen in Bedford Row. Stephen himself, who like Bloom does not appear on the viceroy's itinerary, is not far away, possibly even approaching up Anglesea Street on his way to the Moira Hotel in Trinity Street. This would make him, again like Bloom on Wellington Quay, visible to the viceroy but unmentioned.

Beside Fownes Street is the enormous Central Bank building, designed by Sam Stephenson and completed in 1978. This controversial building was already under construction when it was discovered that its height exceeded by thirty feet the limit laid down by the Corporation planning department. In the end this excess height was slightly trimmed by foregoing the copper roof which was to cover the top of the building and leaving 'undressed' the huge trusses from which the entire building is suspended. The angular framework is visible for a considerable distance over the Dame Street skyline.

Part of the Central Bank site was previously occupied by the handsome Commercial Buildings, in which was located the Bodega wine store where Ben Dollard had been with John Henry Menton (before walking down Crown Alley, through Merchant's Arch and across the metal bridge in *WR xiv*). Menton himself now stands 'filling the doorway of Commercial Buildings'. The façade of the building which faces onto the plaza is a replica of the

Commercial Buildings front, at right angles to the original position. On the Dame Street front is a round stone plaque of a sailing vessel named *The Ouzel Galley*. The plaque, which was originally placed over the inside of the door where Menton stands, commemorated a ship which was posted missing at sea in 1695 and on which insurance was duly paid. Five years later it returned, having escaped, together with some considerable booty, from the hands of pirates. The Ouzel Galley Society, formed to settle the disposal of the treasure, remained until 1888 to settle other mercantile disputes, and from 1799 met here in the Commercial Buildings.

Next to the plaque, on the left at 11 College Green, was the site of Larchet's hotel and restaurant, where Stephen spent some of the afternoon and early evening drinking. Before this he was in Trinity Street (opposite, on the right) at the Moira Hotel beside Dame Lane, now a vacant site.

The Telecom Eireann offices on the corner of Anglesea Street are on the site of the old Jury's Hotel, which was demolished in the mid-1970s. Its Victorian bar, complete with fittings, was transported in its entirety to Pelikan-strasse in Zurich and reopened under the name of the 'James Joyce Pub'. The hotel is mentioned in *Ulysses*, one of about sixty licensed premises which share that distinction, but there is no indication that Joyce ever went in there.

The next block was formerly occupied by Daly's Club, of which the central section, designed in 1790 by Francis Johnston, survives. The Club was not only the most luxurious in Dublin but also reputed to be the most profligate. The rather more demure Kildare Street Club was founded as a polite alternative.

'Where the foreleg of King Billy's horse pawed the air Mrs Breen plucked her hastening husband back from under the hoofs of the outriders.' The Breens, who have failed to meet Menton in his office, are now on their way to Collis and Ward's at 31 Dame Street in search of a different solicitor. As we learn on page 246, Breen then meets Tom Rochford who sends him to long John Fanning; and from the subsheriff's office he continues up to

Green Street courthouse. The equestrian statue of William III referred to here stood in College Green approximately on the site of the present statue of the poet Thomas Davis. The statue, which also features in a comic story in 'The Dead', was unveiled in 1701 and became the subject of repeated attacks. Frederick O'Dwyer notes in *Lost Dublin* that after a bomb explosion in 1836 which 'unseated' King Billy, 'Among the first on the scene was the Surgeon General, Sir Philip Crampton, summoned by a message that an important personage had fallen from his horse in front of the Bank of Ireland.' It was finally blown apart in 1928. The only piece that survives is part of the ornamental plinth by Grinling Gibbons, now on display in the Dublin Civic Museum. Opposite Trinity College the cavalcade turns right from Dame Street, a manoeuvre now forbidden to all vehicles.

24. Foster Place. In this picture, looking across College Green from beside the Bank of Ireland, may be seen King Billy on his horse.

Detour for motorists: continue left past the Bank of Ireland into Westmoreland Street (right hand traffic lane) and double back along D'Olier Street (centre lane) to College Street (left hand lane) and round past the front of Trinity College.

The procession passes the Hely's men outside Ponson-by's at 116 Grafton Street. On the left, opposite Pigott's (now the British Airways office), Mr Denis J. Maginni, who attracted so much attention on O'Connell Bridge on page 194, is 'unobserved' by the viceroy. By the wall of the Provost's house on the corner of Nassau Street, Blazes Boylan 'offered to the three ladies the bold admiration of his eyes and the red flower between his lips'.

209   The cavalcade turns left along the railings of Trinity College, listening to the music played by the 'brazen highland laddies' in College Park, where the College races are under way. On the right, near the corner of Dawson Street, they pass Mr Solomons the optician in the Austro-Hungarian viceconsulate; on the left at the far end of the railings, Cashel Boyle O'Connor Fitzmaurice Tisdall Farrell, returning from Merrion Square, stares across the carriages along the street at Mr Solomons' far-off head, aided by his 'fierce eyeglass'.

The carriages drive straight on into Clare Street without passing the back gate of Trinity in Lincoln Place where Hornblower the porter touches 'his tallyho cap'. Up until a few years ago the Trinity porters all wore hard riding hats with peaks. In Merrion Square they pass Master Dignam on his way home to Sandymount. Outside Holles Street hospital they pass the blind stripling opposite Broadbent's fruit shop (2 Lower Mount Street). Across their path goes the man in the brown macintosh, eating dry bread; he is next seen nearby in Burke's pub at closing time, where we hear that he is known as 'Bartle the Bread'. From Mount Street they cross the canal bridge (a famous 'Joycean slip' – it is the Grand Canal, not the Royal Canal) and drive on across Haddington Road (at the next traffic lights), where 'two sanded women halted themselves, an umbrella and a bag in which eleven cockles rolled to view with wonder the lord mayor and lady mayoress without his golden chain'.

The two women have come up from Sandymount Strand most probably by way of Bath Street, Church Avenue, Londonbridge Road, Bath Avenue and Haddington Road. Their observation gained an unusual complexity on Bloomsday 1982 when, in the re-enactment of *Wandering Rocks*, the parts of Lord and Lady Dudley were taken by the then Lord Mayor of Dublin (complete with golden chain) and the Lady Mayoress (to whom, romantically enough, he had got married the previous weekend).

The route leads straight on along Northumberland Road and past Lansdowne Road on the left. The house admired by Queen Victoria has not been identified, but Hart and Knuth have located at 14 Lansdowne Road the house of Benedetto Palmieri, part-original of Almidano Artifoni, who gives the final salute with his 'sturdy trousers swallowed by a closing door'.

It may be noted that, despite the assurance on page 207 that 'the viceroy was most cordially greeted on his way through the metropolis', he is in fact met with almost total indifference. The few 'cordial' greetings he does get either fail to be communicated or are given by mistake.

The viceroy continues towards Ballsbridge. To the right of his route is the circular American Embassy building, designed in 1964. His final destination is the Royal Dublin Society showground between Anglesea Road and Simmonscourt Road. The handsome buildings date from 1925, when the RDS moved their headquarters from Leinster House.

From the RDS you may drive on along the main road through Blackrock, Monkstown and Dun Laoghaire to Sandycove for Tour 1, or left down Serpentine Avenue to Tritonville Road to connect with Tour 2. Alternatively, you may leave Ballsbridge by Sandymount Avenue (passing W. B. Yeats's birthplace at No. 2 on the right) or by Shelbourne Road, where from March to August 1904 Joyce was living on the upper floor of No. 60, on the right.

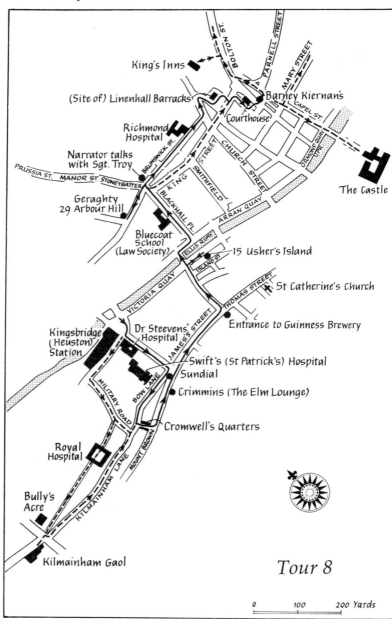

King's Inns

(Site of) Linenhall Barracks

Barney Kiernan's

Courthouse

Richmond
Hospital

Narrator talks
with Sgt. Troy

PRUSSIA ST. MANOR ST. STONEYBATTER

The Castle

Geraghty
29 Arbour Hill

Bluecoat
School
(Law Society)

15 Usher's Island

St Catherine's Church

Entrance to Guinness Brewery

Kingsbridge
(Heuston)
Station

Dr Steevens'
Hospital

Swift's (St Patrick's) Hospital
Sundial

Crimmins (The Elm Lounge)

Cromwell's Quarters

Royal
Hospital

Bully's
Acre

Kilmainham Gaol

Tour 8

0   100   200 Yards

A convenient point from which to start this tour is Heuston Station, beside the Liffey at Kingsbridge. It may be reached by the DART shuttle bus No. 90, which circulates around the quays between here, Connolly Station and Tara Street Station.

Before launching on the Joycean itinerary, it is worth visiting some of the notable buildings in the area, particularly the Royal Hospital, which is within five minutes walk of the station on Military Road (to the left just beyond the station). The hospital, founded in 1680 by James Butler, first duke of Ormonde, 'for the reception and entertainment of ancient, maimed and infirm officers and soldiers,' is perhaps the oldest building in Dublin to retain its original structure. Restored and opened to the public in 1985, it now houses the National Centre of Culture and the Arts. The Great Hall and Chapel are especially impressive. It is open between 12 o'clock and 5 o'clock at weekends and occasionally Tuesday to Friday as well.

The avenue at the far side of the hospital building leads past an ancient graveyard known as Bully's Acre to a striking battlemented gate designed in 1812 by Francis Johnston, which originally stood on the quays at the foot of Watling Street but which was moved to its present location in 1846. Across the road on the far side of the gate is Kilmainham Gaol, built 1787–92 and finally closed in 1924. In its time it housed many celebrated inmates, including the Fenians in 1866, Parnell and his Land League associates in 1881, the Invincibles in 1883 and, in 1916, the Volunteers, several of whose leaders were shot here. With its classic prison interior it has often been used for films. It is now open to the public daily in summer months and on Wednesday and Sunday afternoons for the rest of the year.

Follow the outside wall of the Royal Hospital either from Military Road or from Kilmainham Lane to Bow Bridge. Here a set of steps named Cromwell's Quarters (known previous to 1876 as Murdering Lane) leads to Mount Brown. Turn left here towards James's Street.

Shorter route: Heuston Station to James's Street

If not visiting Kilmainham, follow Steevens's Lane from opposite the station. On the right is Dr Steevens's Hospital, built in 1720 by Thomas Burgh on a bequest from Dr Richard Steevens. Grissel Steevens, the doctor's sister, who had rooms in the hospital, was reputed, according to legend, to have the face of a pig. The building, with its fine quadrangle, housed the oldest public hospital in Ireland until its closure in 1987. At the time of writing its future role is uncertain.

At the top of the lane on the right is St Patrick's Hospital, commonly known as Swift's Hospital after its founder, the celebrated author of *Gulliver's Travels*. Built by George Semple and opened in 1757, it is still a psychiatric hospital and contains some relics of Swift which may be viewed by arrangement.

Turn right along Bow Lane, left up the steps of Cromwell's Quarters, and left again into James's Street.

The Elm Lounge at 27–28 James's Street was formerly Crimmins' pub, from which Tom Kernan has just emerged, glowing with gin and pleasure. As this section begins he has just reached the junction of James's Street with Bow Lane.

196   'From the sundial towards James's gate walked Mr Kernan, pleased with the order he had booked . . .' The sundial on its tall pillar, now somewhat neglected-looking, was built around 1813 by the Dublin Paving Board.

On Mr Kernan's right were Shackleton's offices at No. 35 (now a vacant space between Crampton's and Steel Fixing Services). Mr Kernan is pleased with the way he has persuaded Crimmins (a tea, wine and spirit merchant) to take another order of tea – 'the cup that cheers but not inebriates' – from Pulbrook Robertson, for whom Kernan is an agent. His mind runs back over their conversation 197 about the *General Slocum* disaster, an appalling incident, reported in the day's papers, involving a fire on a riverboat on New York's East River in which 1,021 people, out for the day on a Sunday School picnic, lost their lives.

Mr Kernan pauses to admire himself in 'the sloping mirror of Peter Kennedy, hairdresser' (now the Fish and Poultry shop). The frockcoat of which he is so proud did not attract the attention of Mr Bloom at the funeral that morning, although it is possible that he was not wearing it then. As he looks across the road at someone who looks like Ned Lambert's brother, he sees the only motor car to appear in the whole of *Ulysses*.

25. James's Street. The rooftops in the foreground are those of the Guinness Brewery buildings on the south side of the street. Mr Kernan approaches from further along the street, near the church spire (which has since been truncated). Starting on the south side, he crosses soon after viewing himself in Kennedy's mirror, and walks along the sunny north side to the corner of Watling Street at the extreme right.

Walking on along the street, he looks ahead towards the site of Robert Emmet's execution, outside St Catherine's

Church in Thomas Street. Emmet was twenty-five years old when he led a band of United Irishmen in an abortive rebellion in 1803. The facts of the uprising were familiar to Dubliners in 1904 after the centenary commemorations of the previous year, though Emmet's burial place is still to be established – Glasnevin, St Michan's, St Paul's and St Catherine's are among the candidates.

Opposite the top of Watling Street is the entrance to the famous Guinness Brewery, founded in 1769 by Arthur Guinness. The visitors' centre is open on weekdays to the public, who no longer need to wait in the waiting room across the street. Crane Street, the next turn to the right, leads to the Guinness Hop Store, a major exhibition centre and home of the brewery's wonderful museum.

198 Mr Kernan, however, turns left opposite the brewery and walks 'down the slope of Watling street', passing the Distillery stores on the right at the corner of Bonham Street. As he passes Island Street he spies the viceregal cavalcade on the far side of the river but is too late to register his greetings.

In interpolations in this section we see Bob Cowley and Mr Dedalus meeting on Ormond Quay, the crumpled throwaway floating past North Wall and Sir John Roger-son's Quay (which appear to move westward in relation to it), and Mr and Mrs Breen walking across O'Connell Bridge en route from Bachelor's Walk to Dame Street.

Just in front of Mr Kernan is Bloody Bridge, so named after the outcome of a riot raised in support of the ferrymen whom it put out of business in 1670. The original wooden bridge was replaced in 1704 by a stone one, which was in turn succeeded by the present metal structure in 1863 under the name of Victoria Bridge. Since 1939 it has been known as Rory O'More Bridge, after the leader of the 1641 rebellion who lived nearby.

Mr Kernan's eventual destination is the Ormond Hotel on the far side of the river, though what route he takes to arrive there on p.227 is not specified. He may have crossed here at the bridge and turned right along the north quays. Before following him, turn right along the south quays on Usher's Island. Here at No. 15 is the house where the

Misses Morkan held their party in 'The Dead', the last story in *Dubliners*. The top storey of the building has been removed, but the rooms on the first floor, described in the story, still survive. John Huston's film of 'The Dead' (1987) used the exterior of the original building and faithful reconstructions of the interior. The ground floor is used as an office by Finnheat, who occupy the building next door. The future of the house is at present doubtful, depending on the outcome of proposals for a new Dublin road scheme.

Return to Bloody Bridge and cross to the north quays. Turn right, and then left up Blackhall Place (directly opposite 15 Usher's Island). On the left is the 'Bluecoat School', properly King's Hospital School, built by Thomas Ivory in 1773. Students in the school, which was founded by royal charter, wore the traditional blue uniforms up to 1923. When the school moved to new premises in Palmerstown the building was acquired by the Incorporated Law Society of Ireland.

Continue up to the top of Blackhall Place to the corner on the left where Arbour Hill meets Stoney Batter. Arbour Hill, as Joyce would have known when writing *Ulysses*, had become a place of particular veneration for Irish nationalism since 1916, when the executed leaders of the Easter Rising were buried here under quicklime at the corner of the barracks, at the far end of the lane. Wolfe Tone and the Sheares brothers were also imprisoned here at the barracks in 1798.

Cyclops, 5 p.m.

240 'I was just passing the time of day with old Troy of the D.M.P. at the corner of Arbour hill there . . .'

The anonymous narrator of this episode – known to scholars as the Nameless One – is a 'collector of bad and doubtful debts'. He has been trying to extract money from Michael Geraghty at 29 Arbour Hill (along the road on the corner with Chicken Lane, now Ardrigh Road), when, after an unrecorded conversation with a member of the Dublin Metropolitan Police, he meets Joe Hynes coming from the City Arms Hotel at 55 Prussia Street (a former residence of the Blooms, between Stoney Batter and the North Circular Road) where he has been reporting on the cattle traders' meeting.

As the narrator explains his business to Joe, we are treated to the first of a series of interruptions in the narrative, written in a variety of 'specialist' styles according to their point of view. Thus the dispute between 241 Geraghty and Herzog is couched in legal jargon of the most pedantic variety, while the description of St Michan's Parish is in the style of neo-Celtic romantic legend.

The pair walk to Barney Kiernan's 'by the Linenhall barracks and the back of the courthouse'. To go by the barracks they would most likely have gone along North Brunswick Street (but see the *Alternative route* below), passing the Richmond Hospital on their left. Founded in 1811, the hospital was rebuilt in its present Tudor style in 1900. It was closed in 1987.

All around them lies 'the land of holy Michan', the parish bounded by the North Circular Road, Dorset and Capel Streets and the river. It is named after St Michan's church in Church Street, with its fifteenth-century 'watch-tower' and its famous vaults where bodies – some of them believed to be as much as eight hundred years old – lie preserved by the dry air, 'as in life they slept'. Among these 'warriors and princes' are the Sheares brothers, executed for their part in the 1798 rebellion, and Lord Leitrim, a particularly hated landlord, who was murdered 242 in 1878. The 'shining palace' is the North City Market off Chancery Street, with its stalls of fruit and vegetables, while 'the herds innumerable' are flocking to the Cattle Market beside the City Arms Hotel in Prussia Street.

Beyond the Richmond Hospital and the convent next door, North Brunswick Street meets Church Street, and formerly continued on the other side where a block of Corporation flats now stands. Cross Church Street here, turn left up the hill and then right into Coleraine Street which leads behind the flats. Here, rejoin the original route by turning left into Lisburn Street. The Linenhall barracks, which stood to the north of Lisburn Street, were destroyed in the 1916 rebellion and have been replaced by housing. At the end of Lisburn Street turn right along Lurgan Street and left onto North King Street.

Alternative route via North King Street. The above route depends entirely on taking the phrase 'by the Linenhall barracks' to mean that the narrator and Joe actually passed the barrack building. On the other hand, the more direct route from Stoney Batter to Barney Kiernan's, along North King Street, still passes within a short distance of the barracks, and this is possibly what the narrator may have meant. To the right of North King Street is an extensive cobbled area called Smithfield, the ancient Haymarket of Dublin, now mainly known for horse trading.

Follow North King Street beyond Church Street and turn right down Halston Street, past the back of Green Street courthouse. This building, where the Central Criminal Court is located, at that time also housed the Recorder's Court. Robert Emmet's trial was held in the courthouse, and a monument to him was erected in 1903 in the little park (site of the infamous Newgate Gaol) at the bottom of the street. Cross the park into Green Street and cross again to the corner of Green Street and Little Britain Street. Just beyond the demolished building on the corner is a hairdresser's shop at No. 9. Barney Kiernan's pub, which stood here, also originally comprised Nos. 8 and 10.

In the pub they meet another nameless person merely referred to as 'the citizen', who is generally believed to be based on Michael Cusack, founder of the Gaelic Athletic 243 Association. Joe buys three pints of Guinness with the 244 money that he drew from the cashier in the *Freeman* before 245 lunch, and the citizen accepts the drink while reviling the *Freeman*. He also pours scorn on the *Irish Independent* for its British orientation.

'As they quaffed their cup of joy', Alf Bergan comes in and hides behind the snug. Bob Doran is discovered 'snoring drunk' in the corner; it is not clear whether or not he has visited another pub in the Liberties (the direction in which he was heading on page 202) before coming here.

Alf points out through the door at Mr and Mrs Breen, who have come up from the subsheriff's office to the court-house, looking for libel action over the matter of the anonymous postcard. Alf, who works in Fanning's office, has apparently followed them up Capel Street to see the fun. He gets a 'pony' – a third of a pint of Guinness – from Terry the barman and hands over a penny in payment. Victorian pennies were, of course, common in change three years after her death, and were still in good circulation up to 1971 when old pennies became redundant. A Joycean commentator, who shall remain appropriately nameless, interpreted the word 'testoon' as a coronation-mug, involving Alf and Terry in a mysterious exchange of drinking vessels.

26. Barney Kiernan's. This is a late picture of Barney Kiernan's, where cases in the nearby Criminal Court were traditionally re-argued over a few pints.

The citizen spots Bloom 'prowling up and down out-side' and Alf produces some hangmen's letters. Before the others can read them, however, alarm is caused by Alf's casual remark that he saw Paddy Dignam 'not five minutes ago' in Capel Street. Joe Hynes, who saw Dignam buried that morning, disillusions Alf, and Bob Doran begins to weep drunkenly about Dignam. A remark by the narrator clearly identifies him with Mr Doran of 'The Boarding House' in *Dubliners*, who married his landlady's daughter.

Bloom, who has been waiting around in Green Street to meet Martin Cunningham, comes warily in past the citizen's dog and is pressed by Joe to have a drink. In the end he accepts a cigar.

The original of this episode in the *Odyssey* tells how Ulysses and his men were captured by the Cyclops, a one-eyed giant, and kept in his cave to be eaten one by one. Ulysses plied the giant with drink, telling him his name was 'Noman', and when the Cyclops fell asleep he blinded him with a burning stick. The other giants heard the Cyclops' cries but went away when they were told 'Noman has wounded me'. Ulysses and his men escaped from the cave and taunted the giant as they sailed away. Enraged, the Cyclops hurled a huge rock after them, which fortunately missed its target.

Various elements of the story are worked into this episode – nameless people, references to blind eyes and single eyes, treating with drink and so on. The citizen's 'tunnel vision' hatred of anything that is not Irish is another form of monocularity. Bloom's cigar, of course, takes the place of Ulysses' flaming stick.

250 The hangmen's letters give rise to a conversation about capital punishment, which in turn gets the citizen going
251 on his favourite topic, great Irish nationalist heroes and
252 martyrs. Interpolated at this point is a melodramatic account of the execution of one such hero. F. L. Radford★ has pointed out that the passage derives much from descriptions of Robert Emmet's execution, and that elements of this and some of the other interpolations in *Cyclops* can be traced to newspaper accounts of the following events in 1903: the centenary of Emmet's rising on 23 July; King Edward VII's visit to Ireland, 21 July to 1 August; the death of Pope Leo X on 20 July, his funeral and the election and coronation of his successor Pius X; and the huge demonstration on the centenary of Emmet's
253 execution, 20 September. Rumbold the executioner is named after one of Joyce's enemies, the British consul in

★'King, Pope and Hero-Martyr: *Ulysses* and the Nightmare of Irish History', *James Joyce Quarterly*, vol. 15, no. 4.

254 Zurich in 1917, and the hero's 'blushing bride elect' owes much to Emmet's girlfriend Sarah Curran, who married an English officer of good family two years after the execution.

255 The citizen, Bloom and Joe get talking about the Irish language and the Gaelic League, and the citizen speaks to
256 his dog in Irish, eliciting a few growls in reply. Joe offers to buy another round of drinks, which the citizen and the
257 Nameless One readily accept; Bloom, however, declines, explaining that he is just waiting for Martin Cunningham to bring him to Dignam's house. That he has something else weighing on his mind is indicated by his Freudian slip about 'the wife's admirers'.

258 Bob Doran passes on drunken condolences to Mrs Dignam and leaves the pub. With the new pints the others start talking about the foot-and-mouth disease and the
259 cattle traders' meeting. Bloom is dismayed to hear that Nannetti is off to London, as he had hoped to arrange with him the renewal of Keyes's advertisement. Another mat-
260 ter dear to the citizen's heart, the revival of Gaelic games, is discussed. Bloom attempts to put a word in for more cosmopolitan sports like tennis but is drowned out by the citizen's rendering of 'A Nation Once Again'. The name of
261 Blazes Boylan crops up in connection with the boxing match which he organised; Bloom, painfully aware that Boylan is indulging in a particular form of athletics at that moment, tries unsuccessfully to steer the conversation
262 back to tennis. Inevitably the forthcoming concert tour is mentioned and the narrator notices Bloom's discomfort.

J. J. O'Molloy and Ned Lambert enter the pub. J.J. has now got money, apparently from Ned, for whom he buys a whiskey. In return for the loan he has done Ned a favour at
263 the courthouse, probably, as the narrator suspects, 'getting him off the grand jury list'. They bring the others up to date on the Breen story, the latest news being that Corny Kelleher has advised Breen to have the handwriting on the postcard examined. Alf Bergan is accused of sending the postcard, and does not altogether deny it. He appears to go rather quiet when J. J. O'Molloy, the barrister, gives his opinion that Breen has got grounds for

264 a libel action. 'Who wants your opinion?' thinks the narrator to himself, half expecting the lawyer to claim his 'six and eightpence' for advice. Just then the Breens pass the door again with Corny Kelleher.

265 The citizen begins to mutter about foreigners 'coming over here to Ireland filling the country with bugs', and Bloom, at whom the remark appears to be directed, pretends not to have heard. Instead he reminds Joe about the money still owed to him, 'telling him he needn't trouble about that little matter till the first but if he would just say a word to Mr Crawford'. Having lost Nannetti, he still hopes to get Myles Crawford's co-operation in the renewal of the ad.

266 The citizen, still trying to provoke Bloom, mentions the affair between Dermot MacMurrough and Dervorgilla which first brought 'the Saxon robbers' to Ireland. Alf and Terry are giggling over a modern-day adulteress in the *Police Gazette*.

'So anyhow in came John Wyse Nolan and Lenehan with him with a face on him as long as a late breakfast.' Nolan has been at the meeting about the Irish language in City Hall; Lenehan, who was last seen leaving the Ormond Hotel at four o'clock, has met him on the way somewhere, having also found out the result of the Gold

267 Cup race. Throwaway, the outsider, has come first and his own tip, Sceptre, is 'still running'. The citizen, meanwhile, is holding forth about Ireland's great resources and

268 her opportunities for trade, ruined by 'the yellowjohns of Anglia'. He looks forward to the day when Ireland will be a nation once again.

269 John Wyse Nolan orders a 'half one . . . and a hands up' for himself and Lenehan, which Terry correctly interprets as a 'small whisky and a bottle of Allsop'. It will have been noticed by now that none of the drinkers ever orders a drink by its proper name; this is typical of the innuendo and inferential language in which the entire episode is

270 written. Encouraged by the others, the citizen inveighs against the Royal Navy and the British Empire 'of drudges and whipped serfs'. Bloom's protest 'isn't discipline the same everywhere?' is ignored as the others hurl abuse at

the British and their European neighbours. Joe buys a
271 third pint for the narrator and the citizen, who show no
sign of returning the favour.

Bloom, goaded into losing his cool, tries to speak out
against persecution and 'national hatred among nations,'
272 but gets laughed at. His claim to be Irish elicits an
expressive spit from the citizen, and he lacks the elo-
273 quence to make his point that life is about love instead of
hatred. Suddenly he breaks off and leaves the pub to see if
Martin Cunningham is at the courthouse.

274 The others settle back to their drinks and the citizen
reads them a skit from the *United Irishman*. Then Lenehan
leaps to a conclusion. '—Bloom, says he. The courthouse
is a blind. He had a few bob on *Throwaway* and he's gone
to gather in the shekels.'

275 The narrator goes out the back to consider this information while relieving himself. He has already consumed two
of the three pints Joe has bought him, and another one
cadged off an unnamed person earlier in Slattery's (Suffolk House in Suffolk Street), and has a good load to let
off.

Back inside, John Wyse Nolan is claiming that Bloom
has been working behind the scenes with Arthur Griffith,
leader of the Sinn Fein nationalist movement. Martin
Cunningham arrives on the castle car with Jack Power and
Crofton, an 'orangeman' or loyalist who appears in 'Ivy
Day in the Committee Room' in *Dubliners*. Crofton,
whose politics would normally put him in opposition to
276 the citizen, sides with the others in denouncing Bloom.
277 Even the reasonable Martin Cunningham fails to defuse
their hatred.

Ned Lambert buys drinks for the three new arrivals,
and Martin Cunningham's toast 'God bless all here'
278 prompts an interpolation describing an enormous procession of saints marching across the city to bless the pub.

279 The narrator, having almost finished his pint, is looking
around in hopes of being offered another one when Bloom
returns. Martin Cunningham, aware of the ugly mood in
the pub, quickly gathers his party onto the jaunting car
280 outside the door. The citizen, with Joe and Alf trying to

hold him back, staggers after them and shouts '—Three cheers for Israel!' attracting the attention of 'all the raga-muffins and sluts of the nation'. Bloom stands up on the car and boldly retorts '—Your God was a jew. Christ was a

281 jew like me.' The citizen grabs the empty biscuit-tin from the pub and hurls it after Bloom, but as his target is heading into the sun he is, like the Cyclops, blinded and causes no injury. An interpolation, however, describes the

282 impact as cataclysmic, leaving in ruins the courthouse and all surrounding buildings.

283 The car gathers speed and is last seen heading south-wards down Little Green Street past Donohoe's pub (now the Molly Malone) 'like a shot off a shovel'.

Bloom now travels to Sandymount, probably via Arran Street, the north quays, O'Connell Bridge and back along the funeral route to 9 Newbridge Avenue.

At the east end of Little Britain Street is Capel Street, where three alternatives present themselves.

A. Turn left and follow Capel Street into Bolton Street. On the left is Henrietta Street, leading to the King's Inns where Chandler works in 'A Little Cloud' in *Dubliners*. Bolton Street continues into Dorset Street, leading to Eccles Street (Tour 3).

B. Turn right along Capel Street and left along Mary Street. On the right is St Mary's Church, founded in 1627 and at present disused. Richard Brinsley Sheridan, Wolfe Tone and Sean O'Casey were among those baptised here. Nearly opposite at No. 45, now the east end of Penney's department store, was the Volta Cinema, which was opened by James Joyce in 1909. It closed in 1948 and the remains of the original frontage were removed recently. Follow Mary Street and Henry Street to O'Connell Street for Tour 6.

C. Turn right and follow Capel Street to the quays near the Ormond Hotel, and across the river up Parliament Street and Cork Hill to Dublin Castle for Tour 5.

APPENDIX I *The Movements of Leopold Bloom and Stephen Dedalus on 16 June 1904*

LEOPOLD BLOOM

8.00–8.45 a.m. *Calypso*:
7 Eccles Street and Dlugacz's.

8.45–9.45 a.m. Eccles Street to Sir John Rogerson's Quay.

9.45–10.30 a.m. *Lotuseaters*:
Sir John Rogerson's Quay to Lincoln Place.

10.30–11.00 a.m. Leinster Street baths; Sandymount tram to Haddington Road and Newbridge Avenue.

11.00 a.m.–12.15 p.m. *Hades*:
Sandymount to Glasnevin. Coaches return mourners to city centre.

12.15–1.10 p.m. *Aeolus*:
Newspaper office; visits Keyes in Bachelor's Walk and returns.

1.10–2.10 p.m. *Laestrygonians*:
Abbey Street to Kildare Street via Davy Byrne's.

2.10–2.55 p.m. *Scylla and Charybdis*:
National Museum, National Library.

STEPHEN DEDALUS

8.00–8.45 a.m. *Telemachus*:
Joyce Tower and Forty Foot.

8.45–9.45 a.m. Joyce Tower to Mr Deasy's school; lesson starting 9.00 a.m.

9.45–10.05 a.m. *Nestor*:
Mr Deasy's school, Summerfield, Dalkey Avenue.

10.05–10.40 a.m. Dalkey to Sandymount via Lansdowne Road station.

10.40–11.10 a.m. *Proteus*:
Sandymount Strand. Ringsend to Irishtown.

11.10 a.m.–12.15 p.m. Walks into town along funeral route. Visits College Green P.O.

12.15–1.10 p.m. *Aeolus*:
Newspaper office; across O'Connell Street to Mooney's in Abbey Street.

1.10–2.10 p.m. Drinking in Mooney's *en ville* (Abbey Street) and *sur mer* (now the Horse and Tram on Eden Quay); proceeds to National Library, probably by same route as Bloom.

2.10–2.55 p.m. *Scylla and Charybdis*:
National Library.

2.55–3.40 p.m. *Wandering Rocks*:
From National Library to Bedford Row,
Merchant's Arch and Wellington Quay.

3.40–4.30 p.m. *Sirens*:
Wellington Quay to the Ormond Hotel,
and thence to Marks's on Ormond Quay.

4.30–5.45 p.m. *Cyclops*:
Via Chancery Street, Greek Street,
Mary's Lane and Little Green Street to
Barney Kiernan's in Little Britain
Street.

5.45–6.00 p.m. By jaunting car from
Barney Kiernan's via (probably) Little
Green Street, Arran Street, north quays,
O'Connell Bridge, D'Olier Street and
Brunswick (Pearse) Street to 9
Newbridge Avenue.

6.00–8.25 p.m. 9 Newbridge Avenue,
and thence to Sandymount Strand via
Leahy's Terrace.

8.25–9.00 p.m. *Nausikaa*:
Sandymount Strand.

9.00–10.00 p.m. Sandymount Strand,
and thence by tram to Holles Street
Hospital.

10.00–11.15 p.m. *Oxen of the Sun*:
Holles Street Hospital, and thence to
Burke's pub and via Denzille Lane to
Westland Row.

11.15–11.35 p.m. Westland Row Station
to Killester Station and back to Amiens
Street Station.

11.35 p.m.–12.40 a.m. *Circe*:
Amiens Street, Talbot Street, Mabbot
Street, Bella Cohen's in Tyrone Street,
and Beaver Street.

12.40–1.00 a.m. *Eumaeus*:
Beaver Street to Amiens Street, Store
Street and Butt Bridge.

2.55–3.40 p.m. *Wandering Rocks*:
Walks to the front gate of Trinity College
and meets Almidano Artifoni. Continues
to Fleet Street and Bedford Row.

3.40 p.m. onwards. Spent some or all of
the next six hours drinking in the Moira,
15 Trinity Street, and Larchet's,
11 College Green, eventually reaching
Holles Street hospital with the medical
students.

10.00–11.15 p.m. *Oxen of the Sun*:
Holles Street Hospital, Burke's pub to
Westland Row.

11.15–11.25 p.m. Westland Row Station
to Amiens Street Station.

11.25 p.m.–12.40 a.m. *Circe*:
Amiens Street to Bella Cohen's and
Beaver Street.

12.40–1.00 a.m. *Eumaeus*:
Beaver Street to Amiens Street, Store
Street and Butt Bridge.

1.00–2.00 a.m. *Ithaca*:
Butt Bridge to Gardiner Street, Gardiner Place, North Temple Street and 7 Eccles Street.

2.00 a.m. onwards. *Penelope*:
Asleep in 7 Eccles Street.

1.00–2.00 a.m. *Ithaca*:
Butt Bridge to 7 Eccles Street, and thence into the unknown.

APPENDIX II *Ulysses:* The Corrected Text

The text to which this guide refers is the 1986 edition of *Ulysses*, which laid down a standard text with identical lines and page numbers in all British and American editions, hardback and paperback.

The 'corrected' edition was made necessary by the fact that every single previous edition contained large quantities of typographical errors, omissions and unintended variations overlooked at the time of the original publication in 1922 and subsequently perpetuated. The task was not just a simple one of referring to the original manuscript of the novel, since Joyce made substantial revisions and additions on typescripts and several sets of proofs, amounting to approximately 25 per cent of the final text. The combination of an American publisher, a French printer and typesetter, and typists of various nationalities, all trying to interpret the difficult handwriting and unpredictable syntax of a half-blind Irish genius, was only part of the story.

The editors of the new edition, in their search for an 'ideal' text, had to spend seven years collating and assessing every known variation on the text of *Ulysses* that could be attributed to Joyce himself. In several cases there was no clear preference between two or more readings and the judgement had to rest on editorial discretion. Few of the more than five thousand alterations to established texts, however, make any great difference to the interpretation of the novel. Most of them are based on punctuation and minor spelling differences, but in some cases phrases and even whole sentences have been restored. Richard Ellmann discusses some of the more interesting corrections in his introduction to the text.

Line numbers relating to each episode are printed in the hardback and 'student' editions of the Corrected Text, but not in the ordinary paperback. For readers who prefer a well-thumbed old pre-1986 model to the glossy new version, quotations in the Guide may be used as signposts to the corresponding pages in *Ulysses*.

APPENDIX III *Joyce's Schema and the Episode Titles*

In 1921 Joyce lent Carlo Linati a schema or plan of *Ulysses* in which he assigned to each episode a title from an episode in Homer's *Odyssey*, a time, a colour, persons, a technique, a science or art, a sense or meaning, an organ of the body and a symbol. Joyce also lent it to Valery Larbaud for a lecture, in order, as he said. 'to help him to confuse the audience a little more'. In 1931 Joyce allowed Stuart Gilbert to publish most of the schema in *James Joyce's Ulysses*, with a number of changes (suggesting that parts of the plan were made to fit the book rather than the other way round). The full text of both versions is reproduced in Richard Ellmann's *Ulysses by the Liffey*.

The information contained in the schema does not convey much in the way of clarification. However, it is referred to occasionally in the Guide where it seems of particular interest. Some of the times given in the plan are misleading, and Joyce himself changed his mind about the times of the later episodes in the second version of the schema. The times quoted in the Guide are taken from the schema only when internal evidence does not suggest otherwise.

The Homeric titles given to the episodes are traditionally used by commentators, although they do not appear in the text of *Ulysses*. Joyce did use them in early drafts and later dropped them, but gave his approval for Stuart Gilbert and Frank Budgen to use the titles in their books. The spelling of some of the Greek names varies according to the commentator.

Bibliography

Bruce Bidwell and Linda Heffer, *The Joycean Way: A Topographic Guide to Dubliners and a Portrait of the Artist as a Young Man*, Wolfhound Press, 1981.

Harry Blamires, *The Bloomsday Book*, Methuen, 1966.

Carole Brown and Leo Knuth, *Bloomsday: The Eleventh Hour – A Quest for the Vacant Place*, A Wake Newslitter Press, 1981.

Frank Budgen, *James Joyce and the Making of Ulysses*, Grayson and Grayson, 1934.

Desmond Clarke, *Dublin*, Batsford, 1977.

Maurice Craig, *Dublin, 1660–1860*, Hodges Figgis, 1952.

Frank Delaney, *James Joyce's Odyssey*, Hodder and Stoughton, 1981.

Richard Ellmann, *James Joyce* (revised edition), Oxford University Press, 1982.

— *Ulysses on the Liffey*, Faber and Faber, 1972.

— *James Joyce's Tower*, Eastern Regional Tourism Organisation, 1969.

Stuart Gilbert, *James Joyce's Ulysses: A Study*, Faber and Faber, 1930.

Oliver St John Gogarty, *It Isn't This Time of Year at All!*, MacGibbon and Kee, 1954.

Clive Hart and Leo Knuth, *A Topographical guide to James Joyce's Ulysses* (revised and corrected edition), A Wake Newslitter Press, 1981.

James Joyce, *Ulysses: The Corrected Text*, Penguin Books/The Bodley Head, 1986.

— *Dubliners: The Corrected Text*, Jonathan Cape, 1967.

— *A Portrait of the Artist as a Young Man*, B. W. Huebsch, 1916.

— *Letters of James Joyce, Vol. I* (ed. Stuart Gilbert), Faber and Faber, 1957.

— *Letters of James Joyce, Vol. II and III* (ed. Richard Ellmann), Faber and Faber, 1966.

Weston St John Joyce, *The Neighbourhood of Dublin*, 1912 (revised edition, 1922, Gill).

Pat Liddy, 'Dublin Today', *Irish Times*.

Frank MacDonald, *The Destruction of Dublin*, Gill and Macmillan, 1985.

Frederick O'Dwyer, *Lost Dublin*, Gill and Macmillan, 1981.

Mary Power, 'The Discovery of "Ruby"', *James Joyce Quarterly*, Vol. 18, No. 2, 1981.

F. L. Radford, 'King, Pope and Hero-Martyr: Ulysses and the Nightmare of Irish History', *James Joyce Quarterly*, Vol. 15, No. 4, 1978.

Danis Rose, 'The Best Recent Scholarship in Joyce', *James Joyce Quarterly*, Vol. 23, No. 3, 1986.

Weldon Thornton, *Allusions in Ulysses: An Annotated List*, University of North Carolina Press, 1968.

Mervyn Wall, *Forty Foot Gentlemen Only*, Allen Figgis, 1962.

Note: This bibliography is not an exhaustive one. Essentially it is a list of those works consulted or cited specifically in connection with the writing of this book. There are, of course, many other books on Joyce and on Dublin which have contributed to my views and knowledge of the subject over a period of years.

Index

This book is a work of fiction. Any references to historical events, real people, or real locales are used fictitiously. Other names, characters, places, and incidents are the product of the author's imagination, and any resemblance to actual events or locales or persons, living or dead, is entirely coincidental.

❧ALADDIN PAPERBACKS
An imprint of Simon & Schuster Children's Publishing Division
1230 Avenue of the Americas, New York, NY 10020
Copyright © 2008 by Simon & Schuster, Inc.
All rights reserved, including the right of
reproduction in whole or in part in any form.
NANCY DREW, NANCY DREW: GIRL DETECTIVE, ALADDIN PAPERBACKS, and related logo are registered trademarks of Simon & Schuster, Inc.
Manufactured in the United States of America
First Aladdin Paperbacks edition December 2008
10 9 8 7
Library of Congress Control Number 2008920582
ISBN 978-1-4169-6827-6

CAROLYN KEENE

NANCY DREW

GIRL DETECTIVE®

SECRET IDENTITY

#33

**Book One in the
Identity Mystery Trilogy**

Aladdin Paperbacks
New York London Toronto Sydney

NANCY DREW

Available from Aladdin Paperbacks

A Case of Cyberbullying Becomes a Little Too Real.

Shannon seemed terribly keyed up, like she'd just drank three espressos. "Well, actually," she said, clicking onto her Internet browser to launch it, "this all has to do with BetterLife. My avatar, Sassygirl48 . . ."

I sighed. "But Maggie said you were having problems at school?"

Shannon closed her eyes and nodded. "That started just a couple days ago. People whispering when I walked into the room, throwing spitballs at me, mean little things. I found out that afternoon that someone posted footage of Sassygirl48 being bullied on uVid."

I'd dealt with plenty of bullies in my life, but they were always easy to confront. It's hard to yell an insult at someone, or throw something at her, and remain anonymous. On the Internet, though, everyone is anonymous. Which makes it incredibly easy to hurt someone's feelings with no repercussions.

I patted her shoulder. "All right," I said. "You have my word that I'm going to find the person who started this and make sure it *ends*. Nobody deserves to be treated like this. Nancy Drew is on the case."

Contents

SECRET IDENTITY

PROLOGUE

Thank goodness her friend picked up the phone on the first ring. "Hey there."

She felt like she might explode from excitement. "Oh . . . my . . . gosh. You will not believe what is happening to me right now."

Her friend sounded wary. "What?"

"Well, I've been playing BetterLife ever since I got home."

"Duh. That's practically all you do these days."

She couldn't help smiling. That wasn't far from the truth. But the virtual-reality site had become *the* place to be over the last couple months; she probably socialized more online than she did in real life. "Stop. So Sassy Girl Forty-eight is at the mall, and guess who started flirting with me there?"

"Santa Claus."

She sighed. "No. Come on, be serious."

There was a pause of a few seconds. "I don't know. Why don't you tell me?"

"Jake!" she squealed and paused, waiting for the news to sink in. "Jake. Jake Seltzer! Isn't that amazing?"

There was another pause. "But he'd have a different username and look, right? I mean, it's a game, not real life. How did you know it was him?"

She sighed again. "Dude, his character in the game looks just like him. He has the blue streak in his hair, and the nose ring. His name is Guitar Lover Fifteen, and you know how Jake likes music. It has to be him!"

"Wow." Her friend seemed to mull over this information for a few seconds. "The guy you have a crush on is flirting with you online? Do you think he knows who you really are?"

"I think he does. He's said a few things about seeing me in real life, or wanting to flirt with me in real life but being too shy." She smiled to herself. Her heart was beating double-time; that's how excited Jake made her. On-screen, his character was smiling at her adoringly. Other virtual characters walked through the mall all around them, but it was like they were the only two people in the world.

Suddenly there was a loud beep, and she glanced at the dialogue box, where a new message from GuitarLvr15 to Sassygirl48 had appeared.

I LIKE UR BLOND HAIR. U R SO PRETTY, U MUST HAVE GUYS FALLING ALL OVER U.

She squealed. "Oh gosh! You won't believe what he just said." She read the message off to her friend, smiling bigger with each word.

"Wow! Is he talking about you or your avatar?"

She turned to the screen. Her avatar, which she'd spent a week designing, looked as much like her as she'd been able to get: long blond hair, brown eyes, petite. She wore the trendiest clothes she could find; when the outfits available on the site looked too boring, she'd designed her own. All in all, the character was her virtual mini-me. But still . . . "I think he's talking about me. He knows who I am, and he's trying to flirt! We're totally meant to be!"

Her friend let out a breath. "This is almost too good to be true! You should write back, 'You're the only guy I care about.'"

The girl giggled, shaking her head. "Ha! I should, really. Do you think?"

"Totally. I'm being serious."

She gulped. Clicking on the dialogue box, she typed:

U R THE ONLY BOY I CARE ABOUT.

She paused, her mouse hovering over the Send button. Was it time to let Jake know about her crush? She'd hesitated all this time because she didn't want to get hurt. But now it seemed clearer than clear that Jake liked her just as much as she liked him.

Quickly, before she could think better of it, she clicked back into the box and added:

IT'S BEEN THAT WAY FOR A LONG TIME.

She clicked send. "Omigod. You won't believe what I just sent." She read the message back to her friend.

"'Omigosh' is right! Well, now he'll know you like him."

She gulped. "Really like him. But does he like me?"

Beep. She felt her stomach clench as she turned back to the computer for his answer. A new comment had appeared in the dialogue box. She almost felt too nervous to read it, but it drew her eyes like a magnet.

I CARE ABOUT U 2. I'VE JUST BEEN 2 SHY TO TELL U IN REAL LIFE.

She gasped.

"What's up?"

"He wrote back." She read his message to her friend, feeling like she might float away. Was this really happening? The guy of her dreams, liking her too?

Beep. Another comment popped up on her screen.

MAYBE WE SHOULD GET TOGETHER IN REAL LIFE SOMETIME.

"Oh wow." She thought her heart might beat out of her chest. "He just wrote more! He wants to get together sometime. In real life."

"Gosh." Her friend didn't sound as excited as she was, but that was to be expected. "That's great, Shannon. I mean, that's really exciting! Are you going to meet him?"

"Duh." She smiled. *Dozens of girls would jump at the chance to date Jake Seltzer,* she thought as she clicked in the dialogue box to respond. *Well, now they'll all be jealous of me.*

Jake's avatar was still smiling at her, waiting for

a response. She made her character nod as she quickly typed, THAT SOUNDS GREAT. JUST TELL ME WHERE AND WHEN. . . .

GuitarLvr15's smile widened. Even in the game, his eyes were bright blue, and they seemed to twinkle extragorgeously as he took Sassygirl48's hand and squeezed it. Her computer beeped again and another message came through.

I KNOW WHO U ARE. I'LL E-MAIL U. WE CAN MAKE PLANS THEN.

"Oh." She couldn't help gasping to her friend, squeezing the phone to her ear. "Oh, he's going to e-mail me! This is so perfect. . . ."

Her friend sounded rushed. "That's great, Shannon. I have to go, though—my mom just called us down for dinner."

"Oh, okay." She felt a little disappointed. She'd wanted to discuss this whole thing until it finally seemed real to her. Still, she couldn't complain. She couldn't stop staring at her computer screen, even though GuitarLvr15 was walking away. "Do you think he'll e-mail me right now? Or will it take a few hours . . . ?"

"I don't know. . . . It sounded like he was going to do it right away."

Shannon smiled. "Okay. I'll tell you what he writes to me."

"Totally. Bye."

"Bye."

She let out a satisfied sigh. It was all so perfect: The guy she'd always known was meant for her actually liked her back. She'd always daydreamed about ending up with Jake, and now it was actually happening.

A little chime sounded as a window popped up on her screen: YOU HAVE NEW MAIL. Her heart quickening, she brought up her account and quickly logged in. *Where should we go on our first date?* she wondered. *Dinner would be great, but what's a romantic restaurant . . . ?*

As the e-mail came up, she scanned the first few lines and felt her heart jump into her throat.

SASSYGIRL48,

DON'T GET YOUR HOPES UP. EVEN IN CYBERSPACE, I WOULD NEVER BE CAUGHT DEAD WITH A STUCK-UP WASTE OF SPACE LIKE YOU.

YOU DESERVE TO BE ALONE——IN THIS GAME, IN REAL LIFE, ALWAYS. YOU DESERVE TO SUFFER LIKE YOU'VE MADE OTHERS SUFFER.

1

HOME SWEET MYSTERY

"**I**s this the sort of romantic dinner you had in mind?" I couldn't help but smile as my boyfriend Ned took my hand and whispered to me as we moved into his dining room for dinner. We'd been apart for a week, since I'd been on a supercomplicated case that had brought me to New York, and had planned to make tonight our official "catch-up date" at our favorite Italian restaurant. But this afternoon Ned had called with a change in plans: there'd been a mix-up with faculty housing at the university, so he volunteered to host a visiting professor from Iran and his family at the Nickerson home. They wanted to have a small dinner to welcome them, and tonight was the only night that worked for everyone.

I leaned in close to him. "Romance, shro-mance. A piece of your mother's apple pie will make up for anything we missed."

Ned chuckled and squeezed my hand. "Maybe so. But we'll have to plan a make-up date."

"Agreed." I squeezed back and smiled.

The truth was, it still felt nice to be back in River Heights and doing all the normal things I like to do that don't involve cab chases or setting things on fire. My most recent case had turned into something bigger and crazier than I ever could have anticipated, and I was enjoying being "Normal Nancy" again, instead of "Action Hero Nancy." Being back in Ned's house felt wonderful. And the Nickersons' new houseguests, Professor Mirza al-Fulani and his daughter, Arij, who was twelve, plus his son, Ibrahim, who was sixteen, just couldn't be nicer.

"So, Nancy," Ibrahim began with a smile as we sat down at the dining room table, "have your travels for investigations ever taken you out of the country? Have you been to the Middle East at all?"

I smiled. The al-Fulanis were from Iran, and I was enjoying Ibrahim's upbeat attempts to understand American culture. "I'm afraid not, Ibrahim.

I don't get the chance to travel all that much, even within the United States. But I would love to visit the Middle East someday. There's so much history there."

Professor al-Fulani smiled at me. "This is true, Nancy. It is still sometimes strange for my children and I to wrap our heads around American history, because your country is so new. So much has changed in only two hundred years, whereas in our part of the world, there are thousands of years of history."

Ibrahim piped up excitedly. "Will we study American history at the high school, Nancy?"

I nodded. "Actually, you will, Ibrahim. It's a required class for juniors."

"Excellent." Ibrahim dug into his salad with a grin, glancing at his sister. "I want to learn as much as I can about this country while we are here. I am so eager to meet my classmates."

Arij smiled and nodded, glancing at Ned and me. "Maybe you could look at the outfit I plan to wear tomorrow, Nancy," she said shyly. "I want to fit in well, and make friends quickly."

I laughed. "I don't know if I'm the best person to give fashion advice, but I'd be happy to offer my opinion!"

Ned squeezed my arm. "Don't sell yourself

short, Nance," he cautioned. "After all, you are the reigning Miss Pretty Face River Heights!"

I rolled my eyes at him. While that was true, I wasn't exactly aching to talk about my short and ill-fated career as a pageant queen, which had been part of the case I'd been investigating in New York City. Still, he was smiling. I knew he found my totally out-of-character pageant win amusing.

"Nancy," Ibrahim said, "I am curious about how you solve cases. You have told us a little about your unusual hobby, and I must ask: Do you wear disguises? Do you ever have to lie to people to get the information you need?"

I squirmed in my seat. Ibrahim's face was warm and open, and I knew his questions were coming from an honest curiosity. Still, I liked to keep my trade secrets and didn't exactly want to confess to bending the truth in the service of, well, the truth in front of Ned's father and a bunch of people I'd just met.

"Let's just say I do what the case requires," I replied, reaching for the bread basket. "Every case is different. More bread, anybody?"

Mrs. Nickerson chuckled.

"Ibrahim and Arij," Ned cut in smoothly, "have you ever been to an American high school before, or will tomorrow be your first time?"

"Oh no," Ibrahim replied, shaking his head. "We have attended school in America before. My father travels often for work, you know, and we have traveled with him for months at a time."

Professor al-Fulani nodded. "My children lived with me while I taught at a university in Wisconsin, and also briefly in Florida. Unfortunately both placements were only for a few months, so they weren't able to settle in as much as they would have liked."

Arij nodded, pushing her salad around on her plate. "Sometimes it's hard to make friends," she admitted, a note of sadness creeping into her voice. "People hear my accent or they see my hijab and they think . . . They think I am something that I am not."

Silence bloomed around the table. I nodded sympathetically, imagining how difficult it must be for Arij and Ibrahim to fit in.

"I don't think that will be the case here, Arij," Ned said in a warm voice. "At least, I hope not. We're a university town, and used to diversity."

Mr. Nickerson cleared his throat. "You have any trouble, Arij or Ibrahim, and you let me know," he added. "Ned and I will do everything we can to make your stay here as pleasant as possible."

Arij smiled. She looked a little relieved. "I can't wait to meet everyone," she said quietly.

"Ibrahim and Arij seem very nice," I remarked to Ned a couple hours later as we stood on his porch to say our good nights. "I think they'll enjoy living here, don't you? I think they'll have a good experience at the high school."

Ned nodded. "I hope so," he admitted. "They're definitely a couple of great kids—so friendly and curious. I think as long as their classmates give them a chance, they'll have plenty of friends."

I nodded. The night was growing darker, and crickets chirped in the distance. I took a deep breath. River Heights, I thought happily. Home.

"So . . . ," Ned began, reaching out to squeeze my hand.

"So," I repeated, looking up at him with a smile. "Dinner? Later this week? Just the two of us?"

Ned grinned and nodded. "I'll call you," he said, leaning over to give me a peck on the cheek. "I'm so glad you're back, safe and sound."

"Me too," I said honestly, squeezing his hand again. "Thank your mom for dinner. It was delicious."

Stepping down onto the driveway, I pulled out the keys to my hybrid car and felt a wave of exhaustion wash over me. I imagined my nice warm bed at home, beckoning me. Without a case or anything urgent on the agenda, I could sleep in a bit tomorrow, too. I sighed, carefully driving through the streets that led me home. What a relief to be back among the people I loved, and with a little downtime.

At home, I parked the car in our driveway and yawned as I walked around to the back door. I felt like I had tunnel vision—all I could see was the route to my bedroom, where I'd soon be off to dreamland. Which is why I didn't notice that the kitchen light was on. And three people were sitting at the kitchen table, watching me curiously.

"Nancy?"

A familiar voice pulled me out of my tunnel vision, and I turned to find an unusual sight: my friend Bess; her twelve-year-old sister, Maggie; and our housekeeper and unofficial member of the family, Hannah, were munching on oatmeal-raisin cookies.

"Bess?" I asked, walking in. What on Earth?

Bess stood, placing her hand on Maggie's shoulder. "We were waiting for you to come home," she said. "Hope you're not too tired, Nance. Because I think we've got a case for you."

CYBERVICTIM

"**S**o, this is someone you know from school?" I asked Maggie as she, Bess, and I made the short drive to the house of one Shannon Fitzgerald. Maggie had told me that Shannon was having a lot of trouble at school and had even stayed home that day. Maggie thought I might be able to help.

Maggie nodded. "I've known Shannon since we were in first grade. And now she's in about half my classes."

Hmm. I flipped on my turn signal and pulled onto Shannon's street. "You said she's losing sleep over the problem."

"That's right." Maggie looked like she felt

15

terrible for her classmate. "She's really having a tough time. I hope you can help her."

"Me too," I agreed, parking in front of the Fitzgeralds' house. "Before we go in, can you tell me anything else? Is this a teacher problem, a problem with bullies . . . ?"

Climbing out of my car, Bess and Maggie exchanged perplexed glances. "It's probably easier to show you in person," Bess explained, touching my shoulder. "Let's put it this way: It's nothing we had to deal with when *we* were in middle school."

Hmm, again. I'd been exhausted just minutes ago, but now the excitement of a new case had woken me up a little. We walked up the neatly tended pathway to the Fitzgeralds' front door, and Maggie rang the doorbell. A few seconds later a confused-looking middle-aged woman opened the door.

"Hello?"

"Hi," Maggie greeted her smoothly. "We're sorry to come over so late. I'm Shannon's friend, Maggie?"

"Oh yes," the woman said slowly, nodding. "Shannon told us you might be coming by with some friends."

"We just need to talk to her for a few minutes," Bess explained.

The woman looked us over curiously, but didn't protest. "Okay," she said, backing into the house. "Shannon's room is upstairs, the second door on the left. Just don't be too long."

"We won't," I promised. I was still hoping to get to bed by a reasonable hour.

The Fitzgeralds' house was large and impressively neat, with wide stairs leading up to an open balcony that led into a warm, brightly lit hallway. Loud emo music played from behind a door decorated with a million sparkly stickers.

Maggie raised her hand to knock.

Before she could make contact, though, the door opened, revealing a pretty blond-haired girl. I knew she was supposed to be in Maggie's grade, but she looked older—at least fourteen. Shannon wore pink shimmery eye shadow; mascara; and shiny, rose-colored lip gloss. Her highlighted blond hair fell down her back in carefully arranged waves. She was, honestly, the most put-together twelve-year-old *I'd* ever seen. I fingered my own messy ponytail with a frown.

"I thought I heard someone," she said quickly, looking us all over with a frantic energy. "Maggie, is this her? Is this your sister's friend Nancy?"

Maggie gestured for Shannon to let us into her room, and Shannon reluctantly stepped aside, never taking her eyes off our faces. Bess and I sat gingerly on the end of a perfectly appointed queen-size bed, and Maggie settled into a desk chair.

"Shannon, this is my sister, Bess, and her friend Nancy Drew," Maggie announced, pointing to us in turn. "I told Nancy you were having a tough time, but I didn't go into details. I figured you could show us."

Shannon nodded quickly. She seemed terribly keyed up, like she'd just drank three espressos. She walked over to a computer that sat on a modern stainless-steel desk and jiggled the mouse. "Well, actually," she said, clicking onto her Internet browser to launch it, "this all has to do with BetterLife. My avatar, Sassygirl48—"

"Wait a minute, wait a minute," I interrupted, walking over to get a better look at the computer monitor. "What did you just say? BetterLife?"

Shannon turned from the screen to face me, her perfectly shaped eyebrows furrowed with confusion. "You don't know what BetterLife is?"

"Remember, Shannon," Maggie piped up apologetically, "they're older."

"Oh." Shannon pursed her lips, not exactly looking thrilled with this development. "Okay. Well. Let's see. BetterLife . . ."

"Isn't it kind of like a virtual-reality thing?" Bess asked, scooting closer to us on the bed. "Like Second Life, where you create a character in a whole virtual world. George told me about it."

"That's right," Maggie confirmed. "You create a character—it can look like you or not—and you give it a name. Basically you play your character, living in this alternate world and interacting with all kinds of other virtual people."

Shannon nodded. "You have your own virtual job and place to live," she added, as the Better-Life home page came up on her browser and she clicked into the user login box. "And there's a special community for River Heights Middle School, where all the kids from school hang out."

I watched as she typed SASSYGIRL48 in the user-ID box, then clicked down to the password box and entered something with eight characters. "Ta da!" she said, her voice sounding a little hollow and sad as the browser loaded a new page featuring a pretty blond character who looked a lot like Shannon, but even older than how the real Shannon looked. The character was tall and Barbie-ish, with perfect proportions, wearing a stylish pink dress and heels.

WELCOME SASSYGIRL48! The screen greeted us.

The picture on the screen then jumped to life. Shannon's character, the blond, sat nursing a cup of coffee in a mall's coffee shop. All around her, teenage characters chatted, shopped, or just wandered alone. A scroll at the bottom of the page showed Sassygirl48's stats:

HUNGER LEVEL: 8
FRIENDS: 1
JOB: SALON JANITOR
STYLE LEVEL: 7
HAPPINESS: 5

"I don't get it," I blurted.

Shannon looked surprised. "What's not to get?" she asked, leaning over to click on a button that read Messages. "This is my virtual life. Some people go to a coffee shop or a club to socialize, but most kids from my class come on here."

"So to socialize, you sit alone in your room and type on a computer?" I asked, frowning at the screen.

"Not really *alone*," Shannon insisted. "I'm with my friends, just in a different way. There are no limits in a virtual world. We can do anything—

have our own apartments, throw parties, go shopping . . ."

"And why not just go shopping?" I asked. "You know, here? In River Heights?"

Maggie and Shannon just stared at me.

"It's okay, Nance," Bess comforted me, standing up and walking over to pat my back. "I didn't get it either."

"Anyway," said Shannon, clicking the mouse and causing a new window to come up. "Come take a look at this. I think this will help explain why I've been so freaked out the last few days."

I looked over Shannon's shoulder at the screen, where a new page was loading.

MESSAGES, it finally read. An assortment of short personal notes was arranged below the headline, like on a message board.

SASSYGIRL48, read the first one. UR A LIAR N A JERK. WHEN I'M FINISHED NO ONE WILL DARE BE FRIENDS W/U. U DESERVE 2 SUFFER.

I gasped. Who would write something so awful?

It was signed at the bottom: GUITARLVR15.

"Oh my gosh," I said breathlessly.

"There's more," Shannon said simply. "Did you read them all?"

I hadn't. I quickly scanned down the remaining messages.

21

I USED 2 THINK U WERE NICE. NOW I KNOW UR A WASTE
OF SPACE. GET OFF BETTERLIFE. ROZ84

I CAN'T BELIEVE U ACT THE WAY U DO N EXPECT PEOPLE
TO LIKE U. PEOPLE LIKE U R ALWAYS ALONE. BUTTERFLY-
DUST

DID U LIKE THE NOTE I LEFT ON UR HOUSE? I'M LEAVING
1 JUST LIKE IT ON UR LOCKER 2MROW. KILLERJOE4

"What's the note he's talking about?" I asked.
"On your house? On your locker?"

Shannon swallowed, shaking her head sadly. She
clicked on a tiny icon at the bottom of the page,
and soon the screen was filled with the image of
a cute, tidy, brick townhouse in a well-landscaped
development. One jarring detail kept the house
from looking inviting: Someone had spray painted
loser with red paint across the front door.

"Oh my gosh," I repeated.

"Yeah." Shannon nodded ruefully. "And yesterday I found the same word written on my locker
in red marker."

My mouth had dropped open. Weren't computer games supposed to be fun? "Who are these
people?" I asked as Shannon clicked back to the
messages page. "Roz Eighty-four? Butterfly Dust?

Killer Joe Four? Are these people you know?"

"Could be." Shannon shrugged, still looking sad. "Or they could be total strangers. I had never heard of any of them before last week."

I frowned. "Did something happen last week?"

Shannon sighed and closed her eyes, nodding. "Yeah. But I didn't expect it to lead to this."

"What happened?" I asked, glancing back at the screen. The cruel messages seemed to go on forever. Words like *nasty, horrible,* and *stupid* jumped out at me, like little daggers.

Shannon swallowed again. She opened her eyes, and when she spoke, it seemed as if she was trying to divorce herself from what she was saying—like if she thought too hard about it, she might cry.

"There's this boy I kind of like in town. He's older than me; sixteen. We haven't talked much in real life, except when I sometimes go to the coffee shop he works at, and we've had, like, little conversations."

I nodded. "Okay."

"I never thought much about it. I figured he was older, so he'd never be interested in a girl my age. But then one afternoon, I'm playing Better-Life and I come across this character who looks *exactly* like my crush."

I glanced at Bess. She looked just as confused by all this as I was. "Right."

Shannon sighed. "We were at the mall—I mean, the *virtual* mall—and he just came up to me and offered me a sip of his smoothie."

I tried to make sense of that. "A *virtual* sip of his . . . *virtual* smoothie."

Shannon shrugged. "Right. It was strawberry. I took a sip, and then he started talking to me—asking me about myself, where I lived, what I was doing at the mall. And then he started"—she bit her lip—"giving me all these *compliments*."

I nodded. "*Virtual* compliments."

Shannon nodded. "At first, yes. He said he liked my hairstyle, liked my dress. But at some point—I forget what was the first thing he actually said—but I started to realize that he was complimenting *me* me, and not me, Sassygirl48."

I nodded slowly. "Riiiiiight."

She sighed. "I know, it sounds crazy. But he started saying things that you wouldn't know from meeting my character in BetterLife. Like that I play the violin, or that I was voted Class Favorite at school last year. And then he said . . ." She paused, frowning.

"He said . . . ?" I prompted.

She sighed again. "He said he'd seen me

around—by then I was sure he meant in real life—but he'd always been too shy to talk to me."

I frowned. "And this boy is sixteen?"

Shannon shook her head. "I know, I know. It seems crazy now. Why would he use a game to flirt with me? But at the time it just made so much, I dunno, *sense*."

I nodded. I was sure it didn't hurt that the boy was telling Shannon exactly what she wanted to hear. "Then what happened?"

Shannon's face fell. "Then we said we would get together sometime in real life. After that, he took off. And his e-mail came."

I glanced at the screen, having an idea where this was going. "And his e-mail said . . . ?"

Shannon sighed, moving toward the computer and typing an address into her browser. Soon the middle-school's web-based e-mail program popped up. "See for yourself."

I leaned in closer to the screen as the message loaded. Then, there it was:

To: sfitzgerald@rhms.grade6.edu
From: guitarzrcool@fastmail.net
Sassygirl48,
Don't get your hopes up. Even in cyberspace,

I WOULD NEVER BE CAUGHT DEAD WITH A STUCK-UP
WASTE OF SPACE LIKE YOU.
YOU DESERVE TO BE ALONE—IN THIS GAME, IN REAL
LIFE, ALWAYS. YOU DESERVE TO SUFFER LIKE YOU'VE
MADE OTHERS SUFFER.

I gasped.

Bess was right behind me, reading over my shoulder. "Have you talked to the guy?" she asked, frowning at the e-mail's nasty tone. "Have you asked him why he's so angry at you? Or whether it was really him at all?"

Shannon shrugged, looking down into her lap. For the first time since I'd met her, she'd lost her mature sheen. She looked like a sad, freaked-out twelve-year-old kid. "I'm too embarrassed," she said softly.

"Embarrassed about what?" asked Bess. I could tell she was pretty upset that somebody would target someone Maggie's age through the Internet. "You didn't do anything wrong. You don't deserve to be treated like this!"

Shannon kept staring at her lap, and I placed my hand on her shoulder. "It's okay," I said. "It can be hard to confront a bully. Even if you know you don't deserve to be treated like that."

Shannon nodded and sighed. Bess seemed to

soften, and patted her arm. "I'm sorry. It just really upsets me that this happened to you."

Maggie stood up and walked over to the three of us, asking gently, "Do you want to tell them how it's gone since then, Shannon?"

Shannon nodded. "Yeah," she agreed. "Basically, it's gotten worse and worse. The day after I got that e-mail from GuitarLvr15, I got two more e-mails—from people I'd never heard of. They were just like the messages you see there—I'm terrible, mean, whatever."

I nodded. "Wow."

"Yeah." She frowned. "Little by little, people started being meaner to me in the game. They'd yell things when I walked by, or avoid me when I went to hang out and socialize. At first, it was just a few people, but little by little, it seemed like *everyone* got involved. Even people I'd hung out with in the game before—they didn't want anything to do with me." She paused before continuing. "I work at a salon in the game. I mean, Sassygirl48 does. That's how she pays the bills. But a few days ago I went to work, and my boss suddenly just fired me. She said it was for 'conduct reasons,' but she wouldn't give me any details. I walked home, and all the way, people were yelling things at me on the street. A girl I'd never seen before was eating in the park, and she threw her trash at me. When I got home, and . . . You saw what was painted on the house."

I sighed. "I did. But you said . . . Maggie said you were having problems at school?"

Shannon closed her eyes and nodded. "That started just a couple days ago. People whispering when I walked into the room, throwing spitballs at me, mean little things." She sighed. "I found out that afternoon that someone posted footage of Sassygirl48 being bullied on uVid."

I immediately looked to Bess for an explanation, but she had already turned to Maggie for the same reason.

"It's another website owned by the creators of BetterLife," Maggie explained. "It's sort of a greatest-hits type thing. When you're playing the game, it automatically records your game play every fifteen minutes, so if anything really cool happens, you can save it as a video file and post it to uVid so everyone can watch."

I frowned. "You can just post it anonymously? So no one has any privacy, even in this virtual world?"

Shannon shook her head. "No, you have to post it under your username. But it's no one I know. Just another random stranger who hates me on the Internet." Her voice caught, and she looked into her lap again.

I reached out and touched her shoulder. "I'm sorry to make you relive all this, Shannon, but just so I'm clear: You were being bullied online, and then someone made public a video of your bullying, and now you're being bullied at school?"

Shannon started to cry. I glanced at Maggie, and she nodded. "That's pretty much it," she confirmed.

"Well," I murmured, glancing at Bess. She looked as dismayed by all this as I felt.

I'd dealt with plenty of bullies in my life, but they were always easy to confront, because bullying is such a deliberate act. It's hard to yell an insult at someone, or throw something at her, and remain anonymous. On the Internet, though, everyone is anonymous. Which makes it incredibly easy to hurt someone's feelings with no repercussions.

"It sounds like this first boy, GuitarLvr15, is the ringleader. He threw the first stone, so to speak, and he's still involved, right?" I asked Shannon gently.

She sniffled and nodded. "Right. I keep getting e-mails from him."

I sighed. "Shannon," I said delicately, "is there

any reason this boy would want to hurt you? Have you had any interactions in person, or any interactions with his friends?"

Shannon shook her head vigorously. "That's what's so crazy!" she explained. "I'd never had a real conversation with him until that time in the game. And I was so happy!" She let out a sob.

I patted her shoulder. "All right," I said. "Shannon, I wish I could have kept this from happening to you, but it's too late. You have my word, though, that I'm going to find the person who started this and make sure it *ends*. Nobody deserves to be treated like this."

Shannon looked up at me, blinking away tears. "Thank you, Nancy!" she cried. "When Maggie told me about you, I wasn't sure . . . I didn't know if I trusted someone I didn't know with what was happening to me. But you're so nice! I believe you can stop this."

"Believe it," I agreed, reaching for Shannon's hand and squeezing it. "Nancy Drew is on the case."

Maggie, Bess, and I were silent as I drove them back to my house, since they'd left Bess's car there. We all had pensive expressions, each thinking our own separate thoughts.

"The Internet has made so many things easier,"

I murmured finally. "Including being a bully."

Bess sighed. "It scares me that this whole virtual world has been going on for years now, and I just realized today that Maggie has an account. If someone bullied her online, who knows whether me or my parents would even find out."

Maggie rolled her eyes. "Bess," she chided, "don't be such a worrywart. Of course I'd tell you."

I glanced at Maggie in the rearview mirror. "What's Shannon like at school?" I asked. The truth was, I was having trouble picturing her. It was hard to reconcile the pretty, outgoing girl I'd met with the quieter, more vulnerable kids I remembered being bullied when I was in school. Unless she was completely different around kids her own age.

Maggie smiled. "She's great! She has great style, and she dresses like a celebrity or something, and she always had tons of friends. . . . She used to eat lunch with, like, fifteen people, and it was always hard to get a seat at their table. . . ."

Hmmmm. "So she was pretty popular before the bullying started."

Maggie looked at me like that was obvious. "Yeah. I would say, like, the most popular—one of the most popular girls in our grade."

Verrry interesting. "Does she have any enemies?"

Maggie seemed to consider this for a minute, then shook her head. "Shannon isn't any meaner than anyone else. I mean, she's popular, but I think people like her. I don't think she's ever, like, ruined anybody's life or anything."

I nodded slowly, pulling into our driveway. Careful to leave space for Bess to pull out, I parked and turned off the car's engine. "Home again, home again," I sang lightly.

Bess moaned and sat up in the passenger seat. "Speak for yourself," she retorted, opening her door. "Come on, kiddo. I've got a date with my bed that I'm not going to miss for anything." She looked back at me. "Thanks, Nancy. You're a lifesaver. I mean it."

I smiled. "Thanks for pointing me in the direction of someone who needs me."

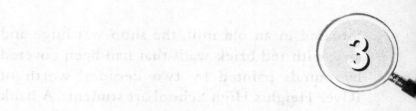

VIRTUAL LIVES

As I showered and dressed the next morning, I had to admit to myself that I was having a little trouble wrapping my head around the whole BetterLife idea. I'd e-mailed Bess and George before bed—I wasn't *hopelessly* computer illiterate—to arrange a time that afternoon for them to come over to help set up a BetterLife identity for me. But for now, I figured, better to stick to the basics of sleuthing: getting out there and asking some questions, person to person.

Barbara's Beans was a cute little coffee shop in downtown River Heights that was popular with the middle-school and high-school crowds.

Situated in an old mill, the shop was huge and airy, with red brick walls that had been covered by murals painted by two decades' worth of River Heights High School art students. A bank of computers was tucked into the right wall, just inside the doors, and they were always filled with kids e-mailing, IMing, or even occasionally—Gasp!—doing homework. Today, though, there was only one kid I was interested in—and he was *behind* the counter.

I scanned the menu. "I'll take a medium—I mean, um, a doppio . . . I mean, a cappuccino with, um, caramel and cinnamon flavoring—"

My target smiled at me. Honestly, he looked a little intimidating, with a ring in his nose and a cobalt blue streak dyed into his shaggy, angular haircut. Up close, his eyes had a warm twinkle that I was sure had influenced Shannon's crush on him. "Milk?"

I nodded. "Yes, please."

He chuckled. "No, I mean what kind of milk would you like. Whole, skim, two percent, soy—"

"*Not* soy," I interrupted him. A few months before, Bess had tried to get George and I on the soy milk bandwagon, as she'd called it, with disastrous results. "Um, whole milk is fine, thanks."

He smiled and nodded. "Decaf? Half caf?"

I nodded. "Caffeinated."

He punched a few numbers into the register. "Don't take this the wrong way," he said with in a just-between-us tone, "but I get the sense you're a bit of a coffee novice."

I'm sure my face fell. "Is it that obvious?"

He smiled. "Did you know that a doppio means a double—two shots of espresso?"

I shook my head. "No! Just one is fine, thanks." I drank coffee maybe a couple times a week. Two shots of espresso and they'd be peeling me off the ceiling.

He nodded. "That'll be three fifty, please."

I handed over the money, glancing up at him out of the corner of my eye. "I have a confession to make," I said. "I'm not just here for the coffee."

He didn't look all that surprised. "No? The computers are right over there," he replied, gesturing.

I shook my head. "No, I mean, I need to ask you some questions."

He looked surprised. "About what?"

"A young girl who's being bullied online," I said slowly, pausing to gauge his reaction. "You wouldn't know anything about that?"

Perhaps this barista was a part-time actor, but I had to admit that he honestly looked stunned by my question, and more than a little lost. "No." He frowned, shaking his head as though to clear it, and placed my money in the cash register, then closed the drawer. "Let me just get someone to cover for me. *Kylie!* Give me a minute, then I'll meet you at that table over there." He pointed at a small table tucked into a private corner surrounded by plants.

I sat down where he told me to, and a minute or two later, a redheaded girl came out from the back and took Jake's place at the counter. I could hear the whirring and gurgling of the espresso machine, and after another minute or so, Jake appeared at the table, holding a foamy cappuccino in a wide, red coffee cup. "Here you go," he said, placing the drink in front of me. "I'm Jake, by the way."

I nodded in greeting. "I'm Nancy."

He settled into the seat across from me. "Now, what were you saying? Something about a girl being bullied?"

I decided to start at the beginning. "Are you familiar with the game BetterLife?"

Jake snorted. It surprised me, and I cast him an annoyed glance over my cappuccino.

"I'm sorry," he said. "It's just . . . that's like asking, 'Have you heard of this restaurant called McDonald's?' I thought everyone had heard of BetterLife."

I stiffened, sipping my drink. "I hadn't," I corrected him. "At least, not until last night. But anyway—"

"Here." Jake suddenly reached out with a napkin and swiped at the tip of my nose. "You had foam. Sorry. Now what about BetterLife?"

I paused, feeling a little silly. Here I was, someone who'd never heard of what was apparently the most popular computer game of all time, and I couldn't even seem to drink a cappuccino properly. Still, I needed to get to the bottom of what Jake knew. "Do you have a character on BetterLife?"

Jake nodded. "Sure."

I sighed. Jake seemed like a nice enough kid, but now I braced myself for the inevitable. "So why have you been attacking Shannon online? She insists she never did anything bad to you, but tell me your side of the story."

But Jake looked confused again. "Who?" he asked. "I'm sorry. Just who do you think I am?"

I frowned. "I think you're Jake Seltzer," I replied. "Here in River Heights. But in the world of BetterLife, I think you go by GuitarLvr15."

I waited for a flash of recognition to pass behind Jake's eyes, but he still looked confused. "Who?" he asked, shaking his head. "Listen, Nancy, I think you have the wrong guy. I'm not sure why you think I'm this Guitar Lover kid. . . ."

"Because he looks *just like you*," I replied, starting to feel a little frustrated. "And he's the ringleader of an angry mob that's targeting a young girl online. You just said you have a BetterLife avatar?"

"Sure." Jake nodded, and started to stand up from his seat. "Hey, why don't we go over to the computers? I can show you my BetterLife character, and maybe you'll believe me when I say I have no idea who this Guitar Lover is."

"Okay," I said hesitantly. I was beginning to feel really confused. If Jake really wasn't Guitar-Lvr15, did that mean someone had purposefully designed the character to look like him? Either to throw Shannon off track, or make her feel like a bigger fool because she'd been humiliated by her crush?

Over at the computers, Jake settled down in front of the huge monitor of a Mac and pulled over a chair for me. "Okay," he said, clicking on the Internet browser icon and briskly typing in the BetterLife URL. It took a few minutes to load, but then the same welcome screen I remembered from last night popped up, an aerial view of a virtual town with a login box on the right. I watched as Jake typed in "BionicEd" and a password, which I read as *bobdylan*. A new page loaded, and slowly we focused in on a tall, thin, somewhat nerdy-looking young man in a scientist's lab coat and thick, black-framed glasses. He sat in a small bedroom with two sets of bunk beds that resembled the dorm rooms at River Heights University.

"This is Bionic Ed," Jake said. "He's a chemistry major at BetterLife University. He loves noodling around with chemicals and someday, he's going to invent an alternative to plastic that's just as durable but totally biodegradable."

I nodded. On-screen, BionicEd stood up from his desk and exited the room. "Is that your dream?" I asked.

Jake frowned. "No," he replied, as if I'd just suggested he dreamed of being the world's first nose-ringed opera singer. "It's BionicEd's dream."

By now, BionicEd was crossing a sunny, well-manicured courtyard that looked similar to, if not exactly like, a courtyard at River Heights University. "This doesn't even look like the same world as the game Shannon was playing," I observed. Where was the idyllic suburban town, the virtual mall, the townhouse?

"That's because it's probably not," Jake replied. A raven-haired beauty wearing surgical scrubs with stiletto heels paused near BionicEd. "There are tons of different forums on BetterLife. They're all completely separate; like their own little worlds. Once you have a character in one, you can move between different forums, but most people don't. I don't hang out in the middle-school or the high-school forum. People are too immature there. BionicEd really belongs in a university setting."

I stared at the screen. "This is the university forum?"

Jake nodded. "RHU, baby!" He'd been typing furiously to "talk" to the dark-haired girl:

HI, HEY WHAZZUP. NUTHIN MUCH, JUST STUDYING; I MISSED U.

Suddenly the girl leaned forward and planted one on BionicEd, right on the lips. BionicEd responded with enthusiasm, and suddenly I felt myself blushing, not quite sure what to do when two virtual characters were virtually making out in their virtual world right in front of you.

"Um . . . Is she your girlfriend?" I asked.

Jake nodded as the characters finally came up for air. "Her name is Doctor Lovely. She's premed. We're always together."

I glanced at Jake out of the corner of my eye, taking mental stock. "You're how old? Sixteen?"

Jake nodded. He was typing again. U LOOK ESP LOVELY 2DAY.

I cleared my throat, feeling like a huge fuddy-duddy. "Aren't you a little young to be dating a college student?"

Jake finally looked up from the computer then, looking at me with what seemed like pity. "*I'm* not dating her," he corrected me. "BionicEd is."

"Oh." I looked at the floor, wondering how I'd possibly missed all this stuff. "But in real life, you're just friends."

Jake shrugged, turning back to the computer. "I've never met DoctorLovely before in my life," he replied. "I don't even know who she is, really. She could be a middle-aged father of six for all I know. But in the BetterLife world, she and BionicEd have a thing going on."

I sighed. This was all really going over my head, and I wasn't making any headway on Shannon's case. "So in BetterLife, you don't have to show any proof that you are who you say you are?"

Jake shook his head. "Nope. Why?"

"I mean . . ." I paused, biting my lip. "I could sign up for, say, a community for people retired from the circus, and nobody would ever check that I really was in the circus?"

Jake glanced up, frowning. "That's right," he said, turning back to type more to DoctorLovely. "Although I don't think that community exists."

I sighed again. "And nobody has a problem with that?" I asked.

Jake sighed, glancing from me to the computer screen. He quickly typed GTG to DoctorLovely, then clicked the mouse on to the computer's sleep mode. The screen went from full color to black, and while BionicEd probably continued to move—kind of wandering around the courtyard now, aimless—it was clear that Jake was no longer controlling him. "Why would anyone have a problem with it?" Jake asked me.

"It just seems a little misleading," I replied. "If I sign up for the middle-school community, other users would probably assume I'm in middle school. And besides, if the game is completely anonymous, it means no one is responsible for their own actions."

Jake nodded. "And if I sign up for the university community, and I get along fine with everyone and everyone's fine with that, and it never goes beyond the computer screen . . . So what?"

"The problem is when it goes *beyond* the computer screen. Like the situation I came to talk with you about. A young girl is being harassed in the middle-school forum, and it's gotten so out of control that now people are bullying her in real life."

Jake nodded again. "Like what kind of stuff?"

I glanced at the computer screen. "It would actually be easier to show you." Sitting down in front of the computer, I glanced at my watch. Shannon had given me her username and password last night as well as permission to go into her e-mail if need be, and she had promised me she'd go to school today, meaning she couldn't be playing BetterLife right now. After I woke up the computer, I clicked on a button that said Log Out and was brought back to the initial login screen. Quickly I typed in SASSYGIRL48 and Shannon's password, GLITTERY, and was brought to a screen where Shannon's character sat sadly in a small bedroom.

"She must be home," I murmured. "How do I get her to leave the house?"

"Here." Jake took the mouse from me and with a series of clicks, navigated Sassygirl48 out of her house and onto her lawn.

"Now turn around," I said, and Jake clicked a compass that changed the view on the monitor to the exterior of Sassygirl48's townhouse.

"Wow," he murmured.

The grafitti I'd seen the night before, *loser*, was still spray painted across the house, and now two front windows were broken, as if someone had thrown rocks through them. Sassygirl48's cute house was quickly turning into a dump.

"What's that in the mailbox?" I asked, pointing to a bright white envelope. Jake clicked on it, and the letter appeared on-screen.

DEAR SASSYGIRL48,

YOU HAVE ALWAYS BEEN A GOOD TENANT, BUT RECENTLY, THE NOISE AND NASTY ELEMENT YOU HAVE BROUGHT TO THE DEVELOPMENT ARE SIMPLY TOO MUCH FOR YOUR NEIGHBORS AND ME TO BEAR. I MUST ASK YOU TO VACATE THE PROPERTY BY FRIDAY. IF YOU DO NOT, I WILL PLACE YOUR BELONGINGS ON THE FRONT LAWN AND CHANGE THE LOCKS. I HOPE YOU WILL TAKE THIS ACTION AS ENCOURAGEMENT TO RECONSIDER THE COMPANY YOU KEEP.

SINCERELY,

YOUR LANDLORD

HAMSTERMAN03

"Hamster Man?" I asked.

"It's another player," Jake explained. "When you get wealthy enough in the game, you can buy property and rent to tenants."

"Just like in real life."

"Just like in real life," Jake echoed. "And just like in real life, landlords can evict you."

I shook my head. "Wow." On-screen, noises seemed to be coming from the street—shouts and angry growls. Suddenly a tiny white ball hurled through the air and attached itself to Sassygirl48's shoulder.

"Spitballs," said Jake. He clicked a button, and Sassygirl48 turned to face two girls, one had long, lustrous red hair, sparkling green eyes, and—

"Is that a cow?" I asked.

"Yeah." Jake nodded. "In BetterLife, you can have any pet you want. You can domesticate any animal."

I nodded. The other girl had long, black hair and elaborate, catlike eye makeup. A purple tattoo—a Celtic knot— stood out on her arm.

Beep!

Suddenly a message appeared on-screen.

A MESSAGE FROM ILOVEDUBLIN:
U WASTE OF SPACE, WHY DID U COME TO SCHOOL 2DAY?
EVERYONE IN COMPUTER LAB THINKS U SHOULD GO HOME.

"Whoa," Jake murmured.

Beep. Another one appeared.

A MESSAGE FROM MOOMOOGIRL:
YEAH, NO1 LIKES UR FACE OR UR ATTITUDE. STAY HOME
AND CRY INTO UR CORNFLAKES, LOSER.

"I think I've seen enough," Jake murmured, moving the arrow over to the Logout button.

"Wait," I cautioned, grabbing his arm. "Can you look up another user in the middle-school community?"

Jake frowned. "Kind of," he replied. "If Sassygirl48 has dealt with GuitarLvr15 before, I can call up an image of their last interaction."

I nodded. "That works. I want you to look up GuitarLvr15."

Jake looked doubtful, but clicked on a Search History icon and entered the username. Instantly, a short video popped up of a character that looked like Jake's twin—right down to the black concert T-shirt, nose ring, and blue streak in his hair—shoving Sassygirl48 at the mall.

"That was just yesterday," I said, reading the time stamp on the screen.

"Wow," Jake muttered, squinting at the screen. "*Wow.* That really could be me."

"Yeah," I agreed. "And you're sure you have nothing to do with it?"

Jake shook his head. "It's not me," he replied. "But if you figure out who it is, let me know. They're totally stealing my look."

The video came to an end, and Jake glanced up at me sadly before clicking the Log Out button. "Poor girl," he murmured. "That has to be hard."

"And you're sure you don't know Shannon Fitzgerald?" I asked.

Jake's face totally changed. He went from sadness and pity to shock and amazement, all in a couple seconds. "That's *Shannon Fitzgerald*?" he asked, his mouth dropping open. "Whoa. Yeah, I guess it did kind of look like her."

"Why are you so surprised?" I asked. "Look, whoever this Guitar Lover person is, he flirted with Shannon online before completely turning on her and ringleading a mob of bullies."

"And you thought . . . Oh wow." Jake shook his head. "She thought it was me flirting with her. And then me bullying her."

I nodded. "Can you blame her?"

He shrugged. "It looks just like me," he agreed. "And a lot of kids in the middle school . . . They create avatars that look just like them. Them, in computer form."

"Right." I sighed. "But you didn't."

Jake looked up at me, sympathetic now. "Why go through all the trouble of creating a new character who looks and acts just like you?" he asked. "The game is for fun, for you to try something different. Isn't that the whole point of playing? Not to lead *your* life, but a *better* life?" He sighed. "Besides. Even if that character was me, there's no way I would ever flirt with Shannon Fitzgerald."

My ears perked up. "No? Why?"

Jake made a face. "Let's just say, I've heard she has a mean streak."

Hmm. "What do you mean?"

"She's superpopular, and she loves making fun of the less popular kids. Just last week, I heard she tripped some poor girl in the cafeteria, in front of everyone, supposedly because their English teacher had chosen to read this girl's essay out loud. Shannon called her a teacher's pet. Some kids were talking about it while I was working."

My eyes widened. *This* was interesting. Could this person have turned the bullying around on Shannon and retreated online to do it?

"What's this girl's name?"

"Sarah O'Malley." Jake frowned, standing up

from the computer. "Sheesh. I guess no one really deserves to be harassed online, but if you're Shannon Fitzgerald. . ." He paused. "Maybe it's time she saw what life's like for the other half."

CYBERSLEUTHING

A few hours later, Bess and I flanked George as the three of us sat down in front of my computer.

"Okay, so we're going to create Nancy a BetterLife character, so she can be right in the middle of things. Before we begin," George said, wiggling her fingers in what I guessed were pretyping and clicking exercises. "You guys *really* had never heard of BetterLife before this? *Really?* For real? I've been on it for months."

I wrinkled my nose indignantly. "For real," I confirmed. "Why? Is it all over the evening news or something?"

"I've been too busy working and keeping up

with fashion trends to waste time on the Internet," Bess retorted with a sniff, reaching over to tug a piece of George's faded blue T-shirt. "Unlike *some* people."

George shook her off, shaking her head. "Okay, okay," she said, firing up my Internet browser. "I just find it a little strange that my two very smart best friends have somehow missed out on this phenomenon, which was on the cover of *Time* magazine last week...."

"It was?" I asked. Wow. I'd thought this was just something teenagers liked.

George nodded, typing the URL for Better-Life into the browser's search field. "It's available free on the Internet, but the creators have been making a ton of money through advertising. And next month they're introducing a subscription service that will allow users access to special features—wardrobe and career upgrades, special talents for your character, making it easier to make videos; that kind of thing. They're expected to make *billions*."

"Huh," I murmured as the login screen loaded. "Will you still be able to play the current version for free?"

"Yeah." George frowned at the login screen, then clicked a button right below the password box: Create User. "But trust me, the upgrades sound awesome enough that nobody will want to be caught dead on the free version."

A new screen popped up, with BUILD YOUR AVATAR! written across the top. A somewhat bland-looking blond guy stood in the middle of the screen, with arrows on either side of his hair, face, body, and shoes. George clicked on a button marked Gender, and selected Female. The blond guy turned into a cute blond lady. Then George clicked on a box marked Age, and selected 11-15, glancing sideways at me. "Since we're going to put you in the middle-school community," she explained.

"Fine with me," I agreed. On-screen, the lady became a fresh-faced teenager.

Then George started clicking on the arrows that surrounded the character. After about fifteen minutes, we'd created a cute girl with a strawberry-blond ponytail and blue eyes, clad in a white T-shirt, blue cardigan, and tweed pants with sneakers. "Nancy style," Bess said approvingly. Once we'd selected her appearance, a new screen charged us with naming our character's hobbies and interests.

"How about dancing?" George asked.

"And shopping," Bess added.

I cast them a skeptical glance. The last time I'd gone shopping, a different president had been in office.

George shrugged, typing the hobbies into the correct fields on-screen. "You can't just say sleuthing, Nance," she chided.

"Yeah," Bess piped in. "Suspicious much?"

Finally we were brought to a screen that asked us to name our new character.

"How about Twinkletoes14?" Bess asked.

"Or why don't you just call me Wheresthe-Mall?" I joked.

George shook her head, smiling. "Let's try something simpler," she suggested. Clicking in the box, she typed "VirtualNancy" and clicked the Submit button.

A happy chime sounded, and when the screen reloaded, it proclaimed:

CONGRATULATIONS! YOU HAVE CREATED VIRTUALNANCY. AFTER YOU CLICK ACCEPT, YOUR CHARACTER WILL BE DROPPED INTO THE TOWN'S CENTER WITH $500. WE SUGGEST THAT SHE IMMEDIATELY FIND A JOB AND AN AFFORDABLE PLACE TO LIVE. ONCE SHE HAS THESE TWO THINGS, START EXPLORING! REMEMBER, BETTERLIFE IS JUST LIKE REAL LIFE, BUT BETTER—ANYTHING IS POSSIBLE!

"All right, guys," George announced, clicking the Accept button. "Here goes nothing."

VirtualNancy was dropped into the middle of a virtual town center that looked a little, but not exactly, like River Heights. George explained that in the game, your character could, by buying a newspaper, find jobs but only the ones for which she was "qualified" would pop up—and since VirtualNancy was a newbie, that wouldn't be many. Within a few minutes VirtualNancy had checked out the paper and secured an unglamorous job sweeping up in a hair salon. A trip to the virtual real estate office placed her in a drafty studio apartment on the edge of town—the only place poor VirtualNancy could afford.

"I feel so bad for her," Bess murmured as Virtual-Nancy huddled under a dirty quilt to stay warm. "Virtual Nancy shouldn't have to live like this!"

George shook her head. "It's all part of the game, Bess," she assured her cousin. "Everyone starts out in humble circumstances. You work your way up."

Sure enough, after just a few days of work (a day in BetterLife seemed to go by in about half an hour), VirtualNancy had earned enough to buy a clean comforter and some nicer furniture.

"In a few days she'll be offered a better job, as

long as she keeps showing up on time and being polite," George explained. "Soon she'll be able to rent a nicer apartment. Don't you worry."

It only took a couple minutes to reach the entrance to the virtual River Heights Mall. Inside, the mall looked incredibly realistic: familiar-looking stores with slightly different names carried all sorts of clothes in the latest styles while gift stores, toy stores, and specialty stores filled in the remaining stalls. Airy, skylighted spaces encouraged shoppers to linger, and VirtualNancy passed three huge, beautiful fountains on the way to the food court.

"The food court is where the action is," George advised us. "It's where all the characters hang out."

I cast a suspicious glance her way. "You don't hang out in the middle-school community of BetterLife, do you?"

George rolled her eyes. "Of course not. But all the River Heights communities are configured to look the same—except for the university, because that's made to look like a campus. You don't think the creators have time to program individual worlds for each community in each city, do you?"

I looked at George blankly.

"Never mind," she said with a sigh. "Anyway, the food court is the place to be."

Virtual Nancy reached a large, open, well-lit space furnished with modern plastic tables and chairs, and filled almost to capacity with chatting teenagers. Along the walls, virtual restaurants offered burgers, Chinese food, tacos, sandwiches, ice cream, and coffee. But it looked like fewer than half the shoppers were actually there to eat; most tables held no food, but all the seats were filled with kids.

"Wow," I murmured breathlessly. "There are so many of them! Does this mean this many middle-school kids are still up playing BetterLife?"

George nodded. "Pretty much," she confirmed. "When you log out, your character kind of goes into survival mode wherever he or she is; she'll still go to work, eat, and sleep, but she won't socialize or go out to entertain herself. Which means all of these characters are being actively controlled."

I shook my head in amazement. There had to be hundreds of kids in the food court—at least half the kids who attended the middle school.

"What do we do?" I asked.

Bess peered at the screen. "Can we sit down at a table and mingle?" she asked. "Maybe some of these kids know about the Shannon situation."

George nodded, and walked over to a nearby table where a few seats were free. Within seconds she'd asked one of the girls there for permission to sit down, and soon VirtualNancy was having a pleasant conversation with two girls and a boy about last night's episode of *America's Next Top Project Runway*, with lots of input from Bess.

I HAVEN'T SEEN U AROUND BEFORE, one of the girls, Junebug67, said to VirtualNancy. R U NEW HERE?

George glanced at me.

"I am," I dictated to her, "but I know Sassygirl48."

George typed my message out on the keyboard and hit Submit.

The other girl, KylieGal, and the boy, JackOf-All8, abruptly stood up from the table. As they began to walk away, Junebug67 gave me a hasty apology.

SORRY. GTG.

And she left too.

"GTG?" I asked.

"'Got to go,'" supplied Bess, sounding a little exasperated. "Honestly, Nance, even I know that one."

Normally I would have been offended, but a familiar figure had caught my eye in the game. "Wait! Over there, by the yogurt stand. Can you look in that direction?" I asked George, pointing to a familiar blue-streaked head. She clicked a direction on a compass that appeared at the lower right of the screen, then a magnifying glass with a plus sign—the symbol for zooming in. Soon we had a better look at the kids in front of the yogurt shop, and I jumped in my seat.

"That's him!" I cried. "GuitarLvr15! Let's go talk to him!"

George quickly directed VirtualNancy across the food court and over to GuitarLvr15. She clicked on his character and then on a button marked Talk Privately.

"What do I say?" she asked, pausing with her hands over the keyboard.

I swallowed. I actually had no idea how to start a conversation with a virtual middle-school boy.

Luckily Bess jumped into the fray. "Say, 'I'm Nancy. I like the streak in your hair,'" she directed.

George typed that in, then hit Submit.

It seemed like an eternity before my computer beeped, and a message from GuitarLvr15 appeared.

THX. R U NEW HERE?

I glanced at George.

"Yes," she typed. "I just started playing today. What's ur name?"

She glanced over at me, waiting for my approval before she hit Submit. "Good," I said with a nod. "But can we switch places so I can do the talking?"

George smiled and shrugged. "You *are* Real Life Nancy," she agreed.

We switched seats, and just as I sat down, the computer beeped with GutiarLvr15's reply.

MY NAME IS GUITARLVR15. DO U GO 2 RHMS?

I gulped and typed as fast as I could.

I DO. WHAT'S UR REAL NAME?

"Nance," George murmured in a cautious tone.

MY NAME IS GUITARLVR15. WHAT GRADE R U IN?

I wasn't about to accept that as an answer.

8TH GRADE. WHAT'S UR REAL NAME? U CAN TELL ME

George shifted uncomfortably. "You might want to let it go. . . ."

Beep.

MY NAME IS GUITARLVR15. DROP IT. WHAT DO U LIKE 2 DO 4 FUN?

I couldn't let this go.

I LIKE 2 ASK QUESTIONS. WHO R U?? I KNOW JAKE.

I was typing so fast, Bess and George were having trouble keeping up. Just as I hit the Submit button, George jumped up. "Nancy! Don't!"

Within seconds there was a horrible sound, like a car crash or a bomb going off. Suddenly VirtualNancy stood alone in front of the yogurt shop. GuitarLvr15 and his friends had vanished.

A window appeared in the middle of the screen: **GUITARLVR15 HAS BLOCKED YOU FROM TALKING TO HIM.**

"What??" I cried.

Bess looked crushed as George sighed. "It's a feature of the game," George explained. "You can block anyone from privately talking to you for twenty-four hours."

My mouth hung open. "But then . . . How—

how do Shannon's harassers manage it?" I asked. On-screen, more and more people were walking away from VirtualNancy. I wondered how much of that was due to my interaction with Guitar-Lvr15, and how much was due to the fact that I'd told someone I was a friend of Sassygirl48. "Couldn't she have just blocked them?"

George shook her head. "It's a design flaw in the game. Blocking only applies to private conversations. You can still e-mail someone—everyone has an e-mail address listed in their profile—or you can say something publicly. That's how Shannon's bullies operate."

I sighed, pushing back from the desk and crossing my arms in front of my chest. Poor Virtual-Nancy was an outcast at the mall. My first foray into the virtual world had been a failure. "I think I'm ready to log out and come back to the real world," I muttered.

I stood up, and George took over to log out VirtualNancy and close my Internet browser. "I'll leave you basic directions, Nancy," she offered. "You can get on again tomorrow or whenever you have time, and hopefully you'll have better luck."

I nodded as Bess and George both stood up and

started collecting their things. "I hope so," I said. "Because days might go by fast in the BetterLife world, but I bet time feels like it's crawling for poor Shannon."

FRIEND TO ENEMY?

My cell phone woke me up way too early the next morning. Bess, George, and I had played with VirtualNancy until far later than my usual bedtime, and I was zapped. But when I fished my phone off the nightstand and saw that it was Ned calling, I had to pick up.

"Hello?"

"Don't tell me you're still in bed, Nance," Ned greeted me with a chuckle.

"It's that obvious, huh?" I struggled to sit up in bed, and cleared my throat to get the frogs out.

Ned laughed. "Let's just say it's clear you didn't get up for your usual sunrise jog this morning, okay?"

I smiled. Ned knew me pretty well; he knew

that at sunrise, jogging was about the *last* place he could expect me to be. "What's up?" I asked. "Or were you just calling to say hello?"

"*Actually* I do have a reason," Ned replied. "I'm going to a lecture here at the university tonight, and I thought you might like to join me. It's not the most romantic date night, I know, but maybe we could get dessert afterward?"

"That sounds fun," I replied. "What's the lecture about?"

"It's being given by these two Internet entrepreneurs. Their names are Robert Sung and Jack Crilley. Have you heard of them?"

Robert Sung and Jack Crilley. I searched my brain. "Um, no."

"They created something called BetterLife," Ned explained. "It's a virtual world game that you play on the Internet. You create a character, and then—"

"You control this character's life through the game," I supplied. "Get a job, a place to live, socialize. Oh, I know all about BetterLife."

"You do?" Ned sounded surprised. "Don't take this the wrong way, Nancy, but I didn't have you pegged as an online gamer."

I laughed. "Um, not quite." Tossing back my covers, I swung my legs off the bed and stretched.

"But in the last couple days? Let's just say I got a crash course. I will *definitely* join you for that lecture tonight."

Ned and I chatted for a few more minutes, talking about Shannon's case, the subscription plan for BetterLife, and, finally, how Arij and Ibrahim were faring at school (well, it seemed). After a few minutes Ned had to run to a class, and I decided it was time for me to shower and start my day . . . with a visit to Shannon Fitzgerald.

It was Saturday and relatively early, so I was pretty sure Shannon would still be at home. Nonetheless, I texted her to make sure it was okay.

SURE, she texted back. EAGER 2 HEAR WHAT U'VE FOUND OUT.

I took my time driving over to her house, wondering if she'd be so eager to hear about what I'd found out if she knew that her crush had described her as a mean girl and a bully. I still wasn't 100 percent sure that Jake was a reliable source of information, and I wanted to give Shannon the benefit of the doubt. Besides, Maggie had described her as a nice, well-liked girl. I figured I needed to ask Shannon some questions myself.

"Hi, Nancy," Shannon greeted me cheerfully as

she led the way up to her room. She was dressed in a comfy-looking track suit, with her cornsilk-blond hair piled into a messy bun at the top of her head. She looked more natural than sparkly with no makeup on, but it was still clear that Shannon was a beauty. And from what I remembered of middle school, it still struck me as strange that *she* was the target of bullies.

Shannon opened her bedroom door to reveal a petite, curly haired brunette lounging on her bed, flipping through magazines. "This is my best friend Rebecca," Shannon introduced. "We had a sleepover last night. Hope you don't mind she's here, but Rebecca's like my sister—anything I know, she knows."

I nodded and gave Rebecca a little smile. "Hi, Rebecca," I greeted her. "I'm sure Shannon appreciates you sticking by her through this tough time."

Rebecca widened her eyes. "I *know*, right?" she asked, shaking her head with disbelief. "Some kids can be so cruel. I used to love playing BetterLife. But I just don't get it."

Shannon gestured to her iPod, which was sitting on her desk, connected to some shiny pink speakers. "Rebecca brought over music by this new band. What did you say they were called?"

Rebecca smiled. "Flat Macaroon," she replied. "Aren't they amazing?"

I tuned in to the music. It *was* nice—a mellow arrangement of guitars and synthesizers with a smooth-voiced lead singer crooning about springtime. It was an interesting choice for someone Rebecca's age—a little more sophisticated than I would have expected. "I like it," I agreed. "What's this song called?"

"'Blue in the Springtime,'" Rebecca replied. She shuffled off the bed and walked over to the iPod. "Here. I can turn it off, though, so you guys can talk."

We all took a seat on Shannon's bed, and she looked at me expectantly. "So?" she prompted. "What have you found out?"

I sighed. "Well, there's good news and bad news," I replied. "The main thing I learned is, Jake Seltzer isn't GuitarLvr15."

Shannon and Rebecca turned to each other, mouths dropping open.

"But he *has* to be!" cried Rebecca, shaking her head. "The blue streak! The music thing! Who else could it be?"

I shook my head. "The thing is, he does play BetterLife, but not in the middle-school community. He has a character in the university game that looks nothing like him. He showed me himself."

Shannon suddenly turned pink. "You talked to him about me?" she asked.

I nodded. "Well . . . yeah. I had to find out whether it was really him. And I showed him GuitarLvr15 in the game, but he said he has no idea who they really are, or why they would steal his look. He also seemed honestly surprised by what you're going through."

Shannon looked confused. "But . . . but . . . the things he said when we flirted. . . ."

"He says that wasn't him," I said, reaching out to touch Shannon's arm.

If Shannon looked mortified by this information, Rebecca looked almost angry. "Could he be lying?" she asked me pointedly. "I mean, isn't it likely that if he was making Shannon's life miserable, he wouldn't just come out and tell you?"

I sighed. "He could be," I allowed, "but I believe him. His reactions when we spoke seemed genuine. Shannon"—I turned to her and softened my voice—"when you flirted with GuitarLvr15 . . . That conversation . . . Do you remember him saying anything concrete, anything that would make you think it *definitely* had to be Jake flirting with you?"

Shannon looked lost. "No," she admitted, biting her lip. "I mean, at the time, signs all seemed to say it was definitely him. I was just so *sure*. But looking back . . ." She looked up at her ceiling, trying to remember, then sighed and looked down at her comforter. "Everything I remember for sure . . . Now I realize it could have been anybody." She swallowed. "Or anybody who wanted me to *think* I was talking to Jake."

I nodded, thinking this over. Shannon seemed truly crushed. It was hard to reconcile this fresh-looking, vulnerable tween with the manipulative girl Jake Seltzer had described to me. But I had to ask.

"Shannon," I said gently. "In the course of investigating the case I've heard . . . something else. Something I need to run by you."

Shannon turned to me, looking a little unsure. "Okay," she agreed. "Anything. Go ahead."

"Someone told me . . ." I sighed. "Someone told me you could be mean to the less popular girls in your grade."

Shannon's vulnerable look quickly turned to surprise—and then anger. "What?" she asked. "Who? *Who* told you that?"

I shook my head. "That doesn't matter," I replied. "One story they told me was that you tripped a girl named Sarah O'Malley in the cafeteria. You called her a teacher's pet, because a teacher had read her essay aloud in class."

Shannon looked stunned. "That's—that's ridiculous!" she stammered.

"*Totally* ridiculous," Rebecca agreed, looking even angrier than before. "Shannon would never! What a stupid thing for someone to do!"

"Look," I said, holding up my hand for quiet. "I'm not judging you. No matter what you did, nobody deserves to be treated the way you're being treated. But if it *did* happen, if you *did* act less than nice to someone at school, that may lead to some suspects. Maybe someone is mad at you and trying to get you back."

Shannon scowled but turned to Rebecca, seeming to consider this.

"Look, it's just not true," Rebecca insisted. She'd looked friendly when I first entered the room, but now she was looking at me like I was lower than dirt. "Sarah did trip in the cafeteria. But she tripped over her own two feet, then blamed Shannon. It just really stinks that this rumor actually made it around school and got to whoever you talked to."

"It's true," Shannon confirmed. "I would never, in my life, be that mean to someone on purpose. I can't believe people are spreading lies about me! Why would I need to act like that to feel cool?"

I looked from Shannon to Rebecca and back, trying to take all this in. They both looked utterly sure of themselves. So sure, in fact, it made me suspicious. It almost seemed like they were getting *too* defensive. I didn't know what to believe.

Shannon's eyes narrowed as she studied my face. "You don't believe me, do you?"

I was caught off guard. "That's not it, I—"

But Shannon didn't miss a beat. "You can ask her yourself," she went on coldly. "Sarah and I used to take dance class together on Saturday mornings. I know she's still in the class. It's down in the shopping center on River Street, and it lets out at eleven. She has long, dark hair and green eyes." She glanced at her watch. "If you hurry, you can just make it."

I glanced at my watch: 10:39. The River Street Shopping Center was about fifteen minutes away. I had an uneasy feeling about this—Rebecca and Shannon were still giving me a strange vibe—but it *did* seem like the easiest way to resolve who was telling the truth: Jake or Shannon. And once I knew that, I'd have a better idea who might be the bully here.

I stood up. "I'll do that," I agreed. "It's not that I don't trust you. It's just—"

"You'd better hurry," Shannon cut me off, leaning back on her bed and fixing me with an icy look. "You don't want to miss her."

I grabbed my purse and headed for the door.

"*Buh*-bye," Rebecca called after me, reaching over to turn the iPod back on.

Nice. I hurried down the stairs and out the front door, shaking my head as I unlocked my car and settled myself in the driver's seat.

How had I somehow become the villain?

The River Street Shopping Center was a fancy name for a ragtag strip mall a few blocks from downtown River Heights. Sammie Lee's Dance Studio was on the far right, and as I drove into the parking lot at 10:56, I could see the class still stretching to the rhythm of a slow ballad.

I let out my breath, realizing then that I'd been holding it for a while. I made it!

As I pulled into a space facing the mirror-lined studio, I could tell the music had stopped and class was coming to an end. Girls stretched and started gathering their things, stopping to chat in small groups. I spotted one girl wearing a black leotard, pink-striped tights, and purple leg warmers; her chestnut-colored hair was tied in a messy bun at her neck. She looked flushed and happy as she chatted with a curly-haired redhead and a pretty Asian girl. She walked over and grabbed a purple backpack from a communal pile at the front of the room; fishing around in it, she pulled out a small cell phone and started clicking through messages. Her smile faded as she became focused on her phone and her green eyes grew serious.

That has to be her. Sarah O'Malley. I sighed, turning off my car's engine and opening my door. Would Sarah be cooperative?

I climbed out of my car and strolled over to the dance studio's entrance. Girls were already spilling out, talking and laughing. Some of them glanced my way curiously, but nobody said anything. Finally, the girl I'd pegged as Sarah walked out, a serious look on her face as she scanned the parking lot, probably looking for her ride.

"Hey!" I called, trying to get her attention. "Are you Sarah?"

She glanced at me. Interestingly she didn't look all that surprised. "I am," she said warily. "Who are you?"

"I'm Nancy." I smiled, trying to seem friendly. "Can I talk to you for a second? I just have a couple questions to ask."

Sarah glanced at the parking lot one more time, and shrugged. "Sure," she said. "My ride's not here yet."

"Let's sit over there." I gestured to a picnic table that sat in a small area of grass outside a barbecue joint. Sarah nodded and we walked over. She didn't seem all that enthused to talk to me, but she didn't quite seem annoyed, either.

We sat and I smiled again. "Listen, I'm sorry to bother you. It's just that I've been talking to a classmate of yours, Shannon Fitzgerald?"

"Sure, Shannon." Sarah nodded to let me know she knew Shannon, but her expression gave away nothing. I couldn't tell if Shannon was a close friend or an enemy—or someone Sarah only passed occasionally in the hallway.

"You may know this already," I continued, "but Shannon is being harassed online. In a game called BetterLife. Do you know it?"

Sarah shrugged. "I've heard of it," she said simply. "I'm not much for online gaming."

"Okay." I paused. "Listen, I'll get to the point of why I'm talking to you . . . I was told by who I thought was a reliable source that Shannon can be a little mean to other girls at school."

Sarah blinked and looked down at the table. She didn't look very excited to talk about this subject.

"Specifically," I went on, undaunted, "I was told that there was an incident between the two of you in the cafeteria. That a teacher of yours had read your essay out loud in class that day, and Shannon called you a teacher's pet and tripped you." I paused again. Sarah was still staring at the table, stone-faced. "In front of everyone," I added.

Sarah was silent for almost a minute before she spoke, so quietly I could barely hear her. She looked past me, toward the parking lot. "You heard wrong," she told me.

"What do you mean?" I pressed. "It never happened at all? Or someone misheard what happened?"

Sarah swallowed, but didn't look up. "You misheard it," she said. "I tripped myself. I can be clumsy. Shannon had nothing to do with it."

She still wouldn't look me in the eye. It was unnerving. "Nothing at all?" I asked.

"Nothing at all." Sarah finally looked up, frowning at me. "Was there anything else? My mom's going to be here any minute."

Was there anything else? No, not really, except that I was getting a funny vibe from Sarah. Something seemed off about her story, something I couldn't quite put my finger on.

"Nothing else," I replied, flashing a bright smile as I glanced into my purse. "Well, actually, I *do* have another question for you, but it has nothing to do with Shannon."

Sarah actually smiled a little bit, looking relieved. "Okay," she agreed. "What is it?"

"Can I borrow your cell phone?" I asked hopefully, giving her a little just-between-us-girls smile. "I told my boyfriend I'd give him a call to set up our date tonight, and then I stupidly left my phone at home." I shook my head. "Do you have one? I promise it will only take a second."

Sarah shrugged. "Oh, sure." She reached into her purse and pulled out a metallic-purple cell phone. "But once my mom comes, I'll need to go."

"No problem," I said, nodding. "I'll be fast. I just need to get the address of the restaurant where I'm meeting him from my car."

I walked over to my car with Sarah's phone, then opened the door and climbed into the driver's seat, trying to look like I was searching for a piece of paper. Actually, though, I wanted to get a better look at Sarah's cell phone. I have lots of experience snooping on different kinds of phones, but it took me a few tries to locate the Sent/Received Texts option on Sarah's.

Finally I found it. Sent Texts. There was nothing recent. Received Texts. There was just one today, from a familiar-looking number.

IF N E 1 ASKS. . . U BETTER NOT SAY N E THING ABOUT WHAT HAPPENED IN THE CAFTERIA. U TRIPPED URSELF, U KLUTZ.

It was from Shannon.

For a moment I just sat there and stared at the text, amazed. So Shannon really did have a "mean streak," as Jake had put it. She had tripped Sarah in the cafeteria. . . . And worse, Sarah was frightened enough of Shannon to lie for her about it.

What kind of person was I working for?

I bit my lip, glancing at Sarah, who still sat at the picnic table. She stared down at the sleeve of her hoodie as she picked at a loose thread. She looked unhappy. I decided not to say anything to her about the text. She didn't strike me as the cyberbullying type, and goodness knew Shannon had her pretty freaked out if that text was any indication.

I got out of my car and walked back to the picnic table. Feeling jittery, I started flipping the tiny cell phone over and over in my hand.

"Thanks," I told Sarah when I reached her. "You're a lifesaver." I held her cell phone out to her.

And then I saw it, on the back of the phone.
A shiny decal: a Celtic knot.
Just like the girl who had harassed Shannon in
BetterLife.

MAKING ENEMIES

I decided not to say anything to Sarah about the Celtic knot decal. It wasn't enough evidence to really accuse her of anything, and I wanted to have more information before I confronted anyone. That night, I met Ned in the lobby outside of the university auditorium, eager to learn more about the two creators of BetterLife.

"Nancy!" Ned cried as he spotted me through the huge and growing crowd. Apparently we weren't the only two people interested in hearing what Robert Sung and Jack Crilley had to say. "I'm so glad to see you. Listen, I—"

"Nancy?" A familiar, friendly, accented voice

piped up behind Ned, and soon Ibrahim maneuvered around some university students to join us. "How nice to see you again! How have you been?"

"Hi, Nancy!" No sooner had Ibrahim appeared than his sister Arij popped up behind him.

"The outfit you helped me pick out for my first day was a big hit! But I may need your advice again. Fashion is very complicated in middle school."

I smiled at Ibrahim and Arij, honestly happy to see them but also a little surprised.

"I'm sorry, Nance," Ned murmured, taking my arm and swiftly leaning up to whisper in my ear. "I wasn't planning on bringing them, but when I mentioned the lecture, they seemed so intrigued by it. They don't know many people in town yet, and I think they're suffering from a little cabin fever. I know this isn't the date we planned on."

"It's fine," I whispered back, squeezing Ned's arm. "We'll make up for it later." I turned to Ibrahim and Arij, raising my voice to its normal level. "It's good to see you two again! How's school going?"

After fifteen minutes of updates—it seemed both Ibrahim and Arij were *really* enjoying their time in the River Heights school system—we all settled into a center row about halfway back from the stage.

"So explain this to me again," Ibrahim said brightly, looking at the huge crowd around us. "What is BetterLife and why is it so popular?"

Ibrahim looked expectantly at me, but it was Ned who replied first.

"It's an online community," he explained, "a virtual world game. You create a character and control everything about him or her, including his job and living situation. But most people use BetterLife to socialize. You can hang out and meet people just like in real life, but from the comfort of your own home."

Arij nodded, looking fascinated. "And do you and Nancy have these BetterLife characters?" she asked.

"Well—" I started, at the same time Ned replied, "I do, but I don't play very often."

I turned around in surprise. "You *do*?" I asked Ned, who looked a little sheepish. "I didn't realize you played BetterLife. Are you part of the university community?"

Ned shrugged. "When I started at the university," he explained, "*everyone* was getting on BetterLife. I figured I'd give it a try. It's fun, but I never really got into it like a lot of people."

I was still a little surprised that my boyfriend, who doesn't spend much time online by any means—had a secret online identity. "And you—did you meet people through BetterLife?" I asked.

"Occasionally. Just as friends, though, sometimes with similar interests. That's one nice thing about the online community: It makes it very easy to find people who have common interests."

Hmm. I knew I shouldn't be jealous. Ned is the most trustworthy guy I know. Still, I wondered how I had missed out on this whole BetterLife bandwagon.

"You said you played too?" Arij asked, turning to me.

"Oh." I pulled my thoughts back to the present, and turned to Arij with a smile. "I actually just created a character to help me investigate a case I'm working on. So I'm still a newbie."

"A noob . . .?" Ibrahim frowned, perplexed by the unfamiliar vocabulary.

"I'm sorry. I'm still new at it, is what I meant," I clarified.

"It sounds like a wonderful idea," Arij murmured, looking excited.

"It does," Ibrahim agreed. "I would like very

much to go home and try this game myself! It sounds like a good way to meet friends in a new town."

"Oh," I said, shaking my head quickly, "I'm not sure about that, Ibrahim. People can be cruel online. And it's very easy to lie about your identity, so not everybody is what they seem."

Ibrahim shrugged. "Isn't that true in real life, also?" he asked. "You might think that someone is your friend, when in fact they say terrible things about you when you're not around. Or perhaps someone lies about liking opera to seem smarter. Everyone has secrets."

"But I—" I started to argue with Ibrahim, but stopped myself. He *did* have a point. And surely Ibrahim and Arij would be careful online. They both seemed like smart kids.

"Oh look," Ned said, nodding toward a trio of men who were stepping onto the stage. "I think that's them—Jack Crilley and Robert Sung. And there's my computer-science professor to introduce them."

A bearded, salt-and-pepper-haired man stepped up to the microphone. "Greetings," he announced. "I want to thank everyone for coming tonight. I'm Professor Frank of the computer-science department, and I'm here to introduce two men who have revolutionized the way we socialize with one another, make friends, and express ourselves to an increasingly diverse Internet population. Who here has a character on BetterLife?"

Almost the entire audience raised their hands. "Wow," Ibrahim whispered to me.

"Before BetterLife," Professor Frank continued, "socializing on the Internet was largely limited to impersonal and difficult-to-police chatrooms, and social networking sites where your entire persona is represented by a two-dimensional, text-heavy profile." He smiled, turning to glance at the BetterLife entrepreneurs. "Robert Sung and Jack Crilley changed all that. Now, through BetterLife, everyone can live a complete, three-dimensional life on the Internet. Sometimes, as the name suggests, a life that is even better than the 'real' one. As many of you know, in three weeks BetterLife will begin to offer a subscription service, so that users can pay for an enhanced online experience. It is estimated that more than five million users will pay for this service, making our two guests very rich men." The two young entrepreneurs chuckled uncomfortably, and Professor Frank glanced at them and laughed too. "Many of the students in this auditorium will probably soon be turning over a bigger portion of their paychecks to these two inventors. Ladies and gentlemen, I give you two visionaries: Robert Sung and Jack Crilley."

The applause was almost deafening as the two surprisingly young men—a small Asian man with a goatee and a taller, gawky redhead—stepped up to the podium.

"Helloooo, BetterLifers!" the redhead, who I assumed to be Jack, cooed into the microphone. The response was amazing. People were yelling and cheering, as if Sung and Crilley were a football team who had just won the Super Bowl, instead of two skinny computer programmers.

I glanced at Ned. "This should be interesting," I whispered.

Ned nodded, looking a little taken aback himself. "Something like that," he agreed.

"So as you can see," Robert Sung was explaining two hours later, after he and Jack had shared with us every detail of their childhoods, adolescence, and early adulthood years. "BetterLife has revolutionized the gaming industry, Internet networking, and, indeed, the way people socialize in general."

"Robert and I are a little uncomfortable with the term *genius*," Jack broke in, trying to look humble, "but we do recognize the importance of what we've done here. Without BetterLife, we would all be limited by the scope of our off-line—some would say *real*, but we don't believe interactions in BetterLife are any less real—lives."

The duo was quiet for just a moment, and for what seemed like the thousandth time that night, applause swept through the auditorium. I caught Ned's eye.

"You would think they were rock stars!" I muttered.

Ned nodded. "Or they just announced that we're skipping midterms this year," he whispered back.

I turned to my other side, and saw that Ibrahim and Arij were watching the programmers with starry-eyed expressions.

"It sounds like they have really changed the world, Nancy!" Ibrahim said eagerly, when he caught my glance. "I can't wait to get home to create my character."

"Me too!" Arij agreed.

"You two just be careful on there," I whispered. "In this game, you can't be sure anything is what it seems."

Finally the applause died down, and Robert

moved toward the microphone again. "Are there any questions?"

I threw my hand in the air. I certainly had a few questions for these two. After listening to two hours of how brilliant and dedicated and revolutionary BetterLife was, I wanted to hear what they had to say about a few of its flaws.

Unfortunately for me, many other members of the audience had questions, too. They ranged from, "How can you tell when someone's hitting on you in BetterLife?" to "In the university community, in the science building cafeteria, what is the code to get two drumsticks instead of one? My friend did it once, and I've never been able to figure out how."

Robert and Jack seemed flattered, and were patient with everybody. Many of the questions from the audience ended with, ". . . and I just think you two are brilliant," so I don't exactly think the Q & A was hard on their already-healthy egos.

"You there, in the yellow sweater," Jack said finally, pointing in my direction. "With the reddish hair. What was your question?"

I stood up. "What is your feeling on the lack of background checks in BetterLife?" I asked.

The two young men just stared at each other

blankly, as though I'd asked my question in Martian. "Background checks?" asked Robert. "I'm not sure what you mean. People are playing a game here, not running for political office."

A chuckle ran through the crowd.

"I *mean*," I replied, "that it's very easy to misrepresent yourself on BetterLife. You can change your age, your gender, even your appearance. I could log on right now as a sixty-year-old square dancer from Philadelphia, and you would never know I was anything different."

Jack actually looked annoyed at my comment. "Well, miss," he replied sharply, "that's part of the *game* of BetterLife. It wouldn't be a better life if it were the exact same one you were already living, would it?"

Again, the crowd chuckled. I stood my ground, though, waiting for more of a response. Finally Jack continued.

"On BetterLife, people can try out other ages, genders, identities. It's a game. And I don't know who you are, miss, but the Internet is a free society that will police itself. If a game becomes unpleasant to play, people will stop playing and the website will die. Neither Robert nor I would feel comfortable violating our members' privacies with these 'background checks' you're talking about, so they're not going to happen. And I think somehow our members will be just fine. Next question?"

"Wait!" I cried, holding up my hand. "Doesn't allowing people to create new identities with no accountability encourage people to be cruel to one another, to do and say things they'd never get away with in real life?" I asked. "If we met on the street, I would never call you a horrible name because you might see me again; you might tell other people I know that I behaved badly. But in the game, if I'm hiding behind some made-up identity, why couldn't I be cruel to you? Or anybody? By the time you figure out who I am, I'll already have created an entirely new character."

Jack shook his head, looking disgusted with me. "I'm done here. Next question?"

"*Furthermore,*" I broke in, "when you start your subscription service, you'll have to collect personal information from your members: billing information, credit card numbers, addresses. Why not just use that information when people are being harassed online?"

Jack looked like he'd been sucking on a lemon. He glanced at Robert, who shook his head, and then said curtly, "Clearly some of our audience members don't grasp the idea of freedom and the right to privacy. I think we've answered all the questions we're going to tonight. Thank you for coming."

A buzz of disappointment ran through the crowd as the two programmers suddenly moved away from the microphone and walked offstage. Students turned to one another with disbelief—and to me with disgust.

"Thanks for nothing, weirdo," huffed a blond girl behind me. "I'll never learn how to make my character famous now."

People began gathering their things and moving toward the exits. I turned sheepishly to Ned. "Do you think she meant famous in real life, or famous in the game?" I asked quietly.

Ned just shook his head. "For some of these people, Nance," he replied, "I think there is only the game."

I glanced toward the door. The lecture was being followed by a reception in the lobby, where Robert and Jack were supposed to mingle with the crowd. I hoped that some of the audience would have their questions answered there, but I still wanted *my* question answered also. It wouldn't make anyone happy, but I felt I had to try to speak with Jack and Robert again, and figure out what they really knew about the security lapses in their game.

Ned, Ibrahim, Arij, and I followed the crowd toward the lobby. Ibrahim and Arij kept up a bubbly discourse about the amazing features of BetterLife, and how they planned to control their characters.

"I think Little Arij will be a dancer," Arij was saying. "She'll take lessons three times a week, and hopefully after a few months she will get a job on Broadway."

Ibrahim shook his head. "My character will be just like me," he insisted. "Perhaps taller, and perhaps he will have a mustache. But we will share the same interests and the same personality. That way, everyone I meet in the game can also be my friend in real life."

Ned wrinkled his nose. "A *mustache*, Ibrahim?" he asked. "I think that may be the wrong call."

Ibrahim looked startled. "Perhaps a full beard, then?" he asked. "Or . . . I know. A soul patch?"

Just then I spotted Robert Sung and Jack Crilley, escorted by Professor Frank, trying to quietly enter the lobby through an unmarked door. But within seconds, whispers erupted throughout the crowd and a small mob of adoring fans began to form around them.

"Excuse me," I murmured, wandering away from Ned, Ibrahim, and Arij and trying to angle my way through the crowd to get to the two founders.

"And so, after that, I really had a much easier time meeting people and had much more confidence," a pretty, dark-haired girl with glasses was explaining to Robert and Jack as I stepped closer. "I really credit your game with changing my life."

"That's amazing," Robert replied gently, patting her shoulder. "I really think that—"

Suddenly Jack spotted me in the crowd and began freaking out. "Stop her! Stop! I don't want to talk to her, I don't want to talk to that girl! She was hostile in the Q and A!" He pointed right at me, and Professor Frank looked me over, an uncomfortable expression on his face. Robert also looked uncomfortable. It was like neither one of them really wanted to tell me to get lost, but they didn't know what else to do.

Finally Robert cut through the awkwardness by gently placing a hand on Jack's shoulder. "Come on, Jack," he coaxed. "Let's just hear what she has to say." He turned to me, smiling sheepishly. "Forgive Jack," he apologized. "He's just very passionate about our creation. He can be sensitive to criticism."

I nodded understandingly. "I can see that," I replied. "Look, I don't want to ruin your night. Clearly your creation *has* changed a lot of lives for the better, and no one can take that away."

Both creators nodded, Jack's expression softening a bit. "I appreciate you saying that," he murmured.

"It's just . . . I'm working with a young girl, who's now being harassed and bullied through BetterLife," I explained. "I know the game wasn't invented for this purpose, but it *does* make the whole process much easier, since the game is so anonymous. Almost everyone in the middle school is playing."

Robert nodded. "That's an unfortunate misuse of our game," he said.

"Listen," I coaxed. "This girl is having her house vandalized—in the game—and getting all kinds of private messages and e-mails that contain language I wouldn't wish on my worst enemy." I paused. "I know you want to protect the users' identities, but knowing what's going on in this case, is there any way you could share the identity of the head bully?"

Jack glared at me. "Who says we have it?" he demanded.

I sighed. "I've played BetterLife," I explained.

"I know you take basic contact information from users. Anything you could give us would be helpful to narrow down—"

But Jack was already moving away, shaking his head. "I'm sorry, miss," he replied curtly. "The Internet is a reflection of our society: People are people, and just as people bully in real life, people will bully on the Internet. Logging onto a computer doesn't improve your character."

"But this is worse than—"

Jack scowled, and cut in again. "Robert and I strongly believe in the Internet being a free society," he insisted. "We will not share that information with you, or anyone. Period. I'm leaving now."

He turned to leave the lobby, and I held up my hands. "Forget it. Don't leave on my account," I said, backing away. "*I'll* leave. You guys mingle with your fans." I gestured for the other students and audience members to take my place, and slowly disentangled myself, until I was on the outer reaches of the mob.

"*Nancy!*" A hand reached out and grabbed my arm, and I turned, relieved to see Ned.

"Hey," I said with a sigh. "Well, I think I just officially—"

But Ned frowned, cutting me off. "Where've

you been?" he asked. "You just wandered off. I've been looking all over for you. I need to get Ibrahim and Arij home. They have school tomorrow."

I glanced behind Ned to see Arij and Ibrahim awkwardly drinking punch and watching our conversation. "I'm so sorry," I said honestly. "I went to ask Robert and Jack some more questions; I thought you heard me."

Ned shrugged. "Never mind," he said, touching my shoulder. "I was hoping we'd get some time alone tonight," he went on, gesturing to Ibrahim and his sister. "But . . ."

I nodded sympathetically, squeezing his arm. "I guess it just wasn't meant to be." I shrugged. "It's okay. We'll make another date, and catch up later."

He leaned over and kissed the tip of my nose. "You're the best, Nance," he said softly, then led me back to Ibrahim and Arij.

Ibrahim was holding a handout from the lecture with a pen poised above it, ready to write something down. "Nancy," he said eagerly, "you have a BetterLife ID, right? Ned said he has one, but it's for the university community. I'd like to keep an eye on Arij, so we would both be joining the middle-school community. That's where you play, right?"

I smiled and nodded. "Sure. It's VirtualNancy. You can look for me at the mall."

Ibrahim grinned, writing on his paper. "You bet I will, VirtualNancy," he said with a smile. "I look forward to having you as a virtual friend."

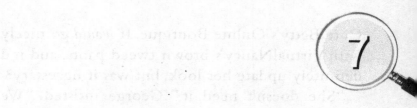

VIRTUALLY REJECTED

"**N**ancy, come on," Bess was pleading with me the next day, as once again, she, George, and I sat in front of the computer. "It's only twenty dollars, and it would look so cute on you."

"Not *me*," I corrected her. "On VirtualNancy."

Bess tossed her hands in the air. "Real Nancy, virtual Nancy, whoever!" she cried in frustration. "The point is, VirtualNancy is moving up in the world. She has a new job, a new supercute apartment. Don't you think she should treat herself to a new blouse in celebration?"

I paused, looking on my computer screen at a ruffly yellow blouse that hung in the window of

Cute Betty's Online Boutique. It *would* go nicely with VirtualNancy's brown tweed pants, and it'd definitely update her look, but was it necessary?

"She doesn't need it," George insisted. "We should save that twenty dollars and send Virtual-Nancy to that virtual computer class at the virtual community college. We need to invest in her *future*—not just fritter away her money on trendy clothes."

Bess sighed. "You two, I swear," she muttered to herself. "Maybe with some new virtual clothes, VirtualNancy might get herself a virtual *boyfriend*."

"I heard that," I snapped. "And I'm not in this game for love, I'm in it for *information*."

It had been only a few days since the creation of VirtualNancy, and already her life situation had drastically improved. Through careful and diligent game play (I was spending two or three hours online every day), Nancy had advanced from salon janitor to bookstore manager, and from drafty studio apartment to cute one-bedroom condo with a virtual river view. I had to admit, I was proud of her. Me. Us. Whoever. It was a lot more fun playing BetterLife when your character's life was, well, better.

"Oh wow," George murmured, pointing at a

tiny purple dot on-screen. "That's him! Across the food court! It's GuitarLvr15!"

I looked closer, and sure enough, George was right. Although I'd played several times, I hadn't encountered GuitarLvr15 again since that first night in the food court, when he'd blocked me from talking to him. That block had long since expired, but still . . .

"Should I try to talk to him again?" I asked.

"I guess," Bess replied. "I mean, it couldn't hurt, right?"

"Right." Careful to move slowly and not intimidate him, I moved VirtualNancy slowly and casually across the food court floor. It was still driving me crazy: Who *was* GuitarLvr15? Could he be Sarah? She didn't seem that bold, but possibly . . . Could he be Jake, lying about his true motives? Or could he be someone else entirely?

HI, I had VirtualNancy remark casually to GuitarLvr15. YOU LOOK NICE 2DAY. WANT 2 GET SOMETHING 2 EAT?

It only took a few seconds before GuitarLvr15 began moving away. He made no indication of having received my message, but it was clear that he had. Why else would he move across the food court so suddenly? Clearly, even if the twenty-four-hour block had worn off, Guitar-Lvr15's wariness of VirtualNancy had not.

"Ugh," I muttered to my friends, sighing. "What do we do now? He's the whole reason I'm playing this game, and he won't talk to me."

"Uh, Nance," George replied, pointing at the screen again. "Do you know this kid?"

I looked where her finger pointed, and spotted a tall, skinny, olive-skinned boy with short, dark hair and a triangle-shape patch of stubble on his chin. Suddenly it came to me.

"Ibrahim!" I had VirtualNancy greet him.

NANCY! I WAS COMING TO SAY HELLO TO YOU. HOW ARE YOU? HOW DO YOU LIKE BETTERIBRAHIM4?

I chuckled.

I STILL LIKE THE REAL IBRAHIM BETTER, BUT HE'S PRETTY IMPRESSIVE. ARE YOU HAVING FUN?

It only took a few seconds for Ibrahim to respond.

DEFINITELY. I LIKE THIS GAME VERY MUCH. EVERYONE IS SO FRIENDLY. ARE YOU HAVING FUN, NANCY?

I sighed. "I would be," I typed, then quickly deleted it, deciding not to explain the whole GuitarLvr15 situation to Ibrahim. But then an idea came to me.

I AM HAVING FUN, I typed, BUT I COULD USE A FAVOR IF YOU'RE NOT BUSY.

This time he responded even faster.

ANYTHING FOR YOU, NANCY.

"What are you up to?" Bess asked, casting a suspicious glance my way.

"Isn't this Ned's little houseguest?" asked George. "What do you think he could do for us?"

I began typing.

THERE'S A BOY OVER THERE CALLED GUITARLVR15. I NEED TO KNOW WHO HE REALLY IS, BUT HE WON'T TALK TO ME, BECAUSE HE DOESN'T TRUST ME. HE DOESN'T KNOW YOU, THOUGH. COULD YOU TRY TALKING TO HIM?

It only took a few seconds for Ibrahim's reply to light up my screen.

OF COURSE! I WOULD BE HAPPY TO HELP.

We chatted a bit more, and I briefed Ibrahim on what I needed to know and how to approach GuitarLvr15 without seeming suspicious. We made arrangements to meet in a nearby virtual park, so I could leave immediately and Guitar-Lvr15 wouldn't see me hanging around. As I guided VirtualNancy out of the mall, across the street and onto a park bench, George looked at me skeptically.

"Do you think that's a good idea?" she asked. "Involving him like this?"

I shrugged. "I think I need to use all of the tools at my disposal," I replied. "Besides, Ibrahim is really friendly. I'm not asking him to act out of character by chatting someone up."

George sighed. "I guess you're right," she agreed. "Besides, it's not like VirtualNancy was having a lot of luck."

It was about twenty minutes, real-world time, before BetterIbrahim4 came to meet VirtualNancy at BetterLife Park. George, Bess, and I passed the time by catching up and throwing out ideas for who GuitarLvr15 might be. Unfortunately, besides the absurd guesses—the mayor! Hannah! Bess's mom!—we didn't really have a clue. I was beginning to fear this case just might be unsolvable. How do you catch a virtual crook?

Finally BetterIbrahim4 approached.

HI THERE, I greeted him. HOW DID IT GO?

BetterIbrahim4 shook his head. NOT SO GOOD, he replied. GUITARLVR15 IS VERY TOUCHY ABOUT BEING QUESTIONED, NO?

I pressed the button to make VirtualNancy nod. I SHOULD HAVE WARNED YOU.

Ibrahim explained that his conversation with GuitarLvr15 had started out friendly, with the two exchanging names, ages, hobbies, that sort of thing. GuitarLvr15 told BetterIbrahim4 that he was really into music, and even deejayed sometimes at virtual BetterLife parties. He recommended a few bands BetterIbrahim4 might like, and asked him how he was enjoying the game so far. But when Ibrahim asked his true identity, under the guise of wanting to hang out in real life, GuitarLvr15 turned cold.

I'M GUITARLVR15, he'd told Ibrahim. THAT'S ALL THAT MATTERS.

When Ibrahim pressed on, GuitarLvr15 had threatened him. U'D BETTER DROP IT IF U KNOW WHAT'S GOOD 4 U, he'd said. NOT EVERYONE IN THIS GAME IS AS FRIENDLY AS I AM.

"Is he threatening to have Ibrahim beaten up?" I asked Bess and George, in real life, in the comfort of my bedroom.

Bess shook her head. "I think he's threatening to have *virtual* Ibrahim *virtually* beaten up," she corrected.

"Gosh," I muttered. "This is confusing."

"Although that's sort of what's happening to Shannon, right?" George asked, gesturing to the screen. "She's being seriously harassed online, and it's getting just as bad as being bullied in real life."

"That's true," I agreed, considering. "So if GuitarLvr15 is threatening virtual Ibrahim, I guess that's further evidence that he's a cyberbully. Maybe he harasses a lot of people online, not just Shannon."

I'M SORRY I COULDN'T GET MORE INFORMATION FOR YOU, NANCY, BetterIbrahim4 was apologizing online.

THAT'S OKAY, I typed. I WISH WE COULD FIGURE OUT WHO HE IS, BUT I APPRECIATE YOU TRYING.

Suddenly BetterIbrahim4 whipped a piece of paper out from his jeans pocket. BUT ALL IS NOT LOST! he exclaimed.

?, I typed.

WHEN WE FIRST STARTED CHATTING, Ibrahim explained, GUITARLVR15 GAVE ME THIS FLYER.

I directed VirtualNancy to take the flyer and look at it. The contents took over my screen:

FRIDAY NIGHT SOCIAL AT SAM'S SMOOTHIE SHACK! COME GET YOUR GROOVE ON AT 9 PM THIS FRIDAY NIGHT. ENJOY FREE SNACKS, DELICIOUS SMOOTHIES, AND SLAMMIN' TUNES SPUN BY OUR HOUSE DJ, GUITARLVR15. DON'T BE SHY—YOU MIGHT MAKE SOME NEW FRIENDS!

Simple illustrations of music notes, a smoothie, and dancing kids decorated the sides.

HE IS DEEJAYING FRIDAY NIGHT, Ibrahim explained. MAYBE IF YOU GO TO THE PARTY, YOU WILL LEARN SOMETHING USEFUL.

"He's right," George agreed. "It couldn't hurt to observe GuitarLvr15 in a more social setting. Maybe you'll get some clues."

"Good idea," I agreed, thanking Ibrahim on-screen. "I guess I have a date with my computer then."

I said good-bye to BetterIbrahim4, then set VirtualNancy on the path home so I could get some dinner in her and put her to bed. She had to work early the next morning; no more time for socializing tonight. As we passed by a playground, though, I spotted a familiar character out of the corner of my eye.

"That's her!" I cried. "The bully with the Celtic knot tattoo that looks just like the decal on Sarah's phone!"

I directed VirtualNancy into her path, and Bess

looked uneasy. "Are you sure you have enough evidence to . . ."

SARAH, I typed, addressing ILoveDublin. IS THAT YOU? Several seconds went by before I got a response.

WHO'S ASKING?

I bit my lip. I KNOW WHAT REALLY HAPPENED WITH SHANNON, I wrote. YOU CAN TRUST ME. Taking a deep breath, I positioned the mouse over the Send button and clicked.

Crash. That horrible sound effect blared once more, and a window came up: ILOVEDUBLIN HAS BLOCKED YOU FROM TALKING TO HER.

The girl with the Celtic knot tattoo was gone, and VirtualNancy stood alone on an empty street.

"You know," I said to Bess and George, "I think I may just come across better in real life."

BULLIES AND VICTIMS

After a few more fruitless BetterLife games—where VirtualNancy was promoted once more, and bought a really nifty hybrid convertible, but learned nothing more about GuitarLvr15—I was ready to go back to sleuthing the old-fashioned way: by asking questions in person.

And so I climbed into my car and headed to Bess's house.

As I parked in Bess's driveway, my phone beeped twice, indicating two new text messages. I was happy to see that the first was from Ned.

DINNER TONIGHT? FLAVIO'S, JUST YOU AND ME?

I smiled. A cozy dinner at our favorite Italian restaurant sounded like the perfect night to me. MEET YOU THERE AT 8? I texted back.

YOU'RE ON, Ned replied after a few seconds. CAN'T WAIT TO SEE YOU.

Trying to wipe the dopey smile off my face, I checked the second text message. It was from Shannon.

R U EVER GOING TO SOLVE THIS? SCHOOL IS SOO HARD.

Well, that wiped the smile off my face. It also reminded me that I still had no clue who Guitar-Lvr15 was, or how I would find out. Typing quickly, I made arrangements to meet Shannon at her house later that afternoon. Hopefully I would have some more information by then. If not, I could probably spend at least an hour telling Shannon all the things I *didn't* know.

Shoving my phone into my purse, I climbed out of my car and headed to the door, lightly pressing the doorbell. After a few seconds, Bess appeared. "Hey," she greeted me. "She's in the kitchen, waiting."

I followed Bess down the short hallway to their small, warm yellow kitchen. Maggie was sitting at the table, engrossed in the very activity I'd just been involved in: furious texting. I was amazed as I watched her fingers fly over the tiny keys of her cell phone. Texting was definitely an art I hadn't quite mastered yet.

"Hi, Maggie," I greeted her.

She glanced up. "Oh, hi, Nancy," she said with a crooked smile. "Bess said you wanted to talk to me?"

I nodded, sitting next to her at the table. Bess offered me a drink or a snack, but I declined. "I have a few questions for you," I said to Maggie.

"Okay," she replied, looking a little nervous.

"Before we start, I just want to be clear," I cautioned her, "there are no wrong answers here, okay? I just need you to be completely honest. If I'm going to help your friend Shannon, I need to have all the information."

Maggie nodded slightly, looking a little caught off guard. "Um, okay," she replied.

"I need to know the truth," I said, looking Maggie in the eye. "Is Shannon *ever* mean to people at school?"

Maggie bit her lip. "She's not, not really," she said after a few seconds. "I mean, people take her the wrong way sometimes. But when you get to know Shannon, you see how totally great she is!"

"Okay," I said quietly. "So Shannon can be

misunderstood. Can I ask you about a specific incident, though?"

Maggie shrugged. "Sure, if you want."

I leaned a little closer. "Did Shannon trip a girl named Sarah O'Malley in the cafeteria?" I asked.

Maggie looked horribly uncomfortable. Finally she looked down at the table. "Yeah," she said, as though I was torturing this out of her. "But it wasn't as bad as people made it out to be. Besides, Sarah totally had it coming!"

"Maggie!" cried Bess sharply, looking concerned. "How on Earth would you have something like that coming?"

"Sarah totally stole Shannon's *boyfriend*!" Maggie replied, a little triumphantly.

"Wait a minute, wait a minute," I broke in, trying to replay everything Shannon had told me in my mind. I could swear she'd never said anything about having a *boyfriend*. "Who was this boyfriend? A boy at school?"

Maggie nodded her head. "Yeah, but he was older," she replied. "He's sixteen. He works at the coffee shop downtown."

I frowned. "Jake Seltzer?" I asked.

"Yeah, that's him."

I sighed, glancing at Bess. "Jake wasn't Shannon's boyfriend," I corrected Maggie.

But Maggie just looked at me pityingly. "Not *officially*," she replied, and I could suddenly hear Shannon's voice in every syllable. "But he was totally into her. They had a thing. It was only a matter of time before they started going out."

I glanced at Bess. Her expression told me that she was having the same reaction I was: This did not sound like Maggie. Was she just parroting what Shannon had told her?

"Okay," I said, deciding not to press the issue. "You said that Sarah made a move on him? How did that happen?"

Maggie gave me a confidential look. "She used to go to the coffee shop, like, every other day," she explained. "And she would just order a coffee and sit there for hours."

Bess blinked, glancing from Maggie to me and back. "And?" she pressed.

Maggie looked at her blankly. "And that's it." She turned to me. "She was totally going there just to flirt with Jake. Everyone knows it."

"So let me get this straight," Bess responded, beginning to sound exasperated with her little sister. "Sarah had the nerve to go to a coffee shop, order coffee, and drink it? In front of a boy that Shannon was *not* dating? That's why Shannon tripped her in the cafeteria?"

Maggie frowned at Bess, then looked down at her hands. "She was going there to flirt with Jake," she replied insistently, her voice losing steam with every word. "Everyone knows it," she added in a whisper.

I glanced knowingly at Bess, then reached over and touched Maggie's hand. "Is Shannon nice to you?" I asked her.

"Of course she is," Maggie replied, not looking up. "Shannon is, like, one of my best friends."

Bess scoffed. "And what do you get to do as Shannon's best friend?" she asked. "Carry her backpack? Deliver nasty notes?"

Maggie glanced up and glared at her sister. "You just don't get it," she retorted.

I touched Maggie's hand again. "Maggie," I coaxed, "have there been any other incidents like the one with Sarah in the cafeteria? Any other girls who flirted with Jake, or did something else to upset Shannon?"

Maggie swallowed and looked back at her hands, hesitating.

"I'm not asking to get Shannon in trouble," I clarified. "I'm asking so I can have all the information and solve her case faster. No matter what Shannon did, nobody deserves to be harassed like she's being harassed now."

Maggie met my eyes then, considering my words, and sighed. "There was this one other girl," she replied. "I'm not sure why she and Shannon don't get along, but they don't. Anyway, she has this cow-patterned backpack, and in an assembly one day she went up to receive an award, and Shannon got everybody to start mooing at her."

Bess looked disgusted. "Is she overweight?" she asked.

Maggie shook her head. "No, she's actually really tiny," she replied. "It's just that she likes cows. And I guess Shannon thought it would be funny."

"What's this girl's name?" I asked.

"Gloria Suarez," Maggie replied. "She lives right on our block."

I got the address from Maggie, thanked her for her honesty, and stood up to go.

"You and I have to talk," Bess told her sister.

Maggie cringed. "I thought there were no wrong answers!" she cried. "I thought I couldn't get in trouble for this."

"You're not *in trouble*," Bess assured, standing up and squeezing Maggie's shoulder. "I think we just need to have a talk about what makes a friend, a friend." She glanced at me, and smiled. "Good luck, Nance."

"Thanks," I replied. "And really, thanks for your honesty, Maggie. I think this will be helpful."

Gloria Suarez's house was just three doors down from Bess's, a tidy ranch-style home with a rose garden outside and black-painted shutters. When I rang the doorbell, a petite, long-haired woman answered the door.

"Yes, this is the Suarez household," she confirmed. "You'd like to talk with Gloria? What is this about?"

"Actually, I'm trying to get to the bottom of a bullying incident at school," I explained. "I thought Gloria might be able to answer a few questions."

Mrs. Suarez looked horrified. "Gloria would never bully anyone," she insisted. "She's a quiet, good-natured girl. She keeps to herself."

I shook my head. "I don't think she's the bully," I clarified. "I just thought she might be able to answer questions about an incident she witnessed."

Mrs. Suarez looked thoughtful. "Okay," she said finally. "I'll take you to her room. But just for a few minutes."

I smiled. "Thank you. It shouldn't take much longer than that."

We walked down a short hallway, and Mrs. Suarez knocked on a door covered with soft-pencil drawings of animals and cartoons cut out from the Sunday paper. "Gloria?" she asked. "Someone is here to see you."

After a few seconds the door swung open, and I looked down at a tiny figure with long, black hair. Gloria was a good six inches shorter than I was, and her tiny frame was swallowed up by a huge T-shirt that showed a cow wearing a Statue of Liberty crown, with the words MOO YORK CITY stamped below it. She glanced up at me with confusion.

"I'm Nancy Drew," I greeted her. "Can I bend your ear for a few minutes?"

Gloria nodded mutely.

"I'll leave you alone," Mrs. Suarez said. "Gloria, let me know if you need me." She walked back down the hall to the living room.

Gloria looked up at me. "Um, come in," she said with a voice so soft I had to strain to hear it. It was like a dairy farm had exploded inside her room. Cow figurines, cow photos, stuffed cows, and cow-themed bedding all competed for attention. An actual cow-patterned *computer* sat on a small red desk—the only non-cow item in the room.

"Listen," I explained, "I don't want to take up too much of your time. I just wanted to ask you about a specific incident I heard about from one of your classmates."

Gloria looked at me skeptically. "Okay," she agreed.

"I've heard from a few sources that Shannon Fitzgerald can be a little mean sometimes," I said. "And I heard about one specific incident that involves you. I guess there was an assembly—"

Gloria's face paled, and she looked away.

"—an assembly where you had to go up to get an award," I went on. "And Shannon thought it would be funny if she got everyone to moo at you. Did that really happen?"

Gloria swallowed and shrugged. "Who'd you hear that from?"

I tried to meet her eye. Finally she looked at me, and I attempted to look trustworthy. "A reliable source," I replied. "See, I don't give away my sources. If you tell me what really happened, I won't tell anyone."

Gloria looked at me, seeming to consider this. She still looked so uncomfortable. "It happened," she said, in a voice just above a whisper. "But it was no big deal," she added, her voice rising as she looked away. "Shannon messes with everyone.

I'm sure she was just trying to make a joke."

I kept staring at her, trying to make eye contact again, but she turned away and started fiddling with a cow doll on her bed.

Shannon must cut a pretty scary figure at school, I thought. Nobody's willing to cross her.

"Okay," I said agreeably, hiking my purse strap up on my shoulder, as though I was getting ready to leave. "Just one more question: Do you know of a game called BetterLife?"

Gloria met my eyes then, just briefly, then turned and looked away. "What's it called?" she asked vaguely.

"BetterLife," I replied. And you know what it's called, I continued in my head. She was definitely familiar with the game. I could tell by the way she'd looked at me; I'd caught her off guard.

She shook her head. "I dunno, I think I've heard the name before," she said.

"It's a virtual-reality game," I explained to her, playing along. "You create a character, then live a whole virtual life online. I just created a character myself, actually. But you don't play?"

She shrugged. When I kept watching her, she shook her head. "No, I don't play."

You're lying. I took a deep breath. "Okay, then. Well—"

"Gloria?" Suddenly Mrs. Suarez appeared at Gloria's bedroom door, looking awkward. "I'm sorry, I didn't mean to interrupt. It's just that Gloria's friend is here to play."

Gloria glared at her mother. "*Mom*, we don't *play* anymore."

Mrs. Suarez smiled sheepishly. "Right, I'm sorry, *mija*."

I winked at Mrs. Suarez. "I was just leaving," I explained. "Thank you, Gloria, for answering my questions."

Gloria just stared at me. It took a steely look from her mother for her to reply, "You're welcome."

Hiking up my purse strap again, I followed Mrs. Suarez back down the hallway and to the front door. A young girl was waiting in the living room, staring at a game show on the television.

She glanced up as Mrs. Suarez and I passed, and I gasped at the same time she did.

Gloria's friend was Sarah O'Malley.

CONFESSIONS

I climbed into my car with a sigh, shaking my head. Sarah O'Malley and Gloria Suarez—two girls who were publicly humiliated by Shannon Fitzgerald—were friends. What were the chances? And what were the chances that these two friends had commiserated over their embarrassment, and decided to get revenge on Shannon?

I suddenly flashed back to my first experience on BetterLife, when Jake had shown me his character in the coffee shop. When I'd logged on as Shannon to show him what was happening to her, *two* bullies had been messaging her, wanting to know why she'd come to school that day. One was the girl I believed to be Sarah, with the

Celtic knot. And the other . . . Hadn't she had a pet cow?

Knock, knock, knock. I was startled as someone knocked on my driver's-side window, inches from my ear. When I finally calmed down and looked out, I saw Sarah and Gloria gesturing for my attention.

Wary, I lowered the window. "Yes?" I asked.

Sarah glanced at Gloria, and then looked to me hesitantly. Neither one of them seemed eager to continue the conversation. Finally, Sarah, fiddling nervously with an iPod clipped to her belt, announced bluntly, "We did it."

"You did?" I cried, the meaning of what she was saying almost overwhelming me. Was it possible that after all my questioning and noodling around in BetterLife, the culprits would just drop themselves into my lap?

Gloria nodded. "We bullied Shannon," she confirmed. "Some of the stuff you saw online— that was us."

"So which one of you is GuitarLvr15?" I asked.

Sarah looked concerned. "*Neither* of us," she admitted. "That's why we wanted to tell you. Gloria and I participated in the bullying, but we didn't start it."

I frowned. "Okay. Then who did?"

Gloria squirmed. "GuitarLvr15 did," she replied.

I sighed. This was getting frustrating. "And he is . . . ?" I prompted.

Sarah and Gloria exchanged shrugs. "We don't know," Sarah told me. "We only interact with him online. We don't really know anything about him, except that he hates Shannon."

"Wait a minute, wait a minute." I tried to make sense of all this. "How did you get involved in the bullying, then? How did you even find out this was going on?"

"He e-mailed us," Sarah replied, nervously pulling the plug for her headphones in and out of her iPod, over and over. "The day Shannon tripped me in the cafeteria, I got this e-mail from guitarzrcool@fastmail.net," she said.

I nodded. "That's the address Shannon got the first nasty e-mail from, and a few since then."

Sarah went on. "The e-mail said Shannon had been mean to too many people for too long, and it was time for her to taste some of her own medicine."

I nodded. "And?"

Gloria cleared her throat, speaking up. "A few days later, when she had everybody moo at me, I got the same e-mail," she said.

I furrowed my brow. I still felt like I was missing

something. "What did it tell you to *do*?" I asked. "If you were tired of getting bullied by Shannon, what action were you supposed to take?"

Sarah and Gloria exchanged glances. "It just told us to keep an eye on uVid," Sarah explained, "to look for videos with Shannon's character, Sassygirl48. It said they would give us the idea."

My mind was whirring. GuitarLvr15 wasn't only bullying Shannon, he was recruiting an army to help. "And what did you see on the videos?"

Gloria shrugged. "Sassygirl48 getting yelled at by random strangers. Sassygirl48 getting fired. Sassygirl48 having her house spray painted, and getting nasty letters."

Sarah nodded. "After a few days of watching those videos, we both got another e-mail from guitarzrcool. 'You can join in any time,' it said."

"Join in the bullying, is what he meant," I clarified.

"Right," agreed Sarah.

"And did you?" I asked, giving them both hard looks.

They both looked uncomfortable.

"I did," admitted Gloria. "You have to understand, I'm not a mean person. I've never bullied anyone in real life."

"But online's different," I supplied, not doing

a very good job of hiding my disappointment in these girls.

"Not just that," Sarah broke in. "You have to know how nasty Shannon can be. It's like you're not even a *person*, like you're lower than a speck of dirt on a worm. That's what she makes me feel like."

"Me too," Gloria agreed.

"I just—I didn't mean for things to go as far as they did," Sarah explained. "I never thought it would get this big. I just wanted her to experience being the bullied one, for once. I wanted to make her feel like she makes me feel."

I looked at Gloria. She nodded, ashamed. "Yeah," she said sheepishly. "Me too."

I sighed. It was like a nasty bullying cycle—from Shannon to these girls, then back to Shannon. No one felt any better for their nastiness; everyone felt worse.

"What about the others?" I asked. "Clearly you're not the only two helping GuitarLvr15. So are all of the other BetterLifers victims of Shannon, too? Trying to get revenge?"

Sarah swallowed. "Some of them are. I mean, she's been mean to a lot of people," she replied.

I nodded. "Okay. That's some. What about the rest?"

"I don't even know if they know Shannon," Gloria admitted. "I think some people—some people just saw the videos on uVid, and thought it was a cool thing to do."

Yuck. "Bullying Shannon was *cool*?" I asked.

Sarah shrugged. "Not cool," she replied. "Well, maybe . . . sort of. But more like it was this thing everyone was doing and getting excited about. I think people even tried to one-up one another—doing meaner, more outrageous things."

Gloria nodded. "And then people started being mean to her at school," she said softly.

"And Shannon got so upset she stayed home a few days."

Sarah winced. "Look," she said. "I know what we did was wrong. We're not proud of our-selves."

"You can say that again," I started to reply, then stopped myself, not wanting to sound like their mothers. "Listen, girls. This is very impor-tant. I want you to *promise* me that you'll lay off Shannon. No more bullying—in real life, in Bet-terLife, anywhere."

Sarah and Gloria nodded, looking at the ground. "We promise," they chorused.

"It doesn't make anyone feel better," I went on. "Does it?"

They glanced at each other. "No," Gloria admitted. "I kind of feel worse. I didn't want to freak out Shannon as much as we did."

I nodded. "Good. And to the extent that you can, I want you to encourage the others to stop."

"Okay," they agreed.

I sighed again, putting my keys in the ignition. "I want to thank you both for being truthful with me. If that's it, though, I'm going to go."

Sarah nodded. "What will you do now? About GuitarLvr15?" she asked.

I glanced from one ashamed-looking girl to the other. "I wish I knew," I replied honestly.

"Oh. My. God," Shannon greeted me a few minutes later. We were in her bedroom, and I had just shown up for our scheduled afternoon appointment. "Nancy, what has been going on? Do you have any idea what a nightmare school is for me? Did you know that someone drew all over the back of my new jacket with permanent marker, and people throw *food* at me in the cafeteria?"

"I didn't know that," I admitted. "Look, Shannon, I'm really sorry. No one should have to be treated like that."

Shannon's eyes filled with tears. "They broke

into my house in the game, Nancy. I can't even log on anymore; it's so upsetting. And at school, everyone except Rebecca just stares at me and laughs. When are you going to solve this, so the right people can be punished?"

I took a deep breath. "Listen," I began. "I'm working very hard to solve your case. And the good news is, today I learned who a few of the bullies are, and I think that may lead me to Gui-tarLvr15."

Shannon's eyes widened. "You know who some of the bullies are?" she asked eagerly. "Who?"

Uh-oh. I knew I was working for Shannon, but still, it seemed like the wrong call to tell her about Sarah and Gloria. She'd targeted them for humiliation before, and even if she wasn't as bad as I'd heard—even if Jake, Gloria, and Sarah had all been exaggerating—I would feel terrible if she tried to retaliate against them. Settling down on the edge of Shannon's bed, I tried to change the subject.

"Shannon," I said gently, "would you say you have a temper? Have you ever, say, said anything to a classmate that, thinking about it later, you thought was a little harsh?"

Shannon frowned. She seemed to have no idea where this line of questioning was coming from, and I couldn't blame her. "Uh, *no*," she replied. "I'm really nice at school. To everyone."

I nodded. "Do you know Gloria Suarez?" I asked.

A suspicious look passed over Shannon's face. "Sure," she replied. "We've been in school together since River Heights Elementary. Of course I know her."

I nodded. "The thing is, Shannon . . . I've heard from a few sources that there was an incident at a recent assembly."

Shannon's eyes suddenly seemed to burn with anger, but she quickly gained her composure. "Look, Gloria and I go way back. We're *friends*, okay? And friends rib each other sometimes. I know Gloria likes cows, so when she won the academic award at that assembly, I thought it would be funny if I mooed instead of clapped. When I did it, a bunch of other people joined in."

"It was a joke?" I asked warily.

"*Yeah,*" Shannon replied, a defensive edge to her voice.

I swallowed, choosing my next words carefully. "Sometimes," I began, "we might think we're only joking with someone, but they don't think it's very funny. They feel hurt by it. Do you think that might be the case with Gloria?"

Shannon narrowed her eyes. "This is just like that Sarah thing," she complained. "Did you talk to her? Did you get that straightened out?"

I nodded. "I did talk to Sarah."

"And what did she say?"

"She said she tripped herself," I said truthfully, watching Shannon carefully. She looked triumphant, like this somehow proved her innocent on all counts. "But I think someone may have been telling her to say that."

Shannon glared at me. "Why would you think that?"

I sighed. "Shannon," I said. "I've heard from a few people that you can be a little tough on your classmates. I'm not trying to make you feel bad or tell you that you're a bad person. No matter what, no one deserves to be treated like you're being treated now."

Shannon's lip quivered. "But I . . . But I don't . . ."

I inched closer to her, placing my hand on her shoulder. "You don't what?" I asked.

Shannon's face began to crumple. "I'm not a bully!" she whined, then let out a strangled sob. "I can't believe you're accusing me! I asked you to help me because I'm being harassed, and you're trying to say *I'm* the bad guy!"

"Oh Shannon." I sighed again, rubbing her shoulder as she sobbed. "I'm not trying to say that. I just need the truth. What if you *were* mean to someone, and that someone knows something about what's happening to you now?"

Shannon sobbed. "The only person who knows who's behind this is—is GuitarLvr15," she insisted, shoulders shaking. "Do you know who he is yet?"

I shook my head sadly. "Not yet," I confessed.

Shannon stopped crying for a moment, and her eyes widened. "Do you know anything about him?"

I tried to smile. "I . . . Well, uh . . ." No? I racked my brain, trying to think of any identifying information we'd come up with. He liked to talk to people online? And not give away his identity? He drank virtual smoothies? "He . . . oh! He's really into music!" I said hopefully. "And he deejays sometimes."

Shannon looked at me blankly. "Really into *music*?" she asked disgustedly. "That's, like, everyone in my whole *school*," she scoffed. "Or anyone with an iPod."

Well, that burst my bubble. I shrugged. "I'm sorry, Shannon. That's all I have so far. But I told you when we first met that I would find who was doing this to you, and I intend to do that. I keep my promises."

Shannon blinked, wiping her eyes on her sleeve. "You'd better," she replied softly. "I don't know how much more of this I can take."

SECRET CRUSHES

Sarah O'Malley and Gloria Suarez, I thought, climbing back into my car. Both friends, both victims of Shannon's bullying. I started up my Prius and pulled out of Shannon's driveway. Both upset Shannon in some way, I thought. Gloria probably made Shannon jealous by winning her award . . . Sarah, by talking to Jake.

I stopped at a stoplight, thinking this over. Jake. Maggie had told us that Sarah had "stolen" Shannon's "boyfriend," but it had turned out, all she had done was talk to Jake at the coffee shop. If Shannon was so paranoid that Sarah just talking to Jake set her off, then surely Sarah couldn't be the only girl who had done that. Right? And maybe another girl who talked to Jake would also have been targeted by Shannon for bullying . . .

. . . and might be involved in the cyberbullying of Shannon.

When the light turned green, I made an abrupt U-turn. It was already getting dark, but I had something important to do downtown.

I had a few more questions for Jake Seltzer.

"Nancy! Fancy meeting you here!" A familiar, lightly accented voice greeted me as I walked into Barbara's Beans. I turned to the right, and spotted Ibrahim and Arij sitting at two computer terminals in the corner. They were both smiling, and judging from what was up on their screens, it appeared that they were both engrossed in games of BetterLife.

"Ibrahim, Arij!" I greeted them cheerfully. "How are you guys? How's school?"

Arij spoke up. "Very good, Nancy," she replied. "I've made some new friends, and we eat lunch together every day."

I nodded. "Good, good. Ibrahim, how's Better-Ibrahim4 doing?"

Ibrahim grinned. "Oh, very well, in the game," he replied. "He's gotten a good job at the Better-

Life bank, and I've enrolled him in night school, to get his degree in finance." He lowered his voice. "But unfortunately our friend from the other night has not spoken to him again."

I shrugged. "I guess that's not a surprise."

Ibrahim sighed. "I'm sorry I couldn't be more help, Nancy."

I gently touched his arm. "Don't worry about it," I assured him. "I appreciate what you did. Now if you'll excuse me, I need to speak with someone here."

"Of course, of course," he replied. "Do your thing. But if you have time, say good-bye on your way out."

"Sure."

Ibrahim turned back to his game, and I headed over to the counter. The shop was unusually quiet this evening, and Jake was leaning against the counter, staring into a television mounted on the far wall that was tuned in to MTV.

"Excuse me? Jake?" I asked.

He looked up. "Oh, hey there," he said in a friendly tone. "You again. Need some more BetterLife tips?"

I shook my head. "Actually," I replied, "I wondered if I could ask you some non-BetterLife-related questions."

He smiled. "Shoot. Ask me anything. My life is an open book."

"Well," I said confidentially, "listen. You're a good-looking guy, and you probably have girls coming in here just to talk to you a lot."

Two spots of bright pink appeared on his cheeks. "What? Come on. Whatever." He paused. "Did you ask me something?"

I tried to suppress my smile. "Um, I was really asking if any younger girls had come in here and hung out for a while, trying to talk to you," I explained. "Like, middle-school age. Girls coming in alone and chatting you up."

He looked thoughtful. "Not really," he admitted. "Oh, wait, there was this one girl. Dark hair, dark eyes? She looked about Shannon's age, actually. She used to come in almost every afternoon and order a decaf latte. She would sit right over there." He pointed to a table not far from the counter. "She would nurse that thing for hours. And yeah, she liked to talk. She especially liked to talk about music. Had mad cool taste for a younger girl."

I thought of Sarah—her long dark hair, and the iPod she'd been fiddling with incessantly when she and Gloria had told me they'd bullied Shannon. She took dance lessons, too. It stood to reason that she was into music. Just like Guitar-Lvr15. But that could be a coincidence. Hadn't Shannon said everyone in her class was into music? And Sarah had the ILoveDublin character. Why would she bother with that if she was already ringleading the charge against Shannon as GuitarLvr15?

In any case, Sarah had green eyes, not dark, but that was easy enough to miss. I pulled my attention back to Jake. "She had long hair?" I asked.

Jake nodded. "Yeah, long hair. She still comes in every once in a while, but she avoids me like the plague. She goes right to the computers and, if I'm behind the counter, she'll wait till I go off shift to order anything."

Ever since Shannon humiliated her into submission, I thought. So Maggie had been right about one thing: It seemed Sarah did have a thing for Jake. "Was there anyone else?" I asked hopefully. I so wanted him to say, *Yes, there was this other girl.* I wanted him to put me on the path of someone new. Someone who might be GuitarLvr15.

But he just shook his head. "Not that I can think of," he confessed. "I mean, someone might have come in once or twice. But I didn't notice."

"Right." It was almost completely dark outside. The colorful star-shape light fixtures in the shop filled the space with warm light. Suddenly a thought occurred to me. "Oh no," I muttered, looking at my watch. "Oh no! Thanks, Jake. I gotta go!"

I whirled around and ran for the door. It was 7:47, and my date with Ned was at eight. I barely had enough time to run a brush through my hair and book it to the restaurant. I was definitely going to be late no matter what I did. Fishing my cell phone out of my purse, I started dialing Ned's number to warn him.

"Nancy!" Ibrahim's cheerful voice drifted over from the computer terminal. He was sitting alone now. It looked like Arij had headed home. "Are you rushing home to check out the party at the virtual smoothie shop? GuitarLvr15 starts deejaying in about ten minutes."

The virtual party! "Oh shoot," I said out loud. My big chance to see GuitarLvr15 in a social setting—and hopefully gain some clues to his real-life identity. I'd completely forgotten.

"I . . . well, I . . ." I hesitated at the door. I knew I *should* check out the virtual party. I needed any info I could get on GuitarLvr15, especially after seeing Shannon today and how upset she was about the whole thing.

But . . . It had been so, *so* long since I'd spent

time alone with Ned. And what if I spent all night at the party and didn't learn anything new? Wouldn't I feel terrible for breaking my date?

"Shoot." I plopped myself down at the terminal next to Ibrahim and dialed Ned's number on my cell phone. It went straight to voicemail. He was probably on his way to Flavio's now.

"Ned, I'm so, *so* sorry," I said after the beep. "I don't think I can make it tonight."

PARTIES AND LIES

brahim looked at me curiously as I pressed the End button on my phone. "Did you have plans with Ned?" he asked.

"Yes," I replied with a sheepish smile. "I'm such a bonehead, I forgot about the virtual party on BetterLife. Thanks so much for reminding me, Ibrahim. I would have been kicking myself if I'd missed this."

Ibrahim beamed. "Don't mention it, Nancy," he replied. "I'm sure Ned will understand that your work on this case comes first."

I flashed back to the night of the lecture; Ned had seemed so upset that I'd wandered off and that we hadn't been able to spend any time alone together. "Yeah," I said slowly. "I'm sure he will."

I must not have sounded very convincing, because Ibrahim raised an eyebrow. "Do you think he will be upset?" he asked. "I know he cares for you, Nancy. I'm sure he must be disappointed not to see you. Who wouldn't be?"

I glanced up, startled by the sincerity in his voice. But when I caught his eye, he just smiled warmly. Ibrahim was such a sweet, friendly person. It was nice to have someone in my life who was so supportive and utterly upbeat. "Thanks," I replied, blushing a little. "I'm sure Ned will understand. I mean, he's such a good guy."

"Of course," Ibrahim replied, turning to his computer station. "Shall we get started? It's almost time for the party to start."

"Good idea." I turned to my screen and hastily logged on to BetterLife. When the familiar aerial view of the virtual River Heights came up, I took the mouse and guided it over to the—

"Wait!" I cried, grabbing Ibrahim's arm and pointing to the Username box.

It already had a name in it: GuitarLvr15.

"Whoa," Ibrahim said breathlessly. "The program remembers the last player who logged in from a certain computer. It's meant to make it easier for you to log in if you play at the same computer all the time."

My eyes widened. "So that means . . ."

". . . GuitarLvr15 was playing right on this computer!" Ibrahim and I chorused.

Wow. That meant that GuitarLvr15 was a customer at Barbara's Beans . . . or that he worked there. Suddenly I looked over to see who was working behind the counter: Jake was gone. A short-haired blond was now manning the espresso machine. Jake must have disappeared into the back. We hadn't seen him leave out the front door.

"Hmm," I murmured to myself. "I wonder if there are computers in the back."

"There are," Ibrahim responded, turning eagerly back to face me. "Once, when our father dropped us off here to do our homework, all of the computer terminals were busy, and the manager kindly allowed me to work in the back room until one became available," he explained. "There are two computers back there. They have all of the same programs as these computers, but they're older models."

I bit my lip. Hmm. I remembered the first time Jake had logged on to BetterLife to show me the game. It had been on this very computer! And then I thought of Jake's description of Sarah. The outgoing girl he'd described didn't sound like the reserved young lady *I'd* met. And he'd gotten her eye color wrong.

Which would make sense ... if he'd been making the whole thing up.

"Ibrahim," I began, typing my username and password into the login box, "do you know if it's possible to have two BetterLife IDs at the same time?"

"Of course," Ibrahim responded. He had already been logged on to the game, so he was busy directing BetterIbrahim4 to the virtual mall. "I had several when I was first starting out. It took a few tries to get BetterIbrahim4 just right." He glanced up from the monitor, and smiled.

Nodding, I turned back to my own screen, where I picked up VirtualNancy at her apartment and got her moving to the smoothie shop, too. This was all interesting information. So Jake could be BionicEd ... *and* GuitarLvr15. I glanced back at the counter. Jake was still missing.

But it was time to concentrate on the game ... and the virtual party. BetterIbrahim4 and Virtual-Nancy arrived at the smoothie shop together. Sure enough, GuitarLvr15 was at the DJ booth. Every few minutes someone would go up to talk to him—making requests, maybe—but for the most part, he seemed lost in his own little world.

As a pretty redhead turned away from the DJ booth, I caught a glimpse of GuitarLvr15's T-shirt—and gasped.

"What is it, Nancy?" asked Ibrahim.

"His T-shirt," I replied. "It's a molecular diagram of caffeine."

Ibrahim glanced up at me from his screen, looking curious. "Oh. Does that mean something?"

"It could mean that he's into science," I replied, thinking of BionicEd. "And I happen to know that Jake has an interest in chemistry. Or at least, his other alter ego does."

Ibrahim looked confused. "Okay, but couldn't it also mean that he likes coffee? Caffeine? Get it?"

Oh. I sighed. If GuitarLvr15 was just a coffee fan, that *could* be Jake, who worked at Barbara's Beans, or it could be any of his customers. Probably many of Shannon's classmates among them. "Maybe," I replied. "Anyway, we'd better not try to talk to him. I don't want to make him mad. We can just blend into the background at this party, and observe him in his natural setting."

Ibrahim nodded. "Sounds like a plan."

So BetterIbrahim4 and VirtualNancy both got

strawberry smoothies—BetterIbrahim4's treat—
and settled on a couch to chat and keep an eye
on GuitarLvr15. A few strangers came up to us
and made conversation—nice kids, mostly, who
lost interest when they realized we didn't have
much of an opinion about the teachers at school
or the most recent sport in gym class. (I AM NEW!
Ibrahim explained, and a couple of kids took his
e-mail address to contact him in real life.) Meanwhile, GuitarLvr15 had a few visitors of his own.
As people approached him, I moved my mouse
over their avatars and clicked to view their user-
names.

"Butterflydust," I read. "Killerjoe4. Ibrahim,
these are all people who harassed Shannon in the
game!"

"I guess that's not surprising," Ibrahim replied.
"He is their leader, right?"

"Nancy?"

Suddenly a familiar, warm voice startled me
away from my computer screen. When I turned
around, there stood Ned: dressed to the nines in
a shirt and tie, holding a gorgeous bouquet of
pink roses. "Ned," I murmured breathlessly.

He looked at me with confusion, then looked
to my left. "Ibrahim? What are you doing here?
Where's Arij?"

Ibrahim shrugged. "She went home to begin her reading for her history class," he replied. "I stayed here, to surf the Net a little more."

Ned frowned. "How did she get home? I came to give her a ride."

"She walked," Ibrahim explained. "She said she wanted the exercise. And it's not far."

"I guess not," Ned agreed, looking down at the roses in his hand and then back to Ibrahim. "I thought you had a study group?"

"I did," Ibrahim replied. "It was canceled. The girl who was hosting it came down with the flu."

I looked from Ned to Ibrahim. I had been thrilled to see Ned, but strangely, he didn't look quite so happy. He looked . . . not quite annoyed, but . . . puzzled.

"I'm so sorry I had to break our date, Ned," I apologized. "It wasn't because I wasn't looking forward to it, believe me. It's just that something came up in the case."

Ned met my eye, a confused expression on his face, then looked behind me at the computer screen. "Is that BetterLife?" he asked.

"It is," I answered. "You know the case I'm working on has to do with BetterLife. I told you all about it before the lecture."

Ned swallowed. "I know, but . . . you broke our date to play a computer game?"

My mouth dropped open. I didn't know what to say. "Ned, you know—"

"Never mind," Ned interrupted me, holding up his hand in a my-bad gesture. "Never mind. I know you, Nance. I know that if you canceled, it must be something important." He paused. "I guess I'm just a little surprised to see you here." He glanced from me to Ibrahim. But Ibrahim had turned back to his computer and was directing BetterIbrahim4 to accept the invitation to dance from a curly-haired brunette.

I sighed. On my screen, VirtualNancy sat alone on the couch, sipping her virtual smoothie. Behind her, GuitarLvr15 sorted through a stack of CDs to pick the next tune. Was this really how I wanted to spend my Friday night? I wasn't learning anything new from the game. The one big thing I'd learned tonight was that GuitarLvr15 played from Barbara's Beans and that Jake mysteriously disappeared right around the time GuitarLvr15 was due to start deejaying. Maybe that was enough for one night. "Ned, you know . . . ," I began. "Maybe we should just go to dinner now. I don't know that I'm learning anything new from this virtual party, and—"

Suddenly I stopped. The song that GuitarLvr15 was playing. It seemed so familiar. Where had I heard it before?

And then it came to me. Dark hair, dark eyes. Loves music.

"Omigosh," I blurted, jumping up from my computer terminal and grabbing my purse. "I'm sorry, but—Ibrahim, Ned, I have to go!"

REAL-LIFE ANSWERS

"**W**hat are *you* doing here?" Rebecca greeted me as she opened the door to her bedroom. I'd called Maggie from my car, and she'd gotten me Rebecca's address from the middle-school directory. Rebecca's parents were out, and her older brother, who'd been absorbed in an extremely loud video game, had let me in without much more than a grunt. But Rebecca looked about as happy to see me as you might be to find a cockroach wandering out of your sandwich.

"We need to talk," I said, trying to walk past her into the bedroom.

Rebecca held out her arm to stop me. "I didn't

expect you," she whined. "My room is a mess! At least give me a chance to clean up before you come in."

I had a feeling I knew exactly what she didn't want me to see. I didn't want to be rude, but I *did* want to catch her in the act. "I don't have a lot of time," I insisted, pushing her arm out of the way. "We're all messy. I won't think any less of you." I barged in, Rebecca fluttering behind me, fidgeting and acting nervous.

"Can I—I mean, would you like, you know . . ."

Rebecca was doing her best to distract me, but there was no denying it: a laptop sat open on her desk, and on the screen was the profile for GuitarLvr15. He was still deejaying, but the song that was playing was coming to an end. Guitar-Lvr15 should have been cueing up another song, but he sat motionless. I glanced at Rebecca. She looked at me, seeming hopeful that I wouldn't catch what was going on.

The last notes of the song played, and we were plunged into silence.

I gestured to the computer. "You'd better pick another song," I advised. "Wouldn't want to let GuitarLvr15's many fans down!"

Rebecca's face fell. Caught! She sighed and, instead of walking over to the game, sat down on the bed and put her head in her hands.

"It was you the whole time, wasn't it?" I asked. "You created the character GuitarLvr15 to look like Jake, and get Shannon all excited when he started flirting with her. But all along you planned to humiliate her, and you made her humiliation worse by recruiting an army of cyberbullies."

Rebecca sighed, then looked up, trying to recover herself. "*Why* would I do that?" she asked. "Shannon is my best friend."

"She *was* your best friend," I corrected. "Until you both got a crush on the same guy. When Shannon found out you were hanging out at Barbara's Beans to flirt with Jake—the guy she thought belonged to *her*—she must have done something horrible to you," I mused. "Horrible enough that you didn't dare speak to him at all anymore. What is it that she did to you, Rebecca?"

She looked up at me, meeting my eyes. She looked miserable, like she knew she was caught. Finally she sighed again and said quietly, "She printed out all my personal e-mails."

I gave her a questioning look, and she went on, "E-mails that I'd been sending her all year. Not every single one—just the ones with juicy, embarrassing details. Crushes I'd had, stupid things I'd done, things I'd said about my other friends—things I never meant to go public." She paused. "She printed them all out and stapled them together into this packet. Later, she told me she was printing out *all* her e-mails, trying to make backups in case her computer crashed. But somehow this packet was only the worst of mine." She frowned at me. "She left it in our English classroom right before another sixth-grade class came in. So of course someone found it, and read it, and—" Her voice caught.

"And?" I prompted gently.

She gave me a rueful look, tears forming at the corners of her eyes. "It was all over the Internet by that afternoon."

Rebecca hastily wiped at her eyes while I absorbed this revelation. "And you're sure this was on purpose?" I asked.

She nodded. "Later, I told Shannon I thought it was strange that only *my* e-mails were in the packet, that only *my* e-mails had been left for everybody to see." She frowned again. "She told me maybe I should have stayed away from Jake. I asked why, and she told me she knew *I* knew what she was talking about. We never spoke of it again."

We were quiet for a moment. On Rebecca's computer, sounds of conversation got louder as virtual partygoers started filling in the silence left by the DJ.

"You never spoke of it again," I clarified, "but you hatched a plan to get revenge on her."

Rebecca nodded, staring down into her lap. "It wasn't supposed to go this far," she confessed. "It was just supposed to be me as Jake, making her feel stupid for thinking they could be together in the first place." She looked up at me. "I really meant it to be a few messages from me as him, and then over. She'd learn her lesson, and she'd never have to know it was me."

"But?" I asked.

"But," she continued. "One day I was careless. I was writing her an e-mail from Jake in the computer lab at school. Kind of mean stuff, about how she was so nasty to everyone else, now he was going to be nasty to her. And suddenly I hear a voice from behind me. 'What are you writing to Shannon?' It was Krista Mulgrew."

I nodded. "And who's she?"

"She's this other girl in our grade. Sweet but kind of dorky. She had a crush on this really popular guy, Doug, and Shannon found out about it and told him at lunch one day, right in front of her." Rebecca looked disgusted. "He made this big deal out of how he could *never* like her. Krista ran out of the cafeteria in tears." She paused. "I admitted to her what I was doing, trying to get back at Shannon. And she wanted to be a part of it."

I sighed. "And she had a BetterLife ID?"

Rebecca nodded. "She's Butterflydust."

I shook my head.

"It just grew from there," Rebecca explained. "I guess—I guess I was surprised to see that it really got through to Shannon. I've known her for years, and I've seen her do a lot of terrible things to a lot of people who'd done nothing to her. But it's like she's above it all. She can hurt you but you can't hurt her back." Her eyes flashed. "Well, I found a way to actually hurt her. I know it was wrong, but it felt *good*."

"Do you think Shannon deserved what you girls did to her?" I asked. "To be harassed every day at school, to lose everything—Do you think that was fair?"

"No," Rebecca admitted. "Shannon could be really nasty, but this . . . It went much farther than I meant it to." She paused. "To be honest, lately, I've felt bad about it. But there are so many other people involved now. . . ." She shrugged, looking ashamed. "I guess I just didn't know how to stop it."

"Well," I said, "we're going to figure out a way."

She glanced at the still-motionless GuitarLvr15 on her laptop's screen. I sighed again, going over all of this information in my head. Shannon had been a bully, and Rebecca had bullied her back. But when you added in the Internet factor to bullying, it got completely out of control.

"Can I ask you something?" I finally said.

"Sure," Rebecca agreed.

"If you didn't like the way Shannon treated people, including you," I began, "why not just stop being friends with her?"

Rebecca seemed to think that over. "I guess I wanted to keep my friends close but my enemies closer," she replied. "Besides," she added. "I like being popular."

ONE LAST LOG-ON . . .

The next morning I returned from a nearby meeting with Rebecca, Shannon, and their parents, feeling exhausted. After hearing Rebecca's story, I'd insisted on waiting with her for her parents to return from a movie, so she could tell them everything that had been going on. Naturally they had been horrified, and had set up a meeting the next morning between the two girls and both sets of parents.

"I can't believe it was you," Shannon had sobbed after Rebecca and her parents entered Shannon's kitchen. "You were my best friend! I trusted you!"

"But you were so mean to me!" Rebecca persisted. "You treat me like garbage sometimes,

Shannon. I wanted to show you what that felt like!"

After a long conversation and many tears from both of the girls, Shannon admitted that she sometimes wasn't so nice to her classmates.

"Why do you act that way, honey?" her mother demanded, looking completely shocked by all of these revelations. "What do you get out of being mean to people?"

Shannon's lip quivered as she glanced from her parents, to me, to Rebecca. "It—it—it keeps them from being mean to me first!" she cried, shaking her head and looking away.

"Why would they be mean to you?" asked her father. "You're a lovely, smart girl who's capable of being very sweet to her family and friends."

Shannon started to cry. "I don't believe that," she confessed.

It was a tough conversation, and in the end their parents decided that both Rebecca and Shannon should meet with a counselor for a while, to discuss why they felt they needed to bully each other. Mrs. Fitzgerald also volunteered to call the parents of the other kids involved and arrange a meeting at the school to discuss the rash of bullying at the middle school—and the advent of cyberbullying.

"I think a lot of kids will be grounded from the computer for the next few months," Mr. Fitzgerald predicted.

And that was just fine with me.

Now, I lounged on my bed and dialed up Ned. He answered on the first ring, which was a relief. I was afraid my call would go to voicemail, and I would be left to wonder whether he'd really missed it, or he was still upset about last night and avoiding me.

"Nancy? Is this my favorite detective?"

I smiled. "Ned, I'm so sorry about last night." I explained everything to him—finding Ibrahim at the coffee shop, the virtual party, how I'd realized Rebecca was behind the bullying, and everything that had happened since.

"Sounds like you've had quite an exciting twenty-four hours," Ned observed. "But let me ask about your *next* twelve hours. Dinner tonight?"

I grinned. "Yes, please."

We chatted for a few more minutes, catching up on everything we'd been doing the past few days and making concrete plans for tonight.

"Ned, I'm just so sorry for missing our date last night," I repeated, shaking my head. "You looked so nice, and the roses you brought were beautiful. I'm sorry for being so scatterbrained, and having to cancel."

"Don't worry about it," Ned reassured me. "I have another shirt and tie, and I've put those roses in water for you. We can just take up where we left off tonight, okay?"

I smiled, so relieved that Ned wasn't upset. "Okay."

There was a strange pause. "Just one thing, Nancy," Ned piped up suddenly.

"Sure," I replied. "What is it?"

"Maybe you shouldn't . . . spend so much time with Ibrahim," Ned said gently.

I was caught totally off guard. What? Was Ned jealous? Was he having second thoughts about having the al-Fulanis as houseguests?

"What do you mean?" I asked, but at that very moment Hannah called up the stairs.

"*Nancy!* Bess and George are here to see you."

Shoot. I'd invited Bess and George over to help me with the ceremonial laying to rest of VirtualNancy. Now that I knew who the cyberbullies were, I had no need for her.

"Nancy . . . ," Ned was saying.

"Never mind," I told him. "I'm sorry, Ned. We'll have to put a tack in this conversation. Bess and

George are here. Can we talk about this later?"

There was another funny little pause. "Sure," he said after a few seconds. "I'll call you later, okay?"

"Okay," I agreed, "thanks. We'll talk soon." I hung up the phone just as Bess and George appeared at my bedroom door.

"Hey, Nance. Are you *sure* you want to put Virtual Nancy to rest?" Bess asked, pushing a sheaf of computer printouts into my arms. "I designed some cute new outfits for her that I'm sure would make her superpopular in the game, if you wanted to keep playing. There's a program you can download that lets you outfit your BetterLife character in your own designs!"

"And *Hack* magazine just published this new article about all the upgrades you'll get under the new subscription service!" George exclaimed, pushing a magazine at me. "It really sounds *incredible*. Are you sure you want to quit now?"

I glanced down at the printouts. Bess's outfits were gorgeous and chic. It looked like she had drawn them, and an amazingly accurate portrait of VirtualNancy, by hand. And George's article was filled with highlighted sections, with little arrows pointing to them and "Wow!" scrawled in the margins.

My friends were getting *way* too into this.

"I'm sure," I said, giving them both an apologetic smile. "Thanks for bringing this stuff over, guys. But I was really only on BetterLife to investigate my case. Now that it's solved, I think I'm done with so-called 'better lives.'"

Both Bess and George looked crushed.

"Okay," Bess murmured, reluctantly heading over to my computer.

"If you say so," George added, joining her.

The three of us settled in front of the screen, and I called up BetterLife and logged in.

WELCOME VIRTUALNANCY, the game greeted me. YOU HAVE $345, 4 FRIENDS, AND 22 MESSAGES.

"Twenty-two messages?" Bess asked. "That's kind of a lot, isn't it?"

George nodded. "The most we've ever gotten before was three," she confirmed.

"I guess VirtualNancy is getting more popular as she finds her way," I suggested, feeling a strange sense of pride. "Well, I'll just skim them." I clicked on Messages, then glanced down the list. At the top was an urgent one—from ILoveDublin, or Sarah O'Malley.

"It couldn't hurt to see what Sarah has to say," I said, clicking on the message. We were here to end VirtualNancy's reign, but there was no need to be hasty.

Sarah's message contained no text, only a link to what looked liked a uVid video.

"Hmm," I muttered, clicking on the link. "Maybe something happened with the cyberbullies that she wants me to see."

The video began on a quiet residential street in downtown virtual River Heights. It soon focused in on a tall, dark-haired character. "That's Ibrahim!" I said happily. He was holding a letter and arguing with somebody.

"This seems unlike Ibrahim," I murmured. But then the game panned out, and I could see who he was arguing with.

I gasped.

It was VirtualNancy!

"This never happened!" I cried, turning to George. "I mean, I never played this part! How could there be a video of something I never made VirtualNancy do?"

George shrugged. "Just watch what happens," she advised. "Maybe you did this and forgot about it? That happens sometimes."

Captions of what each character was saying appeared on the bottom of the screen, like subtitles.

WHY WOULD YOU SEND THIS TO ME? Better-Ibrahim4 asked. I THOUGHT WE WERE FRIENDS!

VirtualNancy smirked. I WOULD NEVER BE FRIENDS WITH SOMEONE LIKE YOU, she replied.

"Omigosh," I whispered, glancing at George. "I *definitely* did not do this and forget about it."

George looked worried. "Then I mean—I guess the only other way is if someone hacked into your account and did this?"

PEOPLE LIKE YOU ARE RUINING THIS COUNTRY, VirtualNancy was telling BetterIbrahim4 now. WHY DON'T YOU AND YOUR FAMILY GO BACK TO IRAN?

Even in cyberspace, Ibrahim looked stunned. NANCY! he replied. HOW COULD YOU SAY THESE THINGS?

VirtualNancy turned away then, and pulled something out of her purse. I inhaled. It was a can of spray paint!

"Oh no," I whispered. "I'm not doing this, guys! What do I do? I would never do this!"

VirtualNancy walked away from BetterIbrahim4 and over to the apartment complex they stood in front of. Number 3C, a cozy-looking ground-floor apartment, had the name BetterIbrahim4 posted on the mailbox.

VirtualNancy held up the can of spray paint and pushed the button at the top, releasing a stream of red paint onto the black front door.

Behind her, BetterIbrahim4 cried out in distress.

Bess, George, and I were stunned silent as VirtualNancy wrote her message on the door: GO HOME.

"Oh my gosh," I whispered, my chest aching with sympathy and shame. "Oh, poor Ibrahim. I can't believe this. I would never!"

The video ended.

"Wow," Bess muttered breathlessly.

Silently I closed the uVid window and returned to my message in-box. The page reloaded when I clicked back, and suddenly the number of messages changed: YOU HAVE 65 MESSAGES, the game told me. 17 OF THEM ARE URGENT. "People are probably watching this video right now," I cried. "They think I did that!"

I clicked on the first message. It was urgent, from MoomooGirl—Gloria Suarez.

THAT WAS RACIST AND DISGUSTING. I KNOW WHO U REALLY R, AND I'M LETTING PEOPLE KNOW. U SHOULD BE ACCOUNTABLE 4 UR ACTION.

My stomach fell. "Oh no."

My cell phone began ringing. I had a feeling I was going to have to turn it off soon. If even a tiny fraction of the people who played BetterLife in this town saw this video—and realized Virtual-Nancy was me—I could look forward to a lot of harassment in the next few weeks.

I clicked on the message below Gloria's, my heart squeezing when I saw the sender. It was from BetterIbrahim4, marked urgent.

The message consisted of only one word: WHY?

"I don't know, Ibrahim," I whispered, glancing over at Bess and George. They looked as angry as I felt. "But I'm going to find out!"

165